シリーズ待望の大改訂！！　法律英語の良き伴走者

高速マスター
法律英単語®Ⅰ
2100
［第2版］

法律・基礎編

弁護士　渡部友一郎　著

日本加除出版株式会社

第 2 版　はしがき

「渡部先生の『法律英単語®』シリーズ、机に置いて、使っています！」
　講演会の後、このようなお声掛けをいただくたびに、法律英語学習の一助としてこのシリーズが皆様に愛されていることを実感し、胸が熱くなります。
　2020年に初版を出版してから4年、本書『法律英単語®Ⅰ』は、より充実した内容で第2版をお届けできる運びとなりました。今回の改訂では、従来の約2100語に加え、単語に新たに例文を付け加えています。初版では「単語学習に例文は必ずしも必要ない」という仮説をもとに制作しました。しかし、2022年に出版した『法律英単語®Ⅱ』で例文が大変好評をいただいたことを受けて、この第2版では、例文を導入することにしました。
　これにより、『法律英単語®Ⅰ』と『法律英単語®Ⅱ』は名実ともに姉妹本として生まれ変わりました。本書が法律英語学習のガイドとして皆様の机上に寄り添い、日々の学びや実務にお役立ていただけることを心より願っております。
　本書の改訂に際して、編集部の皆様、とりわけ初版からお世話になり、さらに編集者として成長を遂げられている荻原拓海様とともに、心を込めて作り上げたことをここにご報告いたします。熱意をもって本書を企画・制作に携わってくださった日本加除出版株式会社の盛田大祐様、佐藤慎一郎様、濱中聡子様をはじめ関係者の皆様に深く御礼申し上げます。
　また、本書の印税は、法学教育・研究の発展に寄与するべく、研究への支援及び学恩を頂いた東京大学のロースクールへの寄付に充てさせていただいております。また、私事ではありますが、司法修習生の初任給から毎月3万円を166ヶ月積み立てた500万円を東京大学のロースクールへ寄付する夢が叶い、母校のローレビューの存続に役立てていただけることになりました（2023年には、紺綬褒章を頂きました）。第2版の印税も、また同様に、皆様の後輩たちを含む未来の法律家へ還元される予定です。この書籍が法律英語学習者の良き伴走者となり、そして法学の未来に貢献することを心より願っております。心を込めて作ったこの本が末永く愛されることを願っております。

　2025年 元旦
　　弁護士　渡部友一郎

はしがき

◆問題の所在

　私は、司法試験合格直後の2008年秋、都内の大型書店の書棚を奥へ手前へ行ったり来たりして、何冊かの法律英語（英文契約）の本を手にとった後、これらを棚に戻し、少しため息をつき、途方に暮れていました。目当てのものが思うように見つからなかったからです。

　英国外資系法律事務所にアソシエイト弁護士として内定をもらっていた私は、意気揚々、1年間の司法修習期間中に法律英語の基礎を磨いてやると決意。しかし、TOEICやTOEFLでベストセラーとなっている（最初に誰もが手にとる）高速暗記学習のための「英単語帳」が見つからなかったのです。

◆法律英語の山を一緒に登るガイドが必要

　英語学習を登山に例えると「必須は英単語」。これは中学・高校の英語の定期試験、大学受験を経験してきた誰もが100％納得する指摘です。ところが、「法律英語」については登山の「ガイド」が不在なのです。大学受験山、TOEIC山、TOEFL山にはいるガイド達が、私たちが最も必要とする「法律英語の山」にはいないのです。そのため、私たちは、法律英単語の高速暗記学習に最適ではない方法——英文契約の書籍を買い漁ったり、ビジネスパーソン用の語学学校に通ったり（私も）——を十人十色の方法で非効率に実践してきました。

　その後10年経過しましたが、高速暗記学習のための「法律英単語」の最適解は未だないと考えています。基礎的な法律英単語力があれば皆様のお仕事はきっともっと楽しく楽になるはずです。大学受験山、TOEIC山、TOEFL山——これまで私たちがやってきた最適な方法を用いて「法律英語の山」も一緒に1歩1歩登頂を目指して歩んで参りましょう。

◆問題の解決

　本書は、法律英単語（約2100語）を大学受験、TOEFL/TOEIC教材のベストセラー単語集を参考としており、語彙を記憶し速習することを目的としたロングセラーとなるような「法律英単語帳」を皆様へ提案します。これらの学習書は「反復・継続」することに主眼があり、本書も、反復継続する手元にある単語集を目指します。

◆安心のための訳語選択

　本書の魅力は、法務省が法律英語の学識経験者と実務家を集めた日本法令外国語

訳推進会議が編纂公表した「法令用語日英標準対訳辞書」のシソーラス※に準拠していることです。もともとは私が10年間コツコツ集めてきた仕事用の英単語帳をベースに、英単語の日本語訳を、徹底して、法令用語日英標準対訳辞書に準拠する修正を行いました。これにより、私個人の好みの翻訳ではなく、複数の専門家が審議して合意されたシソーラス※を「基礎」として身につけられます。

◆本書の使い方

　本書の使い方は、上記の制作経緯からも明らかですが、最低限度といえる法律英単語（約2100語）を大学受験、TOEFL/TOEIC教材のベストセラー単語集で私たちが昔やった方法と「同じ」ように、何度も何度も「グルグルまわす」ことにより語彙を記憶し定着させることに特化しています。うまくペンキを塗るコツは薄く何度も塗ること、と同じく、4つのランク毎に、1つ1つ語彙を定着させていく方法が最善の使い方であると考えています。

　また、索引も充実させました。例えば、業務中、「委託」を翻訳することになった場合、「朝、単語を見たのに思い出せない」という際には、日本語の索引を利用して見てください。簡易辞書のように索引から素早く英単語記憶のシナプスを再発火し記憶を強化することができます。

◆御礼

　多くの皆様のお力によって、この書籍を世に送り出すことができたことを心から御礼を申し上げます。この書籍を皆様にお届けできることは、私たちの10年以上の夢だったからです。「この本は多くの方を助けると信じております」というSNSの投稿を見て、誰よりも早くお声掛けいただき、サブスク型書籍として人気書籍に育ててくださった弁護士ドットコム株式会社の松本慎一郎様、橋詰卓司様ほか皆様、そして前例のない書籍を心を込めて企画化し出版してくださった日本加除出版株式会社の盛田大祐様、佐藤慎一郎様ほか皆様に心から御礼申し上げます。この書籍が法律英語の第一歩を踏み出す多くの方の良きガイドとして成長し、ロングセラーとなることを願っております。

　　　　2020年12月　著　者

※ 法令用語日英標準対訳辞書の訳語がネイティブの外国人にとって最も分かりやすい言葉かという点には様々なご意見があることも承知しております。すなわち、渉外系法律事務所に所属し日々外国人クライアントと勤務する先生方は上級者（プロ登山家）として場面に適した良い「訳」をお持ちなのです。しかしながら、本書は、私たちすなわち、法律英語の山の中腹を目指す者にとって最初の登山ガイドであり、まずは2100語をマスターすることに集中するのが最善であると考えています。なお、本文中の"法務省は……"、"法務省の……"といった記述につきましては、いずれも「法務省　法令用語日英標準対訳辞書」によれば"と読み替えてください。

著者紹介

弁護士　渡部　友一郎（わたなべ ゆういちろう）

Life's too short for 'what-ifs'.

経歴
鳥取県鳥取市出身。2008年東京大学法科大学院修了、法務博士（専門職）。同年司法試験合格、2009年弁護士登録（第二東京弁護士会）。英国系グローバルローファームであるフレッシュフィールズ法律事務所、株式会社ディー・エヌ・エー法務部を経て、2015年米国サンフランシスコに本社を有するAirbnb（エアビーアンドビー）のLead Counsel、日本法務本部長。2025年1月よりAirbnbの日本法人の取締役。

受賞
2018年、ALB Japan Law Awardsにて「In-House Lawyer of the Year 2018」（最年少受賞）、2020年、「In-House Lawyer of the Year 2020」を受賞（2度目の受賞は日本人初）、及び2018年から30代で6年連続計8冠（史上初）。

諸活動
デジタル臨時行政調査会作業部会「法制事務のデジタル化検討チーム」構成員、経済産業省「国際競争力強化に向けた日本企業の法務機能の在り方研究会 法務機能強化 実装ワーキンググループ」委員、日本組織内弁護士協会理事、ISO/TC262（リスクマネジメント）国内委員会 作業グループ委員などを歴任。

ウェブサイト
組織内弁護士研究ノート®

※著者のBlogはこちらから！

法律英単語® Ⅰ 2100
RANK1

RANK 1

1	**or less** The duration of the right is 20 years or more and 50 years <u>or less</u>.	**…以下** 権利の存続期間は、20年以上50年<u>以下</u>とする。
2	**etc.** [ətsétərə] The documents required include a passport, visa, <u>etc.</u>	**…等** 必要書類は、パスポート、ビザ<u>等</u>である。
3	**opposite party** The <u>opposite party</u> must respond within 30 days.	**相手方（末尾❶参照）** <u>相手方</u>は、30日以内に、返答しなければならない。
4	**the other party (other parties)** A manifestation of intention becomes effective at the time notice thereof reaches <u>the other party</u>.	**相手方（末尾❶参照）** 意思表示は、その通知が<u>相手方</u>に到達した時からその効力を生ずる。
5	**knowingly** [nóʊɪŋli] The defendant <u>knowingly</u> violated the agreement.	**悪意で（末尾❷参照）** 被告は、<u>悪意で</u>合意に違反した。
6	**hereinafter referred to as "…"** a person that has right to perform an obligation (<u>hereinafter referred to as a "performer"</u>)	**以下「…」という** 弁済をすることができる者（<u>以下「弁済者」という</u>。）
7	**the same applies hereinafter** User(s) refers to the individual defined in Article 1. <u>The same applies hereinafter</u>.	**以下同じ** ユーザーとは、第1条に定義された個人をいう。<u>以下同じ</u>。
8	**objection** [əbdʒékʃən] The lawyer filed an <u>objection</u> to the motion.	**異議** 弁護士は、この申立てに対して、<u>異議</u>を申し立てた。
9	**opinion** [əpínjən] The expert's <u>opinion</u> clarified the issue.	**意見** 専門家の<u>意見</u>は、問題を明確にした。
10	**will** [wíl] The <u>will</u> was duly executed.	**遺言** <u>遺言</u>は、適法に執行された。
11	**intent** [ìntént] The buyer's <u>intent</u> was clear in the contract discussions.	**①意思、②目的** 買主の<u>意思</u>は、契約の話し合いの中で、明確だった。

12	**manifestation of intention**	**意思表示**
	Her email served as a <u>manifestation of intention</u> to resign.	彼女のメールは、辞任の**意思表示**となった。
13	**... or more**	**…以上**
	Business cannot be transacted in either House unless one-third <u>or more</u> of total membership is present.	両議院は、各々その総議員の3分の1**以上**の出席がなければ、議事を開き議決することができない。
14	**entrustment** [intrʌ́stmənt]	**①委託、②委任**
	The <u>entrustment</u> of financial records to the accountant was completed yesterday.	会計士に対する財務記録の**委託**は、昨日、完了した。
15	**consignor** [kənsáinə]	**①（販売・運送等の）委託者（末尾❸参照）、②荷送人**
	The <u>consignor</u> provided all necessary documents for shipping.	**委託者**は、船積みに必要な書類をすべて提供した。
16	**delegate** [déləgèit]	**①（権限を代わって行使することを）委託する、②委任する**
	We will <u>delegate</u> the task to a team member with the most experience.	私達は、最も経験のあるチームメンバーに仕事を**委託する**。
17	**entrust** [entrʌ́st]	**（信認関係の下で事務を）委託する**
	She decided to <u>entrust</u> her legal matters to a trusted attorney.	彼女は、信頼できる弁護士に法律問題を**委託する**ことにした。
18	**general consumers**	**一般消費者**
	The regulation change impacts all <u>general consumers</u> equally.	この規則の変更は、すべての**一般消費者**に等しく影響する。
19	**delegation** [dèləgéiʃən]	**委任（権限の委任）**
	The <u>delegation</u> of duties was announced in the morning meeting.	職務権限の**委任**が、朝のミーティングで発表された。
20	**power of attorney**	**委任状**
	He granted his outside counsel the <u>power of attorney</u>.	彼は、外部弁護士に対して、**委任状**を付与した。
21	**breach** [brítʃ]	**違反**
	The <u>breach</u> of contract led to immediate legal actions.	契約**違反**は、直ちに法的措置につながった。

RANK 1

#	英語	日本語
22	**offense** [əféns] The <u>offense</u> was recorded by security cameras.	①違反、②犯罪 この<u>犯罪</u>は、監視カメラに記録されていた。
23	**violation** [vaɪəléɪʃən] Parking in that spot is a clear <u>violation</u> of local ordinances.	違反 あの場所への駐車は明らかな条例<u>違反</u>だ。
24	**illegal conduct** The company was investigated for <u>illegal conduct</u> last year.	違反行為 その会社は、昨年、<u>違反行為</u>で調査を受けている。
25	**investigation into violation** An <u>investigation into violation</u> of privacy laws is underway.	違反調査 個人情報保護法に関する<u>違反調査</u>が行われている。
26	**illegal** [ìlíɡəl] Selling unlicensed merchandise is <u>illegal</u>.	違法な（末尾❹参照） 非正規品の販売は、<u>違法な</u>行為である。
27	**unlawful** [ənlɔ́:fəl] <u>Unlawful</u> entry into the property will result in arrest.	違法な（末尾❹参照） 敷地内への<u>違法な</u>侵入は、逮捕の対象となる。
28	**penalty** [pénəlti] The <u>penalty</u> for late payment is outlined in the agreement.	違約金 支払いが遅れた場合の<u>違約金</u>は、契約書に記載されている。
29	**seal impression** The document requires a <u>seal impression</u> for validation.	印影 この書類には、認証のための<u>印影</u>が必要である。
30	**seal** [síl] She affixed her <u>seal</u> to the contract as a sign of approval.	印鑑（印章の趣旨） 彼女は、承認の証として、契約書に<u>印鑑</u>を押した。
31	**registered seal certificate** A <u>registered seal certificate</u> must be submitted by the end of the week.	印鑑証明書 週末までに、<u>印鑑証明書</u>を提出しなければならない。
32	**contract for work** The <u>contract for work</u> requires completion.	請負 <u>請負</u>は、完成を要する。

33	**contractor** [ká:ntræktər]	請負人
	The <u>contractor</u> is responsible for completing the project on time.	<u>請負人</u>は、期限内にプロジェクトを完了させる責任がある。
34	**action** [ǽkʃən]	訴え（例：会社法第601条）・訴訟
	The company filed an <u>action</u> against the government.	会社は、政府に対して、<u>訴え</u>を提起した。
35	**sale** [séɪl]	①売買、②売渡し
	The <u>sale</u> of the property must be approved by the board.	不動産の<u>売渡し</u>は、理事会の承認を得なければならない。
36	**management** [mǽnədʒmənt]	運営
	<u>Management</u> of companies is government by the Company Act.	会社の<u>運営</u>は、会社法の定めるところによる。
37	**business** [bíznəs]	①営業、②商法上の営業に対し会社法上の「事業」
	Non-competition after a <u>business</u> transfer could be a blind spot.	<u>事業</u>譲渡後の競業禁止は、盲点となりうる。
38	**operation** [à:pəréɪʃən]	営業
	You should consult with the Public Safety Commission with jurisdiction over the location of the office serving as the base of business <u>operations</u>.	あなたは、<u>営業</u>の本拠となる事務所の所在地を管轄する公安委員会に対して、相談するべきである。
39	**business office**	営業所（末尾❺参照）
	The <u>business office</u> handles all financial transactions for the department in Tokyo.	その<u>営業所</u>は、東京にある部門のすべての経済的取引を処理している。
40	**place of business**	営業所（末尾❺参照）
	The <u>place of business</u> was relocated to improve client access.	顧客へのアクセスを改善するため、<u>営業所</u>を移転した。
41	**business year**	営業年度
	This <u>business year</u> has seen unprecedented growth.	この<u>営業年度</u>は、かつてない成長を遂げた。
42	**trade secret**	営業秘密
	They strictly guard their <u>trade secret</u> to maintain a market edge.	彼らは、市場優位性を維持するため、<u>営業秘密</u>を厳守している。

RANK 1

RANK 1

43. for (the purpose of) profit [práfət]

Juridical persons formed for engaging in business <u>for profit</u> are governed by the provisions of the Civil Code and other laws.

営利の目的

<u>営利の目的</u>で事業を営む法人については、民法その他の法律の定めるところによる。

44. service contract

The <u>service contract</u> clearly outlines all deliverables and timelines.

役務提供委託

<u>役務提供委託</u>契約書には、すべての成果物とスケジュールの概要が明確に記載されている。

45. postponement [pəstpóʊnmənt]

The project's start has seen a <u>postponement</u> due to the lawsuit.

延期

プロジェクトのスタートは、当該訴訟との関係により、<u>延期</u>された。

46. embezzlement [embézəlmənt]

An internal audit uncovered <u>embezzlement</u> by an employee.

横領

内部監査により、従業員による<u>横領</u>が発覚した。

47. commit [kəmít]

The Criminal Code applies to anyone who <u>commits</u> a crime within the territory of Japan.

犯す

刑法は、日本国内において罪を<u>犯す</u>すべての者に適用する。

48. corruption [kərÁpʃən]

The scandal brought the corporate <u>corruption</u> issue to light.

汚職

このスキャンダルによって、企業の<u>汚職</u>問題が明るみに出た。

49. parent company

The <u>parent company</u> consolidated its subsidiaries to streamline operations.

親会社

<u>親会社</u>は、経営の合理化のために子会社を統合した。

50. and [ənd]

The contract specifies the rights <u>and</u> obligations of both parties involved.

及び

※「X、Y及びZ」は「X, Y and Z」と訳す。

契約書には、当事者双方の権利<u>及び</u>義務が明記されている。

51. accounting [əkáʊntɪŋ]

The merger demanded rigorous <u>accounting</u> and financial review.

会計

この合併では、厳格な<u>会計</u>及び財務レビューが要求された。

52. financial auditor

The <u>financial auditor</u> flagged discrepancies for immediate correction.

会計監査人

<u>会計監査人</u>は、直ちに是正するよう、不一致を指摘した。

53	**accounting books**	会計帳簿
	Maintaining accurate <u>accounting books</u> is fundamental for financial health.	正確な**会計帳簿**を維持することは、財務の健全性の基本である。
54	**fiscal year**	会計年度
	The <u>fiscal year</u> conclusion triggers a comprehensive financial review.	**会計年度**が終了すると、包括的な財務レビューが行われる。
55	**dismissal** [dɪsmísəl]	解雇、解任、罷免
	The <u>dismissal</u> of the employee was documented.	従業員の**解雇**は、文書化された。
56	**foreign country**	外国
	Expanding into a <u>foreign country</u> presents both challenges and opportunities.	**外国**への進出は、課題とチャンスの両方をもたらす。
57	**foreign national**	外国人
	Employing a <u>foreign national</u> requires supporting visa and work permit processes.	**外国人**を雇用するには、ビザや就労許可証の手続きを支援する必要がある。
58	**foreign corporation**	外国法人
	The <u>foreign corporation</u> registered its subsidiary under local laws.	**外国法人**は、現地法に基づいて子会社を登録した。
59	**dissolution** [dìsəlúːʃən]	①解散（例：法人または議会）、②出資の一部払戻し
	The board decided on the <u>dissolution</u> of underperforming subsidiaries.	取締役会は、不採算の子会社の**解散**を決定した。
60	**registration of dissolution**	解散の登記
	The <u>registration of dissolution</u> was duly filed.	**解散の登記**は、適正に申請された。
61	**disclosure** [dɪsklóʊʒər]	開示
	<u>Disclosure</u> requirements were met ahead of the meeting.	会合に先立ち、**開示**要件は満たされた。
62	**discovery** [dɪskʌ́vəri]	開示
	The <u>discovery</u> process uncovered new evidence.	新たな証拠が、証拠**開示**の過程において、発見された。
63	**company** [kʌ́mpəni]	会社
	The <u>company</u> announced its annual results yesterday.	**会社**は、昨日、年次決算を発表した。

RANK 1

64	**interpretation** [ìntɚ́ːrprɪtéɪʃən] Legal <u>interpretation</u> varies among different jurisdictions.	（文言の）**解釈** 法**解釈**は、法域によって異なる。
65	**misinterpretation** [mɪsɪntɚ́ːrprətéɪʃən] A <u>misinterpretation</u> of the guideline led to widespread confusion.	**解釈の誤り** ガイドラインの**解釈の誤り**が、混乱を招いた。
66	**company split** The <u>company split</u> aims to enhance operational efficiency.	**会社分割** **会社分割**の目的は、業務効率の向上である。
67	**removal (from position/duty)** [rɪmúːvəl] The board approved the <u>removal</u> of the CFO. But, he remains as a member of the board.	**解職** 取締役会は、CFO（職）の**解職**を承認した。しかし、彼はひきつづき取締役として残る。
68	**termination** [tɚ̀ːrmənéɪʃən] The <u>termination</u> of the contract was mutually agreed upon.	**解約（将来に向かって契約を失効）** 契約の**解約**は、双方合意の上だった。
69	**notice of termination** A <u>notice of termination</u> was issued to the vendor last week.	**解約の申入れ** 先週、この業者に対して、**解約の申入れ**が発出された。
70	**price** [práɪs] The <u>price</u> reflects both production costs and market demand.	**価格（品物の価格・値段）** **価格**は、生産コストと市場の需要の両方を反映している。
71	**value** [vǽlju] The <u>value</u> of the investment has significantly increased over time.	**価格（金銭的価値）** 投資**価値**は、時間の経過とともに大幅に上昇している。
72	**lower instance court** The case is now pending in a <u>lower instance court</u>.	**下級審** この件は、現在、**下級審**で係争中である。
73	**become final and binding** The decision will <u>become final and binding</u> if not appealed within 30 days.	**確定する（裁判・判決等）** 30日以内に異議申立てがなければ、この決定は最終的なものとなり、**確定する**。
74	**final and binding judgment** The period of prescription of a right determined by a <u>final and binding judgment</u> is 10 years.	**確定判決** **確定判決**によって確定した権利については、その時効期間は10年とする。

#	英語	日本語
75	**certified date** The <u>certified date</u> was June 18, 2025.	**確定日付** **確定日付**は、2025年6月18日であった。
76	**confirmation** [kɑ̀:nfərméɪʃən] <u>Confirmation</u> of the payment was received via email.	**①確認、②認可（例：更生計画の認可）** 入金の**確認**は、Eメールで受け取った。
77	**defect** [díːfekt] The returned product had a manufacturing <u>defect</u>.	**瑕疵** 返品された製品は、製造上の**瑕疵**を有した。
78	**negligence** [néɡlədʒəns] <u>Negligence</u> in safety procedures resulted in an accident.	**過失** 安全手順における**過失**が、事故を招いた。
79	**loan** [lóʊn] The bank approved the <u>loan</u> application this morning.	**貸付** 銀行は、今朝、**貸付**の申請を承認した。
80	**loan claim** The <u>loan claim</u> can be classified as a quasi-consumption loan.	**貸付債権** その**貸付債権**は、準消費貸借と分類することができる。
81	**comparative negligence** <u>Comparative negligence</u> was considered in determining liability.	**過失相殺** 責任の決定にあたり、**過失相殺**が考慮された。
82	**creditor** [krédətər] The <u>creditor</u> filed a lawsuit to recover the outstanding amount.	**貸主（末尾❻参照）** **（反対語）借主：debtor** **貸主**は、未払い金を取り戻すために、訴えを提起した。
83	**lender** [léndər] The <u>lender</u> provided favorable terms to the borrower.	**貸主（末尾❻参照）** **（反対語）借主：borrower** **貸主**は、借主に対して、有利な条件を提示した。
84	**lessor** [lésər] The <u>lessor</u> agreed to renew the lease agreement for another year.	**①不動産・物品の貸主（末尾❻参照）、②賃貸人** **（反対語）借主：lessee** **賃貸人**は、リース契約をさらに1年更新することに同意した。

RANK 1

RANK 1

85	**lease** [lís]	①不動産・物品を貸す、②賃貸借
	The <u>lease</u> grants the tenant the use of the property for a specified period.	<u>賃貸借</u>契約は、借主に対して、一定期間の不動産使用を認めるものである。
86	**impose** [ìmpóʊz]	課す
	New regulations <u>impose</u> stricter environmental standards.	新たな規制は、より厳しい環境基準を<u>課す</u>ものである。
87	**lend** [lénd]	貸す
	The library agreed to <u>lend</u> rare books for the exhibition.	図書館は、展覧会のために、貴重な書籍を<u>貸す</u>ことに同意した。
88	**merger** [mə́:rdʒər]	合併
	The <u>merger</u> created one of the largest entities in the industry.	この<u>合併</u>により、業界最大級の事業体が誕生した。
89	**merger agreement**	合併契約
	The <u>merger agreement</u> was finalized after months of negotiations.	<u>合併契約</u>は、数カ月にわたる交渉の末にまとまった。
90	**majority** [mədʒɔ́:rəti]	過半数
	A <u>majority</u> of the board voted in favor of the new strategy.	取締役会の<u>過半数</u>が、新しい戦略に賛成した。
91	**share certificate**	株券
	The <u>share certificate</u> was issued immediately after purchase.	<u>株券</u>は、購入後、すぐに発行された。
92	**share** [ʃér]	①株式、②持ち分
	Each <u>share</u> represents a unit of ownership in the company.	各<u>株式</u>は、会社の所有する権利の単位を表す。
93	**stock** [stá:k]	株式
	The <u>stock</u> market reacted positively to the news.	<u>株式</u>市場は、このニュースにポジティブに反応した。
94	**stock company**	株式会社 ※実務上、(kabushiki kaisha) の併記多し。
	The <u>stock company</u> is planning to expand its operations overseas.	その<u>株式会社</u>は、海外での事業拡大を計画している。

95	**shareholder** [ʃérhòʊldər]	株主
	The <u>shareholder</u> expressed concerns about the dividend policy.	<u>株主</u>は、配当方針について懸念を表明した。
96	**shareholders meeting**	株主総会
	The <u>shareholders meeting</u> is scheduled for the first quarter.	<u>株主総会</u>は、第1四半期に予定されている。
97	**shareholder register**	株主名簿
	The <u>shareholder register</u> has been updated to reflect recent sales.	<u>株主名簿</u>は、最近の売却を反映して更新された。
98	**borrower** [bá:rəər]	借主（末尾❼参照） （反対語）貸主：lender
	The <u>borrower</u> secured a loan to finance new projects.	<u>借主</u>は、新規プロジェクトの資金調達のために、ローンを確保した。
99	**debtor** [détər]	借主（末尾❼参照） （反対語）貸主：creditor
	The <u>debtor</u> is negotiating terms for debt restructuring.	<u>借主</u>が、債務再編の条件を交渉している。
100	**lessee** [lesí]	①不動産・物品の借主（末尾❼参照）、②賃借人 （反対語）貸主：lessor
	The <u>lessee</u> is responsible for minor repairs and maintenance.	軽微な修理及びメンテナンスは、<u>賃借人</u>が行うものとする。
101	**exchange** [ɪkstʃéɪndʒ]	①為替、②交換
	The <u>exchange</u> rate fluctuations impacted the company's profits.	<u>為替</u>レートの変動は、同社の利益に影響を与えた。
102	**Subsection** [sʌ́bsèkʃən]	款
	<u>Subsection</u> 7 details the procedure for filing grievances.	第7<u>款</u>は、苦情の申し立て手続きについて詳述する。
103	**summary court**	簡易裁判所
	The <u>summary court</u> handles smaller, less complex cases.	<u>簡易裁判所</u>は、小規模で複雑でない事件を扱う。
104	**jurisdiction** [dʒʊ̀rəsdíkʃən]	①管轄、②裁判権
	The <u>jurisdiction</u> of the court is determined by the location of the incident.	裁判所の<u>管轄</u>は、事件が起きた場所によって決まる。

RANK 1

105	**court with jurisdiction** The court with jurisdiction over IP disputes depend on local laws.	**管轄裁判所** 知財紛争の**管轄裁判所**は、現地法により異なる。
106	**relevant person** This does not apply when the relevant person is a petitioner for commencement of bankruptcy proceedings.	**関係者、当該者** **当該者**が破産手続開始の申立人である場合は、この限りでない。
107	**company auditor** The company auditor raised questions about the financial statements.	**監査役（末尾❽参照）** **監査役**は、財務諸表について疑問を提起した。
108	**board of company auditors** The board of company auditors will review the audit findings.	**監査役会（末尾❽参照）** **監査役会**は、監査結果を検討する。
109	**account** [əkáʊnt] The account statement shows a balance carried forward from last year.	**勘定** **勘定**の明細書には、昨年からの繰越残高が記載されている。
110	**wholly owning parent company** The wholly owning parent company has a controlling interest.	**完全親会社** **完全親会社**は、支配権を有する。
111	**wholly owned subsidiary company** The wholly owned subsidiary company launched a new product line.	**完全子会社** **完全子会社**が、新製品ラインを立ち上げた。
112	**supervision** [sùːpərvíʒən] The supervision of operations is critical for maintaining quality.	**監督** オペレーションの**監督**は、品質を維持するために、非常に重要である。
113	**supervising body** The supervising body announced new industry regulations.	**監督機関** **監督機関**は、新たな業界規制を発表した。
114	**principal** [prínsəpəl] The principal of the loan is due at the end of the term.	**①元本、②主物、③正犯** ローンの**元金**は、期間満了時に支払われる。
115	**solicitation** [səlìsɪtéɪʃən] The solicitation of new clients increased this quarter.	**①勧誘、②募集** 今期、新規顧客の**勧誘**が増加した。

116	**affiliated company**	関連会社
	The <u>affiliated company</u> was involved in the research project.	<u>関連会社</u>が、研究プロジェクトに参加した。
117	**bill** [bíl]	議案
	The <u>bill</u> was passed by the legislature last month.	この<u>議案</u>は、先月、議会で可決された。
118	**as a result of**	起因して
	<u>As a result of</u> the merger, several positions were made redundant.	いくつかの役職が、合併に<u>起因して</u>、余剰人員とされた。
119	**caused by**	起因して
	The delay was <u>caused by</u> unforeseen technical issues.	この遅延は、予期せぬ技術的な問題に<u>起因して</u>いた。
120	**injured party**	被害者（末尾❾参照）
	The <u>injured party</u> sought compensation for damages incurred.	<u>被害者</u>は、発生した損害の賠償を求めた。
121	**period (of time)** [píəriəd]	期間
	The warranty covers a <u>period of time</u> of one year from the date of purchase.	保証<u>期間</u>は、購入日から1年間である。
122	**term** [tə́:rm]	期間
	The loan <u>term</u> was extended to accommodate the borrower's request.	融資<u>期間</u>は、借主の要望により延長された。
123	**denial** [dɪnáɪəl]	却下
	A request for the examination of a witness may be denied (<u>denial</u> of a request).	証人尋問の請求は、これを却下することができる（請求の<u>却下</u>）。
124	**dismissal** [dɪsmísəl]	棄却（請求棄却、控訴棄却）
	If the court of second instance finds the judgment in the first instance to be appropriate, it shall dismiss the appeal with prejudice (<u>dismissal</u> of an appeal with prejudice).	控訴裁判所は、第一審判決を相当とするときは、控訴を棄却しなければならない（<u>控訴棄却</u>）。
125	**voting right**	議決権
	Each shareholder possesses <u>voting rights</u> proportional to their shares.	各株主は、株式に比例した<u>議決権</u>を有する。

RANK 1

126	**period of time** The project will span a <u>period of time</u> of three months.	期限 プロジェクトの**期限**は、3ヶ月である。
127	**minutes** [mínəts] The <u>minutes</u> of the meeting will be distributed to all members by next week.	議事録 会議の**議事録**は、来週までに全メンバーに配布される。
128	**regulation** [règjəléɪʃən] The new <u>regulation</u> affects all financial transactions within the sector.	規制 新しい**規制**は、業界のすべての金融取引に影響する。
129	**institution of prosecution** The <u>institution of prosecution</u> followed the arrest of the CEO.	起訴（末尾❿参照） CEOの逮捕に続いて、**起訴**が行われた。
130	**Regulation** [règjuléɪʃən] The <u>Regulation</u> on data protection comes into effect next month.	規則（法形式が「省令」の場合） データ保護の**規則**（省令）が、来月施行される。
131	**chairperson** [tʃérpə̀ːrsən] The <u>chairperson</u> called the meeting to order at 10 a.m.	議長 午前10時、**議長**が会議の開会を宣言した。
132	**fundamental human rights** The constitution protects <u>fundamental human rights</u> for all citizens.	基本的人権 憲法は、すべての国民の**基本的人権**を守っている。
133	**duty** [dúːti] Every employee has a <u>duty</u> to comply with company policies.	義務 すべての従業員には、会社の規則を遵守する**義務**がある。
134	**obligation** [àːbləgéɪʃən] The <u>obligation</u> to report any conflicts of interest is outlined in the handbook.	義務 利益相反を報告する**義務**は、ハンドブックに概説されている。
135	**affixing the name and seal** <u>Affixing the name and seal</u> to the document certifies its authenticity.	記名押印 文書に**記名押印**することで、その文書が真正であることを証明する。
136	**suspension** [səspénʃən] The <u>suspension</u> of the license was a direct result of non-compliance.	休止（一時休止）、停止 ライセンスの**停止**は、コンプライアンス違反の直接的な結果だった。

#	English	Japanese
137	**right to reimbursement**	**求償権（末尾⓫参照）**
	Article 442 of the Civil Code provides a <u>right to reimbursement</u> among joint and several obligors.	民法第442条は、連帯債務者間の**求償権**を定めている。
138	**mandatory provision**	**強行規定**
	This is a <u>mandatory provision</u> that cannot be modified or waived.	これは**強行規定**であり、変更又は放棄はできない。
139	**statement** [stéɪtmənt]	**①供述、②陳述、③申告**
	A person who submits a false <u>statement</u> for the purpose of having a criminal punishment imposed upon another person is punished.	人に刑事の処分を受けさせる目的で、虚偽の**申告**をした者は、処罰される。
140	**administration** [ædmìnɪstréɪʃən]	**①行政、②管理**
	The <u>administration</u> is responsible for the day-to-day operations of the facility.	**管理**部門は、施設の日々の運営に責任を負う。
141	**administrative organ**	**行政機関**
	The <u>administrative organ</u> decided to revise the existing local ordinance.	**行政機関**は、既存の条例を見直すことを決定した。
142	**compulsory auction**	**強制競売**
	A <u>compulsory auction</u> is scheduled for properties with unpaid taxes.	税金が未納の物件について、**強制競売**が予定されている。
143	**compulsory execution**	**強制執行**
	<u>Compulsory execution</u> of the judgment will proceed if payment is not received.	支払いがない場合は、判決の**強制執行**が行われる。
144	**administrative guidance**	**行政指導**
	The agency issued <u>administrative guidance</u> to all regulated entities.	同庁は、すべての規制対象事業者に対して**行政指導**を行った。
145	**administrative disposition**	**行政処分**
	The <u>administrative disposition</u> was challenged in court by the affected party.	この**行政処分**は、影響を受けた当事者によって法廷で争われた。
146	**compulsory performance**	**強制履行**
	<u>Compulsory performance</u> may be ordered by the court in cases of non-compliance.	不履行の場合、裁判所によって**強制履行**が命じられることがある。
147	**managing member**	**業務執行社員**
	The <u>managing member</u> is tasked with overseeing the project's completion.	その**業務執行社員**は、プロジェクトの完了を監督するのが仕事だ。

RANK 1

#	Term	Japanese
148	**entrustment of operation**	業務の委託
	The <u>entrustment of operation</u> to a third party requires board approval.	第三者に<u>業務</u>の<u>委託</u>をするには、取締役会の承認が必要である。
149	**permission** [pərmíʃən]	①許可、②認可
	An executor may resign from his or her duties with the <u>permission</u> of the family court.	遺言執行者は、家庭裁判所の<u>許可</u>を得て、その任務を辞することができる。
150	**misrepresentation** [mìsrəprɪzentéɪʃən]	虚偽表示
	The lawsuit was based on allegations of <u>misrepresentation</u> in the advertisement.	この訴訟は、広告に<u>虚偽表示</u>があったという主張に基づいている。
151	**resident** [rézɪdənt]	居住者
	The <u>resident</u> filed a complaint regarding noise disturbances.	<u>居住者</u>が、騒音に対して、苦情を申し立てた。
152	**place of residence**	居住地
	The resident must update their <u>place of residence</u> within 30 days of moving.	入居者は、転居後30日以内に、<u>居住地</u>を更新しなければならない。
153	**denial** [dɪnáɪəl]	①拒絶、②否認
	A <u>denial</u> of the application will be notified within two weeks.	申請が<u>拒絶</u>された場合は、2週間以内に通知される。
154	**refusal** [rəfjúːzəl]	拒絶
	The <u>refusal</u> to comply resulted in further legal action.	法令遵守を<u>拒絶</u>した結果、さらなる法的措置がとられた。
155	**grant** [grænt]	許諾
	The <u>grant</u> of the license was approved by the committee.	ライセンスの<u>許諾</u>は、委員会により、承認された。
156	**rejection** [rɪdʒékʃən]	拒否
	After careful consideration, the committee announced its <u>rejection</u> of the proposal.	慎重に検討した結果、委員会は、提案の<u>拒否</u>を発表した。
157	**imprisonment without work**	禁錮
	<u>Imprisonment without work</u> was abolished in favor of rehabilitation programs.	<u>禁錮</u>刑は廃止され、更生プログラムが採用された。

158	**prohibition** [pròʊəbíʃən]	禁止
	The <u>prohibition</u> on public gatherings was lifted following the improvement in public health.	公の集会の<u>禁止</u>は、公衆衛生の改善に伴い、解除された。
159	**national government organ**	国の機関
	The <u>national government organ</u> is responsible for implementing the new health regulations.	<u>国の機関</u>は、新しい健康に関する規則を実施する責任を負う。
160	**partnership** [pá:rtnərʃɪp]	（民法上の）組合
	The <u>partnership</u> dissolved due to irreconcilable differences between the partners.	<u>組合</u>は、パートナー間の和解しがたい不和のため、解消した。
161	**punishment** [pʌ́nɪʃmənt]	刑
	The <u>punishment</u> for the crime includes a fine.	その罪に対する<u>刑</u>は、罰金を含む。
162	**seal to confirm page continuation**	契印
	The document had a <u>seal to confirm page continuation</u> on every sheet.	この文書には、すべてのページに<u>契印</u>がなされていた。
163	**warning** [wɔ́:rnɪŋ]	警告
	A <u>warning</u> was issued to the company for not adhering to environmental standards.	環境基準を遵守していないとして、<u>警告</u>が、同社に対して、発出された。
164	**police officer**	警察官
	The <u>police officer</u> took the report and began an investigation immediately.	<u>警察官</u>は、通報を受けて、すぐに捜査を開始した。
165	**financial statements**	計算書類
	The company's <u>financial statements</u> were approved.	会社の<u>計算書類</u>は、承認された。
166	**pending** [péndɪŋ]	係属
	Once a judicial decision for a transfer becomes final and binding, the litigation is deemed to have been <u>pending</u> before the court to which it has been transferred since it was first brought to the initial court.	移送の裁判が確定したときは、訴訟は、初めから移送を受けた裁判所に<u>係属</u>していたものとみなす。
167	**auction** [ɔ́:kʃən]	競売
	The <u>auction</u> of the assets is scheduled for next month.	資産の<u>競売</u>は、来月に予定されている。

RANK 1

RANK 1

168	**contract** [ká:ntrækt]	①契約、②契約書
	The <u>contract</u> between the two parties was signed yesterday.	昨日、両者の<u>契約</u>が調印された。
169	**resolution** [rèzəlú:ʃən]	決議
	The <u>resolution</u> to increase capital was passed during the shareholders' meeting.	増資の<u>決議</u>は、株主総会で可決された。
170	**payment** [péɪmənt]	①窓口での支払・決済など、②給付、③払込、④弁済
	The <u>payment</u> must be made within 30 days to avoid penalties.	罰則を避けるためには、<u>支払</u>は、30日以内に行わなければならない。
171	**settlement** [sétəlmənt]	決済
	The <u>settlement</u> is scheduled next Monday.	<u>決済</u>は、次の月曜日に予定されている。
172	**fiscal year end**	決算期（決算期末の期日）
	The <u>fiscal year</u> end is approaching, and all departments are finalizing their reports.	<u>決算期</u>が近づき、すべての部署が報告書をまとめている。
173	**decision** [dɪsíʒən]	決定（末尾⓬参照）
	The <u>decision</u> by the court will be announced next week.	裁判所の<u>決定</u>は、来週公表される。
174	**ruling** [rú:lɪŋ]	①決定（末尾⓬参照）、②判決
	The <u>ruling</u> favored the plaintiff, granting them damages.	<u>判決</u>は、原告を支持し、損害賠償を認めた。
175	**written decision**	決定書
	The <u>written decision</u> detailed the reasons behind the judge's ruling.	<u>決定書</u>には、判事の決定理由の詳細が記されていた。
176	**authority** [əθɔ́:rəti]	権限
	The <u>authority</u> to make such decisions lies with the board of directors.	この決定を下す<u>権限</u>は、取締役会にある。
177	**power** [páʊər]	権限
	The <u>power</u> to enact legislation resides with the national parliament.	立法の<u>権限</u>は、国会にある。

178	**plaintiff** [pléɪntəf]	原告
	The <u>plaintiff</u> filed a lawsuit seeking compensation for damages.	<u>原告</u>は、損害賠償を求めて訴えを提起した。
179	**examination** [ɪgzæmənéɪʃən]	①証拠の取調べ、②身体検査
	The <u>examination</u> of the evidence will take place next Tuesday.	<u>証拠の取調べ</u>は、来週火曜日に行われる。
180	**inspection** [ɪnspékʃən]	①検品、②閲覧、③立入検査
	The <u>inspection</u> revealed several safety violations at the factory.	<u>立入検査</u>では、工場でのいくつかの安全違反が明らかになった。
181	**reduction** [rədʌ́kʃən]	減殺
	Chapter 7 of the Criminal Code provides actions not constituting crimes and <u>reduction</u> or remission of punishment.	刑法の第7章は、犯罪の不成立及び刑の<u>減殺</u>・免除を定めている。
182	**public prosecutor**	検察官
	The <u>public prosecutor</u> decided to charge the suspect with fraud.	<u>検察官</u>は、被疑者を詐欺罪で起訴することを決定した。
183	**public prosecutors office**	検察庁
	The <u>public prosecutors office</u> has a high success rate in prosecuting cases.	<u>検察庁</u>の起訴の成功率は高い。
184	**withholding (at source)** [wɪðˈhoʊldɪŋ]	源泉徴収
	<u>Withholding at source</u> simplifies tax collection for employers.	<u>源泉徴収</u>は、雇用者の徴税を簡素化する。
185	**withholding tax**	源泉徴収税
	The <u>withholding tax</u> on dividends will be reduced starting next fiscal year.	配当金の<u>源泉徴収税</u>が、来年度から引き下げられる。
186	**Constitution** [kɑ̀nstətúːʃən]	憲法
	The <u>Constitution</u> guarantees the protection of individual freedoms.	<u>憲法</u>は、個人の自由の保護を保障している。
187	**right** [ráɪt]	権利
	Every citizen has the <u>right</u> to travel within legal limits.	すべての市民は、合法的な範囲内で旅行の自由を享受する<u>権利</u>を持っている。

RANK 1

188 abuse of right / 権利の濫用
Abuse of right occurs when a legal right is used to cause harm intentionally.
権利の濫用とは、法的権利が故意に害をもたらすために利用されるときに生じる。

189 person entitled to / 権利を有する者
The person entitled to the estate must submit a document within six months.
遺産を受け取る権利を有する者は、6ヶ月以内に書類を提出しなければならない。

190 intention [ìntén(t)ʃən] / 故意
A person lacking knowledge of law does not mean a lack of intention to commit a crime.
法律を知らなかったとしても、そのことによって、故意がなかったとすることはできない。

191 paragraph [pǽrəgræ̀f] / 項
A juridical act in contravention of the provisions of the preceding paragraph is voidable.
前項の規定に反する法律行為は、取り消すことができる。

192 item [áɪtəm] / 号
The provisions of the preceding paragraph apply mutatis mutandis to the notice referred to in paragraph 1, item 3.
前項の規定は、第1項第3号の通知について準用する。

193 act [ǽkt] / 行為（末尾⑬参照）
Even when a final and binding decision has been rendered by a foreign judiciary against the criminal act of a person, it does not preclude further punishment in Japan with regard to the same act.
外国において確定裁判を受けた者であっても、同一の行為について更に処罰することを妨げない。

194 conduct [kɑ́:ndəkt] / 行為（末尾⑬参照）
The conduct of the company is under investigation for potential breaches.
会社の当該行為は、（契約）違反の可能性があるとして、調査中である。

195 agreement [əgríːmənt] / 合意
The agreement between the two companies was reached after months of negotiation.
両社の合意は、数カ月にわたる交渉の末に成立した。

196 official seal / 公印
The document must bear the official seal to be considered legally binding.
法的拘束力を持つとみなされるためには、公印が押印されていなければならない。

#	英語	日本語
197	**public welfare** Laws must be congruent with the <u>public welfare</u> to be enforceable.	公共の福祉 法律が強制力を持つためには、<u>公共の福祉</u>に合致していなければならない。
198	**public interest** The project serves the <u>public interest</u> by providing free educational resources.	公共の利益 このプロジェクトは、無料の教育リソースを提供することで、<u>公共の利益</u>に貢献している。
199	**exercise** [éksərsàız] The <u>exercise</u> of rights must be in accordance with the law.	行使 権利の<u>行使</u>は、法律に従わなければならない。
200	**renewal** [rınúːəl] The <u>renewal</u> of the contract is scheduled for next month.	更新 契約<u>更新</u>は、来月に予定されている。
201	**correction** [kərékʃən] The <u>correction</u> was made to address the discrepancies found.	①訂正、②更正、③補正 今回の<u>訂正</u>は、発見された矛盾に対処するために行われた。
202	**fair** [fér] The trade was deemed <u>fair</u> by both parties involved.	公正な この取引は、関係者双方にとって<u>公正な</u>ものであった。
203	**appeal (to the court of second instance)** [əpíːl] The <u>appeal to the court of second instance</u> was filed on Friday.	控訴 控訴は、金曜日に提起された。
204	**dismissal of prosecution** The <u>dismissal of prosecution</u> was a result of defendant's death.	公訴棄却 <u>公訴棄却</u>は、被告人の死亡によるものだった。
205	**binding effect** A judicial decision for a transfer which has <u>binding effect</u> on the court that has accepted the transferred case.	拘束力 裁判所に対して<u>拘束力</u>のある移送の裁判は、移送を受けた裁判所を拘束する。
206	**charged fact** The <u>charged fact</u> was disputed by the defense attorney.	公訴事実 弁護人は、<u>公訴事実</u>を争った。

RANK 1

RANK 1

207 second sentence
The <u>second sentence</u> of the Article clarifies the responsibilities of the involved parties.

後段
条文の<u>後段</u>は、関係者の責任を明確にしている。

208 high court
The <u>high court</u> is set to review the appeal next month.

高等裁判所
<u>高等裁判所</u>は、来月、この控訴を審理することになっている。

209 oral argument
<u>Oral argument</u> is scheduled for the end of the quarter.

口頭弁論
<u>口頭弁論</u>は、四半期末に予定されている。

210 record of oral argument
The <u>record of oral argument</u> was shared with the attorney.

口頭弁論調書
<u>口頭弁論調書</u>は、弁護士に共有された。

211 date for oral argument
The <u>date for oral argument</u> has been set for March 15th.

口頭弁論の期日
<u>口頭弁論の期日</u>は、3月15日に設定された。

212 conclusion of oral argument
The <u>conclusion of oral argument</u> made the attorney relieved.

口頭弁論の終結
<u>口頭弁論の終結</u>は、弁護士を安堵させた。

213 all oral arguments and the result of the examination of evidence
<u>All oral arguments and the result of the examination of evidence</u> are the basis of judgement.

口頭弁論の全趣旨及び証拠調べの結果
<u>口頭弁論の全趣旨及び証拠調べの結果</u>は、判決の基礎となる。

214 trial date
The <u>trial date</u> has been postponed to accommodate witness availability.

公判期日
<u>公判期日</u>は、証人の都合に合わせて延期された。

215 trial record
The <u>trial record</u> was carefully reviewed by both the defense and prosecution.

公判調書
<u>公判調書</u>は、弁護側及び検察側の双方によって慎重に検討された。

216 open court
The case will be heard in <u>open court</u> next week.

公判廷
この事件は、来週、<u>公判廷</u>で審理される。

217 trial procedure
If the <u>trial procedure</u> has been stayed due to the insanity of the defendant after a trial has begun, the trial procedure must be renewed.

公判手続
開廷後、被告人の心神喪失により<u>公判手続</u>を停止した場合には、公判手続を更新しなければならない。

218 the date of promulgation
<u>The date of promulgation</u> is awaited by all parties involved.

公布の日
関係者は、<u>公布の日</u>を待ち望んでいる。

219	**official document**	公文書
	The <u>official document</u> was sealed and delivered yesterday.	<u>公文書</u>は、昨日、封印され配達された。
220	**(affirmative) defense** [diféns]	抗弁
	The <u>(affirmative) defense</u> argued that the act was done in self-defense.	弁護側は、その行為が正当防衛のために行われたと<u>抗弁</u>した。
221	**public duty**	（具体的な）公務
	<u>Public duty</u> requires officials to act in the community's best interest.	<u>公務</u>は、役人が地域社会の最善の利益のために行動することを要求する。
222	**public service**	（性質としての）公務
	With regard to the application of the Penal Code, the members of a council are deemed to be officials that are engaged in <u>public service</u> pursuant to laws and regulations.	審議会の委員は、刑法の適用については、法令により<u>公務</u>に従事する職員とみなす。
223	**public employee**	公務員
	The <u>public employee</u> carefully drafts documents.	<u>公務員</u>は慎重に書類を作成する。
224	**effect** [ɪfékt]	効力
	A disposition on the petition takes <u>effect</u> when notice thereof is given by a method that is considered to be appropriate.	申立てに関する処分は、相当と認める方法で告知することによって、その<u>効力</u>を生ずる。
225	**cease to be effective**	効力を失う（末尾⓮参照）
	The policy will <u>cease to be effective</u> at the end of the year.	この指針は、年末に<u>効力を失う</u>。
226	**expire** [ɪkspáɪr]	効力を失う（末尾⓮参照）
	The membership will <u>expire</u> unless renewed before the deadline.	会員資格は、期限内に更新しない限り、<u>効力を失う</u>。
227	**become effective**	効力を生ずる
	Renewal of prescription period does not <u>become effective</u> against co-owners unless it is made against each co-owner that exercises the servitude.	共有者に対する時効の更新は、地役権を行使する各共有者に対してしなければ、その<u>効力を生ずる</u>ことはない。
228	**subsidiary company**	子会社
	The <u>subsidiary company</u> was established to enter the Asian market.	<u>子会社</u>は、アジア市場に参入するために設立された。

RANK 1

229	**nationality** [næ̀ʃənǽləti]	国籍
	The nationality of the applicant plays no role in the selection process.	応募者の**国籍**は、選考プロセスに影響を与えない。
230	**criminal complaint**	告訴
	The criminal complaint was filed by the affected party yesterday.	**告訴**は、昨日、被害を受けた当事者によって提出された。
231	**domestic** [dəméstɪk]	国内
	The policy applies to all domestic transactions.	この指針は、すべての**国内**取引に適用される。
232	**individual** [ìndəvídʒəwəl]	個人
	The individual's rights were protected under the new legislation.	**個人**の権利は、新しい法律の下で保護された。
233	**personal information**	個人情報
	The individual's consent was obtained before providing their personal information.	本人の同意が、**個人情報**を提供する前に、取得されていた。
234	**bond (certificate)** [bɑnd]	債券
	The bond certificate is a critical document for the investment.	**債券**証書は、投資にとって重要な書類である。
235	**claim** [kléɪm]	債権
	A claim may be assigned.	**債権**は、譲渡することができる。
236	**creditor** [krédətər]	債権者（金銭債権や倒産法の場合）（末尾⑮参照）
	The creditor must provide evidence of the outstanding debt.	**債権者**は、未払い債務の証拠を提出しなければならない。
237	**obligee** [ɑ̀blɪdʒíː]	債権者（末尾⑮参照）
	The obligee has the right to demand full repayment.	**債権者**は、全額返済を請求する権利を有する。
238	**Supreme Court**	最高裁判所
	The Supreme Court is the final authority on legal matters.	**最高裁判所**は、法律問題に関する最終的な権限を持っている。
239	**demand** [dɪmǽnd]	①（債務履行の）催告、②請求、③督促
	The demand for payment was issued after multiple warnings.	支払**督促**は、複数回の警告を受けた後に発出された。

240	**assets** [ǽsəts]	財産
	The <u>assets</u> of the company are being assessed by the liquidator.	会社の<u>財産</u>は、清算人によって査定されている。
241	**property** [prάːpərti]	財産・財物
	A person who steals the <u>property</u> of another person commits the crime of theft and is punished by imprisonment for not more than 10 years or a fine of not more than 500,000 yen.	他人の<u>財物</u>を窃取した者は、窃盗の罪とし、10年以下の懲役又は50万円以下の罰金に処する。
242	**property right**	財産権
	A <u>property right</u> is extinguished by prescription if not exercised within 20 years from the time when the right became exercisable.	<u>財産権</u>は、権利を行使することができる時から20年間行使しないときは、時効によって消滅する。
243	**reappointment** [rìəpɔ́ɪntmənt]	再任
	The <u>reappointment</u> of the board member was approved yesterday.	取締役の<u>再任</u>は、昨日、承認された。
244	**judge** [dʒʌ́dʒ]	裁判官
	The <u>judge</u> is known for his fair rulings.	その<u>裁判官</u>は、公正な判決を下すことで知られている。
245	**power of judicial decision**	裁判権
	The power of supervision does not affect the <u>power of judicial decision</u> of judges.	（司法行政の）監督権は、裁判官の<u>裁判権</u>に影響を及ぼすことはない。
246	**presiding judge**	裁判長
	The designation of court dates are made by the <u>presiding judge</u>.	期日の指定は、<u>裁判長</u>が行う。
247	**court proceedings**	裁判手続（末尾⑯参照）
	When a motion to challenge has been filed, <u>court proceedings</u> must be stayed.	忌避の申立があったときは、<u>裁判手続</u>を停止しなければならない。
248	**judicial proceedings**	裁判手続（末尾⑯参照）
	Rules of Criminal Procedure must be construed in a manner that ensure the speedy and fair <u>judicial proceedings</u> envisaged under the Constitution.	刑事訴訟規則は、憲法の所期する<u>裁判手続</u>の迅速と公正とを図るようにこれを解釈しなければならない。

RANK 1

RANK 1

249	**debt** [dét] As a general rule, creditors who owe <u>debts</u> to a liquidating stock company cannot effect the set-off.	債務（金銭債務） 清算株式会社に対して**債務**を負担する者は、原則として、相殺をすることができない。
250	**obligation** [à:bləɡéɪʃən] The <u>obligation</u> to report any changes is specified in the contract.	債務・義務（債務一般） 変更の報告**義務**は、契約書に明記されている。
251	**debtor** [détər] The <u>debtor</u> was unable to meet the repayment schedule.	債務者（金銭債権や倒産法の場合） **債務者**は、返済計画を守ることができなかった。
252	**obligor** [àbləɡɔ́r] The <u>obligor</u> is responsible for fulfilling the terms of the contract.	債務者 **債務者**は、契約条件を履行する責任を負う。
253	**financial statements** A stock company must retain its <u>financial statements</u> for ten years from the time of preparation of the financial statements.	財務諸表 株式会社は、**財務諸表**を作成した時から10年間、当該計算書類を保存しなければならない。
254	**insolvency** [ìnsá:lvənsi] Chapter 11 of the Bankruptcy Act provides special provisions when foreign <u>insolvency</u> proceedings exist.	①債務超過（無資力）、②倒産 破産法第11章は、外国**倒産**処理手続がある場合の特則を定めている。
255	**assumption of obligation** The <u>assumption of obligation</u> was formalized in a signed agreement.	債務引受 **債務引受**は、署名された契約書によって正式に実行された。
256	**default** [dɪfɔ́:lt] If there is a <u>default</u> with respect to a claim secured by a mortgage, the mortgage extends to the fruits of the mortgaged immovables derived after the default.	債務不履行（末尾⓭参照） 抵当権は、その担保する債権について**債務不履行**があったときは、その後に生じた抵当不動産の果実に及ぶ。
257	**non-performance** Upon tendering the performance, the obligor is relieved from any and all responsibilities which may arise from the <u>non-performance</u> of the obligation.	債務不履行（末尾⓭参照） 債務者は、弁済の提供の時から、**債務不履行**によって生ずべき責任を免れる。

258	**charged offense**	**罪名（審理対象としての罪名）**
	Arrest warrants must contain the <u>charged offense</u> and other particulars as prescribed in the Rules of Court.	逮捕状には、被疑者の**罪名**その他裁判所の規則で定める事項を記載しなければならない。
259	**retroactively** [rètrəǽktɪvli]	**さかのぼって**
	The law applies <u>retroactively</u> to liabilities arose within the last year.	この法律は、過去1年以内に発生した責任に**さかのぼって**適用される。
260	**fraud** [frɔ́:d]	**詐欺**
	<u>Fraud</u> investigations have resulted in several high-profile arrests.	**詐欺**の捜査の結果、何人もの有名人が逮捕された。
261	**mistake** [mɪstéɪk]	**錯誤**
	A manifestation of intention is voidable if it is based on <u>mistakes</u>.	意思表示は、**錯誤**に基づいている場合、無効となる。
262	**deletion** [dɪlíʃən]	**削除**
	The mistake in the contract led to a mutual agreement for its <u>deletion</u>.	契約書に誤りがあったため、当該誤りを**削除**することで合意した。
263	**attachment** [ətǽtʃmənt]	**差押え**
	The <u>attachment</u> of assets was ordered by the court.	資産の**差押え**は、裁判所によって命じられた。
264	**seizure** [síːʒər]	**①差押え、②押収**
	When there is no rendition for the confiscating of seized objects, the decision to release the <u>seizure</u> is deemed to have been rendered.	押収した物について、没収の言渡がないときは、**押収**を解く言渡があったものとする。
265	**seizure warrant**	**差押状**
	The <u>seizure warrant</u> must be shown to the person who is to be subject to said disposition.	**差押状**は、処分を受ける者にこれを示さなければならない。
266	**transfer of possession by instruction**	**指図による占有移転**
	<u>Transfer of possession by instruction</u> requires written consent in this agreement.	本契約において、**指図による占有移転**には、書面による同意が必要である。

RANK 1

267	**homicide** [háːməsàid]	**殺人**
	Article 199 (<u>Homicide</u>): A person who kills another person is punished by the death penalty or imprisonment for life or for a definite term of not less than 5 years.	第199条（**殺人**）：人を殺した者は、死刑又は無期若しくは5年以上の懲役に処する。
268	**miscellaneous provision**	**雑則**
	<u>Miscellaneous provisions</u> cover various aspects not detailed in main sections.	**雑則**は、本則に詳述されていない様々な部分を補足している。
269	**overtime work**	**時間外労働**
	<u>Overtime work</u> regulations have been updated to improve worker welfare.	**時間外労働**に係る規制は、労働者の福祉を向上させるために改正された。
270	**direction** [dərékʃən]	**指揮**
	Detention warrants are, under the <u>direction</u> of a public prosecutor, executed by a public prosecutor's assistant officer or a judicial police official.	勾留状は、検察官の**指揮**によって、検察事務官又は司法警察職員がこれを執行する。
271	**time of commencement**	**始期**
	The <u>time of commencement</u> for the contract is April 1st.	契約の**始期**は、4月1日である。
272	**security deposit**	**敷金**
	The <u>security deposit</u> will be returned by the end of this month.	**敷金**は、月末までに返還される。
273	**magnetic disk**	**磁気ディスク**
	The "register" means a book in which a registration record is recorded, and which is prepared in the form of a <u>magnetic disk</u>.	登記簿とは、登記記録が記録される帳簿であって、**磁気ディスク**をもって調製するものをいう。
274	**fund** [fʌ́nd]	**資金、基金**
	Chapter 2, Section 5 of the Act on General Incorporated Associations and General Incorporated Foundations provides <u>funds</u>.	一般社団法人及び一般財団法人に関する法律第2章第5節は、**基金**について定める。
275	**death penalty**	**死刑**
	When a case is punishable by the <u>death penalty</u>, the trial may not be convened without the attendance of defense counsel.	**死刑**を審理する場合には、弁護人がなければ開廷することはできない。
276	**accident** [ǽksədənt]	**事故**
	The <u>accident</u> investigation is focused on identifying the cause.	**事故**調査は、原因究明に重点を置く。

277	**immediately following paragraph**	次項
	The <u>immediately following paragraph</u> clarifies the scope of the regulation.	<u>次項</u>は、規制の範囲を明確にしている。
278	**prescription** [prəskrípʃən]	時効（取得時効・消滅時効の両方を含む）（末尾⑰参照）
	The <u>prescription</u> is retroactive to the commencement day.	<u>時効</u>の効力は、その起算日にさかのぼる。
279	**statute of limitations**	時効（末尾⑰参照）
	The <u>statute of limitations</u> is completed upon the lapse of the time periods with regard to crimes causing the death of a person and punishable with imprisonment without work or a greater punishment (except for those punishable by the death penalty).	<u>時効</u>は、人を死亡させた罪であって禁錮以上の刑に当たるもの（死刑に当たるものを除く。）については、期間を経過することによって完成する。
280	**on one's own account**	自己の計算において
	The officer of the listed company has conducted purchases <u>on his own account</u>.	上場会社の役員が、<u>自己の計算において</u>、買付けを行った。
281	**facts** [fǽkts]	事実
	The <u>facts</u> of the case are being closely examined by legal experts.	この事件の<u>事実</u>関係は、法律の専門家によって綿密に調査されている。
282	**de facto**	事実上
	A "cohabiting relative whose living expenses are paid from the same resources" means a person whose relationship with the person is, <u>de facto</u>, that of husband and wife, even though they have not registered a marriage.	「生計を一にする同居の親族」とは、婚姻の届出をしていないがその人物と<u>事実上</u>夫婦の関係にある者をいう。
283	**fact finding**	事実の認定
	<u>Fact finding</u> is crucial for resolving disputes fairly.	<u>事実の認定</u>は、紛争を公正に解決するために重要である。
284	**immediately following Article**	次条
	The <u>immediately following Article</u> provides further details on exceptions.	<u>次条</u>は、例外の詳細を定めている。
285	**guideline** [gáɪdlàɪn]	指針
	A certified organization must endeavor to prepare a <u>guideline</u> that are in line with the purport of the provisions of this Act.	認定団体は、この法律の規定の趣旨に沿った<u>指針</u>を作成するよう努めなければならない。

RANK 1

RANK 1

286	**contribute** [kəntríbjut]	①資する、②出資する
	The terms used in this Regulation carry the meanings of the terms used in the "Act on Anonymized Data That Are Meant to <u>Contribute</u> to Research and Development".	この規則において使用する用語は、「研究開発に**資する**ための匿名加工情報に関する法律」において使用する用語の例による。
287	**subcontractor** [sʌbkáːntræktər]	**下請負人** （例：労働基準法第87条）
	The main contractor has, by written contract, had a <u>subcontractor</u> assume responsibility for the compensation.	元請負人が書面による契約で**下請負人**に補償を引き受けさせた。
288	**enforcement** [enfɔ́ːrsmənt]	（法）執行
	There was the J-FTC's <u>enforcement</u>.	日本の公正取引委員会の（法）**執行**があった。
289	**execution** [èksəkjúːʃən]	執行
	A judge is disqualified from <u>execution</u> of its duties when the judge is a relative of the victim.	裁判官は、裁判官が被害者の親族である場合には、職務の**執行**から除斥される。
290	**implementation** [ìmpləmentéɪʃən]	①実行、②遂行
	The court found the existence of circumstances prejudicial to the <u>implementation</u> of the liquidation.	裁判所は、清算の**遂行**に著しい支障を来すべき事情があることを認めた。
291	**be prohibited**	してはならない（末尾⓭参照）
	Smoking in the office <u>is prohibited</u> for health and safety reasons.	健康と安全上の理由からオフィス内で喫煙**してはならない**。
292	**must not**	してはならない・あってはならない（末尾⓭参照）
	A public prosecutor's designation <u>must not</u> unduly restrict the rights of the suspect to prepare for defense.	検察官の指定は、被疑者が防御の準備をする権利を不当に制限するようなもので**あってはならない**。
293	**branch office**	支店
	The <u>branch office</u> plays a crucial role in regional operations.	**支店**は、地域の運営において重要な役割を果たしている。
294	**must** [mʌ́st]	しなければならない（末尾⓭参照）
	A borrower <u>must</u> make use of the thing in compliance with the method of use specified by the contract.	借主は、契約によって定まった用法に従い、その物の使用を**しなければならない**。

295	**shall** [ʃǽl] All members **shall** attend the annual general meeting.	**しなければならない（末尾⓭参照）** すべての社員は、年次社員総会に出席**しなければならない**。
296	**admission** [ædmíʃən] A document which contains an **admission** of a disadvantageous fact may not be used as evidence.	**①自認・承認、②自白（民事）** 被告人に不利益な事実の**承認**を内容とする書面は、これを証拠とすることができない。
297	**control** [kəntróul] "Parent Company" means any entity which is a corporation who **controls** the management of a stock company.	**支配** 親会社とは、当該株式会社の経営を**支配**している法人をいう。
298	**confession** [kənféʃən] The suspect made a full **confession** during the interrogation.	**自白** 被疑者は、取調べで完全な**自白**をした。
299	**date of payment** The **date of payment** is set for the 30th of each month.	**支払期日** **支払期日**は、毎月30日に設定されている。
300	**payment date** Share option holders may not exercise the share options for subscription unless they pay in the entire amount by the **payment date**.	**支払期日** 新株予約権者は、**支払期日**までに全額の払込みをしないときは、当該募集新株予約権を行使することができない。
301	**suspension of payments** **Suspension of payments** was announced due to liquidity issues.	**支払の停止** 流動性の問題から、**支払の停止**が発表された。
302	**grace of payment** **Grace of payment** was granted to affected customers.	**支払の猶予** 影響を受けた顧客には、**支払の猶予**が与えられた。
303	**inability to pay debts (as they become due)** The company is facing **inability to pay debts as they become due**.	**支払不能** その会社は、**支払不能**に直面している。
304	**capital** [kǽpətəl] The amount of stated **capital** of a stock company is the amount of properties contributed by persons who become shareholders at the share issue.	**資本** 株式会社の**資本**金の額は、株式の発行に際して株主となる者が当該株式会社に対して払込みした財産の額とする。

RANK 1

RANK 1

305 stated capital — 資本金
The <u>stated capital</u> is recorded in the company's commercial registry.
<u>資本金</u>は、商業登記簿に記載されている。

306 outside company auditor — 社外監査役（末尾❽参照）
The <u>outside company auditor</u> discussed the annual financial report.
<u>社外監査役</u>が、年次財務報告書を議論した。

307 outside director — 社外取締役
An <u>outside director</u> was appointed to enhance board diversity.
取締役会の多様性を高めるために、<u>社外取締役</u>が任命された。

308 (corporate) bond [bɑnd] — 社債
The <u>corporate bond</u> issuance was oversubscribed by investors.
<u>社債</u>の発行は、投資家の応募を上回った。

309 rules of employment — 就業規則
<u>Rules of employment</u> were updated to comply with new labor laws.
新しい労働法に準拠するため、<u>就業規則</u>が更新された。

310 employee [emplóιi] — 従業者
The <u>employee</u> handbook contains all workplace policies and procedures.
<u>従業者</u>向けハンドブックには、職場のすべての規則と手続が記載されている。

311 address [ǽdrəs] — 住所
The <u>address</u> change must be reported to the authority.
<u>住所</u>変更は、当局に報告しなければならない。

312 domicile [dάməsàil] — 住所
The legal <u>domicile</u> of the company is its registered address.
会社の<u>住所</u>は、登記上の住所である。

313 gross negligence — 重大な過失
<u>Gross negligence</u> led to a significant financial loss.
<u>重大な過失</u>が、大きな経済的損失につながった。

314 appropriation [əpròʊpriéιʃən] — 充当
The designation of the <u>appropriation</u> of the performance is effected through a manifestation of intention to the counterparty.
弁済の<u>充当</u>の指定は、相手方に対する意思表示によってする。

315 assumption (of office) [əsʌ́mpʃən] — 就任
The new CEO's <u>assumption of office</u> is scheduled for next Monday.
新しいCEOの<u>就任</u>は、来週月曜日の予定である。

#	英語	日本語
316	**inhabitant** [ɪnhǽbətənt] The <u>inhabitant</u> tax is calculated based on the place of residence.	住民（長期的な定住者） <u>住民</u>税は、居住地に基づいて計算される。
317	**principal office** The <u>principal office</u> relocation was completed last quarter.	主たる事務所 <u>主たる事務所</u>の移転は、前四半期に完了した。
318	**allegation** [æ̀ləgéɪʃən] The court may, upon hearing the opinions of the public prosecutor and the defense counsel, set deadlines for clarification of the <u>allegation</u>.	主張（末尾⓮参照） 裁判所は、検察官及び弁護人の意見を聴いた上で、<u>主張</u>を明らかにすべき期限を定めることができる。
319	**argument** [áːrgjəmənt] The <u>argument</u> presented in court was compelling and well-structured.	主張・弁論（末尾⓮参照） 法廷での<u>主張</u>（弁論）は説得力があり、構成もしっかりしていた。
320	**assertion** [əsə́ːrʃən] The presiding official must prepare a written report containing his or her opinion as to whether the <u>assertion</u> of the parties, concerning the facts which will be the cause of the anticipated adverse disposition, is justified.	主張（末尾⓮参照） 主宰者は、不利益処分の原因となる事実に対する当事者の<u>主張</u>に理由があるかどうかについての意見を記載した報告書を作成しなければならない。
321	**claim** [kléɪm] The <u>claim</u> for damages is based on the terms of the agreement.	主張（末尾⓮参照） 損害賠償請求の<u>主張</u>は、契約の条項に基づいている。
322	**application** [æ̀pləkéɪʃən] The <u>application</u> for the trademark will be submitted by the deadline.	①出願、②適用、③申立て 商標の<u>出願</u>は、期限までに提出する。
323	**applicant** [ǽplɪkənt] The <u>applicant</u> must provide all required documents.	①出願者、②申立人 <u>出願者</u>は、必要書類をすべて提出しなければならない。
324	**secondment** [sikɔ́ndmənt] <u>Secondment</u> to the overseas office will begin in July.	出向 海外事務所への<u>出向</u>は、7月から開始する。

#	English	Japanese
325	**class share**	種類株式
	Class share dividends may vary from those of other shares.	種類株式の配当金は、他の株式の配当金と異なる場合がある。
326	**class shareholder**	種類株主
	The class shareholder meeting is scheduled for the spring.	種類株主総会は、春に予定されている。
327	**governing law**	準拠法
	Governing law clauses specify which legal system applies to the contract.	準拠法条項は、どの法制度が契約に適用されるかを規定する。
328	**brief** [bríf]	準備書面
	The legal brief summarizes the case's key points and arguments.	準備書面は、この裁判の重要なポイントと主張を要約したものである。
329	**apply mutatis mutandis**	準用する
	This clause shall apply mutatis mutandis to similar situations not directly covered.	本条項は、直接規定されていない類似の状況にも準用される。
330	**Chapter** [tʃǽptər]	章
	Chapter IV sets out with corporate governance issues.	第4章には、コーポレート・ガバナンスが規定されている。
331	**Article** [ɑ́rtikl]	条
	Article 10 outlines the rights and responsibilities of shareholders.	第10条は、株主の権利と責任について概説している。
332	**reimbursement** [rìːmbə́ːrsmənt]	費用の償還
	Reimbursement for travel expenses is processed within two weeks.	旅行に関する費用の償還は、2週間以内に行われる。
333	**commercial custom**	商慣習
	Commercial custom can influence the interpretation of contracts.	商慣習は、契約の解釈に影響を与えることがある。
334	**commercial registration**	商業登記
	Commercial registration must be completed before starting operations.	営業開始前に、商業登記が完了していなければならない。
335	**commercial register**	商業登記簿
	The commercial register lists all officially recognized businesses.	商業登記簿には、公的に認められたすべての事業が記載されている。

RANK 1

336	**succession** [səkséʃən]	承継
	Succession of business is critical for family-owned enterprises.	家族経営企業にとって、事業の**承継**は極めて重要である。
337	**condition** [kəndíʃən]	条件
	A juridical act subject to a condition precedent becomes effective upon fulfillment of the condition precedent.	停止条件付法律行為は、停止**条件**が成就した時からその効力を生ずる。
338	**evidence** [évədəns]	証拠
	There is evidence collected support the claim of patent infringement.	特許侵害の主張を裏付ける収集された**証拠**がある。
339	**trade name**	商号
	The trade name is a key asset of the business.	**商号**は、事業の重要な資産である。
340	**(final) appeal** [əpíːl]	上告
	The final appeal in the case was broadcasted.	当該事件の**上告**が、報道された。
341	**examination of evidence**	証拠調べ
	Examination of evidence will determine the case's outcome.	**証拠調べ**が勝敗を左右する。
342	**employer** [emplɔ́iər]	使用者
	The employer announced a new wellness program for employees.	**使用者**は、雇用者のための新しい福利厚生プログラムを発表した。
343	**notice of calling**	招集通知
	Notice of calling the annual meeting was sent to all shareholders.	年次総会**招集通知**が、全株主に対して、送付された。
344	**certificate** [sərtífikət]	証書（証明書）
	The certificate of incorporation in the jurisdiction verifies the company's legal existence.	その法域における会社設立**証明書**は、会社の法的存在を証明するものである。
345	**instrument** [ínstrəmənt]	証書（契約書など法律的効果を伴う文書）
	The instrument of transfer must be signed by both parties.	譲渡**証書**には、両当事者の署名が必要である。

RANK 1

346	**listed company**	上場会社
	The <u>listed company</u> is subject to stringent reporting requirements.	<u>上場会社</u>は、厳しい報告義務を負う。
347	**acceptance** [ækséptəns]	①承諾・承認（相続や遺贈の承認の場合）、②引受け（手形の場合）
	<u>Acceptance</u> of the offer must be communicated by the deadline.	申込の<u>承諾</u>は、期限までの連絡を要する。
348	**consent** [kənsént]	承諾・同意
	Clicking <u>consent</u> to the terms is required for the contract to be valid.	契約が有効であるためには、条件への<u>同意</u>クリックが必要である。
349	**assignment** [əsáinmənt]	譲渡（末尾⓳参照）
	<u>Assignment</u> of the contract requires agreement from all parties.	契約の<u>譲渡</u>は、全当事者の合意を要する。
350	**transfer** [trænsfə́:r]	①譲渡（末尾⓳参照）・移転、②管轄違いなどによる移送
	The <u>transfer</u> of assets was completed yesterday.	資産の<u>譲渡</u>は、昨日完了した。
351	**transferor company**	譲渡会社
	The <u>transferor company</u> is merging with its international counterpart.	<u>譲渡会社</u>は、国際的な会社と合併する。
352	**assignor** [əsàinɔ́r]	譲渡者（末尾⓴参照）
	The <u>assignor</u> retains no rights after the assignment is complete.	<u>譲渡者</u>は、譲渡完了後、いかなる権利も保持しない。
353	**transferor** [trænsfə́:rər]	譲渡人（末尾⓴参照）
	The <u>transferor</u> completed the paperwork to move ownership.	<u>譲渡人</u>は、所有権を移転するための書類を作成した。
354	**approval** [əprú:vəl]	①可決、②承諾、③承認
	<u>Approval</u> for the project was received from the board.	プロジェクトの<u>承認</u>を、取締役会から受領した。
355	**examination of a witness**	証人尋問
	<u>Examination of a witness</u> will take place during the trial.	<u>証人尋問</u>は、公判中に行われる。

356	**trademark** [tréɪdmɑ̀ːrk] The <u>trademark</u> application was filed by a patent agent.	商標 <u>商標</u>は、弁理士によって出願された。
357	**trademark right** <u>Trademark right</u> infringement cases are on the rise.	商標権 <u>商標権</u>の侵害事件は、増加傾向にある。
358	**goods** [gʊ́dz] <u>Goods</u> damaged in transit are covered by insurance.	①物、②商品、③運送品 輸送中に破損した<u>商品</u>には、保険が適用される。
359	**proof** [prúːf] <u>Proof</u> of purchase is required for warranty service.	証明 保証サービスは、購入<u>証明</u>を要する。
360	**expiration** [èkspəréɪʃən] <u>Expiration</u> of the patent allows for generic versions.	①消滅、②失効、③満了（末尾㉑参照） 特許が<u>失効</u>すると、ジェネリック医薬品が使用できるようになる。
361	**lapse** [lǽps] The attorney overlooked the <u>lapse</u> of a patent right in absence of an heir.	①消滅（権利の消滅、知的財産権の消滅、末尾㉑参照）、②失効 弁護士は、相続人がない場合の特許権の<u>消滅</u>を見落とした。
362	**Ministerial Order** The <u>Ministerial Order</u> sets forth new industry standards.	省令 <u>省令</u>は、新たな業界基準を定めている。
363	**perform the/one's duty (duties)** Employees are expected to <u>perform their duties</u> with diligence.	職務を行う 従業員は、勤勉に<u>職務を行う</u>ことが求められる。
364	**disposition** [dìspəzíʃən] <u>Disposition</u> of the assets was agreed upon by all parties.	処分 資産の<u>処分</u>は、すべての当事者によって合意された。
365	**signature** [sígnətʃər] The <u>signature</u> on the contract was verified for authenticity.	署名 契約書の<u>署名</u>は、真正かどうか確認された。
366	**in writing** That type of contract must be signed <u>in writing</u> to be enforceable.	書面で その類型の契約は、強制力を持つために<u>書面で</u>署名されなければならない。

RANK 1

367	**ownership** [óʊnərʃip]	所有権
	Ownership in land extends to above and below the surface of the land, within the limits of laws and regulations.	土地の**所有権**は、法令の制限内において、その土地の上下に及ぶ。

368	**owner** [óʊnər]	所有者
	The owner is responsible for maintaining the building's safety standards.	**所有者**は、建物の安全基準を維持する責任を負う。

369	**infringement** [ìnfrínʤmənt]	侵害
	An act a person was compelled to take against imminent and unlawful infringement is not punishable.	急迫不正の**侵害**に対して、やむを得ずにした行為は、罰しない。

370	**new share**	新株
	The company issued new shares to raise additional capital.	その会社は、資本を追加で調達するために、**新株**を発行した。

371	**issue of new shares**	新株の発行
	The issue of new shares is planned to fund expansion.	事業拡大のための資金調達として、**新株の発行**が計画されている。

372	**share option**	新株予約権
	The share option scheme is designed to retain key employees.	**新株予約権**の制度は、主要な従業員を確保するためのものである。

373	**human rights**	人権
	Human rights advocacy is part of the company's social responsibility program.	**人権**擁護活動は会社の社会的責任プログラムの一部である。

374	**determination** [dɪtɜ̀:rmənéɪʃən]	①心証（例：末尾㉒参照）、②決定
	The determination of additional corrective order is pending further evidence.	追加の是正命令の**決定**については、さらなる証拠の提出が待たれる。

375	**hearing** [hírɪŋ]	審尋
	The hearing was postponed due to scheduling conflicts.	**審尋**は、日程の差支えにより、延期された。

376	**interrogation** [ɪntɜ̀rəgéɪʃən]	①審尋、②被疑者取調べ
	Interrogation techniques are being reviewed to ensure fairness.	公平性を確保するため、**被疑者取調べ**の手法が見直されている。

#	Term	Japanese
377	**presumption** [prɪzʌ́mpʃən] The <u>presumption</u> of innocence is a fundamental legal principle.	推定 <u>推定</u>無罪は、基本的な法原則である。
378	**is presumed** A person offering a statement indicating that person to have no knowledge of a fact alleged by the adverse party <u>is presumed</u> to have denied that fact.	推定する 相手方の主張した事実を知らない旨の陳述をした者は、その事実を争ったものと<u>推定する</u>。
379	**promptly** [prɑ́:mptli] In summary court, disputes are to be resolved <u>promptly</u> through simplified proceedings.	迅速に 簡易裁判所においては、簡易な手続により<u>迅速に</u>紛争を解決するものとする。
380	**may not** Marriage <u>may not</u> be annulled.	することができない 婚姻は、取り消す<u>ことができない</u>。
381	**may** [méɪ] If a victim is negligent, the court <u>may</u> determine the amount of compensation for loss or damage by taking that into consideration.	することができる 被害者に過失があったときは、裁判所は、これを考慮して、損害賠償の額を定める<u>ことができる</u>。
382	**does not preclude** A possessory action <u>does not preclude</u> an action on title that legally supports the possession.	することを妨げない 占有の訴えは本権の訴え<u>を妨げない</u>。
383	**be not required to** It <u>is not required to</u> satisfy any formalities such as preparation of a written document in order to form a contract.	することを要しない 契約の成立には、書面の作成その他の方式を具備<u>することを要しない</u>。
384	**must endeavor to** A business operator handling personal information <u>must endeavor to</u> maintain personal data accurate and up to date.	するよう努めなければならない 個人情報取扱事業者は、個人データを正確かつ最新の内容に保つ<u>よう努めなければならない</u>。
385	**tax** [tǽks] <u>Tax</u> implications of the transaction are being analyzed.	税 <u>税</u>務上の影響については、現在分析中である。

RANK 1

386	**claim** [kléɪm]	請求
	The <u>claim</u> for unpaid wages is being processed by HR.	未払い賃金の**請求**は、人事部で処理中である。
387	**request** [rɪkwést]	請求
	The agreement on liquidated damages do not preclude the <u>request</u> for performance.	賠償額の予定は、履行の**請求**を妨げない。
388	**statement of (the) claim(s)**	請求の原因
	The plaintiff may amend the <u>statement of the claims</u> until such time as oral arguments have reached a conclusion.	原告は、口頭弁論の終結に至るまで、**請求の原因**を変更することができる。
389	**object of (the) claim**	請求の趣旨
	The following particulars shall be entered in a complaint: (i) the parties and statutory agents; and (ii) the <u>object of the claim</u> and a statement of the claims.	訴状には、(i) 一当事者及び法定代理人、並びに、(ii) **請求の趣旨**及び原因を記載しなければならない。
390	**acknowledgment of claim**	請求の認諾
	<u>Acknowledgment of claim</u> was received from the opposite party.	相手方から、**請求の認諾**を得た。
391	**waiver of claim**	請求の放棄
	<u>Waiver of claim</u> was signed to expedite the settlement process.	和解手続を迅速化するため、**請求の放棄**の書面に署名した。
392	**in good faith**	①誠実に、②善意で
	Negotiations were conducted <u>in good faith</u> to reach an amicable solution.	交渉は、円満な解決に向け**誠実**に行われた。
393	**justifiable** [dʒʌ́stəfàɪəbəl]	正当な
	The actions were <u>justifiable</u> under the circumstances described.	その行動は、説明された状況下では**正当な**ものであった。
394	**legitimate** [lədʒítəmət]	①正当な、②適法な
	The court found the claims to be <u>legitimate</u> and warranted.	裁判所は、この請求は**正当**であり、理由があると判断した。
395	**proper** [prɑ́ːpər]	正当な
	The procedures were reviewed to ensure they were <u>proper</u> and compliant.	手順が**正当**かつ適法であることを確認するため、見直しが行われた。

396	**legitimate grounds**	正当な理由
	Legitimate grounds for the non-compliance were presented during the hearing.	審尋では、違反に関する**正当な理由**が提示された。
397	**age of majority**	成年
	The age of majority is recognized as 18 in most jurisdictions.	**成年**の年齢は、ほとんどの法域で18歳と認められている。
398	**authenticated copy**	正本（末尾㉓参照）
	An authenticated copy of the judgement was submitted.	判決の**正本**が提出された。
399	**original** [ərídʒənəl]	正本（末尾㉓参照）・原本
	The original document is required for verification purposes.	確認のため、書類の**原本**が必要である。
400	**accountability** [əkáʊntəbìlɪti]	（説明）責任（末尾⓭参照）
	The accountability of directors under the Companies Act is breached by the CEO.	CEOによる会社法に定める取締役の**説明責任**の違反が生じた。
401	**liability** [làɪəbíləti]	責任（末尾⓭参照）
	The company's liability for the accident is being assessed.	事故に対する同社の**責任**は、現在査定中である。
402	**responsibility** [rispὰːnsəbíləti]	責任（末尾⓭参照）
	A guarantor has the responsibility to perform the obligation of the principal obligor when the latter fails to perform that obligation.	証人は、主たる債務者がその債務を履行しないときに、その履行をする**責任**を負う。
403	**responsibility** [rispὰːnsəbíləti]	責務（末尾⓭参照）
	The State shall be responsible for comprehensively formulating measures necessary for ensuring the proper handling of personal information.	国は、個人情報の適正な取扱いを確保するために必要な施策を総合的に策定する**責務**を有する。
404	**effective date**	施行期日
	The effective date of the act is the first of the month.	当該法律の**施行期日**は、その月の1日である。
405	**Enforcement Regulation**	施行規則
	The Enforcement Regulation specifies procedures for applying the law.	**施行規則**は、法律の適用手続を規定している。

RANK 1

406 Enforcement Order — 施行令
The Enforcement Order was issued to ensure compliance with the new standards.
新基準の遵守を確実にするために、**施行令**が出された。

407 measure [méʒər] — ①（具体的）施策、②措置
The State shall take necessary **measures** to ensure the appropriate, prompt processing of complaints.
国は、苦情の適切かつ迅速な処理を図るために必要な**措置**を講ずるものとする。

408 policy [páːləsi] — ①（抽象的）施策、②方針
The Government shall establish a basic **policy** on the protection of personal information.
政府は、個人情報の保護に関する基本**方針**を定めなければならない。

409 rectification [rèktəfəkéɪʃən] — 是正
A reportable fact has occurred despite efforts being made to conduct investigative and **rectification** measures.
調査**是正**措置をとることに努めたにもかかわらず、通報対象事実が発生した。

410 Section [sékʃən] — 節
Section 5 of the document outlines the terms of the agreement.
同文書の第5**節**には、契約条件の概要が記されている。

411 interview [íntərvjùː] — ①接見、②参考人・証人等の取調べ
The suspect in custody may, without any official being present, have an **interview** with defense counsel.
身体の拘束を受けている被疑者は、弁護人と立会人なくして**接見**することができる。

412 incorporation [ìnkɔ̀ːrpəréɪʃən] — （会社の）設立
The **incorporation** of the new subsidiary was completed last month.
新子会社の**設立**は、先月完了した。

413 cause attributable to (someone) — 責めに帰すべき事由
The **cause attributable to** the seller was identified.
売主の**責めに帰すべき事由**が特定された。

414 good faith acquisition — 善意取得
Good faith acquisition of property can protect the buyer's interests.
善意取得は、買主の利益を守る。

415 unknowingly [ənnóʊɪŋli] — 善意で
The item was purchased **unknowingly** by the company.
その商品は、会社が**善意で**購入したものだった。

416	**without knowledge**	善意で
	The transaction was made <u>without knowledge</u> of the fraud.	当該取引は、詐欺について**善意で**行われた。
417	**in good faith and without gross negligence**	善意でかつ重大な過失がないとき
	Any performance made to the transferee company remains effective if the performing party has acted <u>in good faith and without gross negligence</u>.	譲受会社にした弁済は、弁済者が**善意でかつ重大な過失がないとき**は、その効力を有する。
418	**a third party in good faith**	善意の第三者
	<u>A third party in good faith</u> may retain ownership under certain conditions.	**善意の第三者**は、一定の条件下で所有権を保持することができる。
419	**declaration** [dèkləréɪʃən]	宣言
	The <u>declaration</u> was made in accordance with legal requirements.	**宣言**は、法的要件に従って行われた。
420	**immediately preceding paragraph**	前項
	The <u>immediately preceding paragraph</u> shall not apply to the seller.	**前項**の定めは、売主に適用されない。
421	**immediately preceding Article**	前条
	The <u>immediately preceding Article</u> shall not prevent the buyer from claiming damage.	**前条**の定めは、買主の損害賠償の請求を妨げない。
422	**(take an) oath** [óuθ]	宣誓
	The witness agreed to <u>take an oath</u> before giving testimony.	証人は、証言の前に**宣誓**することに同意した。
423	**first sentence**	前段
	The <u>first sentence</u> of Section 2, Article 10 of the Act clarifies the scope of the regulatory provision.	法第10条第2項**前段**は、規制規定の範囲を明確にしている。
424	**appointment** [əpɔ́ɪntmənt]	選定
	The <u>appointment</u> of the representative director at incorporation are determined by a majority of the directors at incorporation.	設立時代表取締役の**選定**は、設立時取締役の過半数をもって決定する。
425	**election** [ɪlékʃən]	①選任、②選挙
	The <u>election</u> of committee members will take place next week.	委員の**選挙**は、来週行われる。

RANK 1

426 possession
[pəzéʃən]

Possession of the disputed asset is currently under Kanagawa City.

占有

係争資産の**占有**は、現在、神奈川市のもとにある。

427 possessory right

The transfer of possessory rights is effected by the delivery of the thing possessed.

占有権

占有権の譲渡は、占有物の引渡しによってする。

428 due care of a prudent manager

A co-owner must use the property in co-ownership with the due care of a prudent manager.

善良な管理者の注意

共有者は、**善良な管理者の注意**をもって、共有物の使用をしなければならない。

429 set-off
[sétɔ̀f]

Set-off of the outstanding debts was agreed upon by both parties.

相殺

未払い債務の**相殺**は、両当事者によって合意された。

430 search
[sə́ːrtʃ]

A thorough search of the premises was conducted as part of the investigation.

捜索

捜査の一環として、敷地内の徹底的な**捜索**が行なわれた。

431 general provisions

The general provisions of the Act include the purpose of the Act.

総則

その法律の**総則**には、法律の目的が含まれている。

432 inhéritance
[ìnhérətəns]

Inheritance disputes are to be resolved in accordance with the will.

相続

相続争いは、遺言に従って解決される。

433 share of an estate

The share of an estate left to each beneficiary is detailed in the document.

相続分

各受益者に残される**相続分**は、文書に詳細に記載されている。

434 service
[sə́ːrvəs]

The subject of the contribution may be services.

①送達、②労務・役務

出資は、**労務**をその目的とすることができる。

435 reasonable period of time

A reasonable period of time for delivery is stipulated in the contract.

相当の期間

納品までの**相当な期間**は、契約に定められている。

436 donation
[dənéɪʃən]

The donation of cars to Ishikawa Prefecture was made anonymously.

贈与（末尾⓭参照）

石川県に対する自動車の**贈与**は、匿名で行われた。

437	**gift** [gíft]	贈与（末尾⑬参照）
	The <u>gift</u> was a significant contribution to the fund.	この**贈与**は、基金への大きな貢献となった。
438	**donor** [dóʊnər]	贈与者
	With respect to gifts with burden, the <u>donor</u> provides the same warranty as that of a seller, to the extent of that burden.	負担付贈与については、**贈与者**は、その負担の限度において、売主と同じく担保の責任を負う。
439	**lawsuit** [lɔ́ːsùːt]	訴訟・訴え（末尾㉔参照）
	The <u>lawsuit</u> seeks to recover damages for breach of contract.	この**訴訟**は、契約違反に基づく損害賠償請求である。
440	**litigation** [lìtəgéɪʃən]	訴訟・訴え（末尾㉔参照）
	<u>Litigation</u> against the manufacturer is based on product liability.	メーカーに対する**訴訟**は、製造物責任に基づいている。
441	**complaint** [kəmpléɪnt]	①訴状、②苦情
	The <u>complaint</u> was filed last week.	**訴状**は、先週、提出された。
442	**counsel** [káʊnsəl]	訴訟代理人
	<u>Counsel</u> counterargued the assertion.	**訴訟代理人**は、その主張に反論した。
443	**litigation representative**	訴訟代理人
	In summary court, with the court's permission, a person who is not an attorney at law may be named <u>litigation representative</u>.	簡易裁判所においては、その許可を得て、弁護士でない者を**訴訟代理人**とすることができる。
444	**court costs**	訴訟費用
	<u>Court costs</u> are to be borne by the losing party, as per the court's ruling.	**訴訟費用**は、裁判所の決定に従い、敗訴した側が負担する。
445	**distribution of profits and losses**	損益分配
	<u>Distribution of profits and losses</u> among partners is governed by the partnership agreement.	パートナー間の**損益分配**は、パートナーシップ契約によって規定される。
446	**damage** [dǽmədʒ]	損害
	The company must pay <u>damage</u> compensation for the harm caused.	会社は、引き起こされた被害に対する**損害**賠償を支払わなければならない。

RANK 1

RANK 1

447 compensation for loss or damage — 損害賠償
Unless a particular intention is manifested, the amount of the <u>compensation for loss or damage</u> is determined with reference to monetary value.

損害賠償は、別段の意思表示がないときは、金銭をもってその額を定める。

448 liquidated damages — 損害賠償額の予定
<u>Liquidated damages</u> were specified in the contract for early termination.

早期の契約解除については、契約書に**損害賠償額の予定**が明記されていた。

449 court of first instance — 第一審裁判所
The <u>court of first instance</u> has scheduled a hearing for the case.

第一審裁判所は、この裁判の審問を予定している。

450 consideration [kənsìdəréɪʃən] — 対価
<u>Consideration</u> for the contract was agreed upon by both parties.

契約の**対価**は、両者で合意した。

451 value [vǽlju] — 対価
The <u>value</u> of the project is over 10 billion Japanese Yen.

このプロジェクトの**対価**は、100億円を超える。

452 resigning (resignation) — 退職・退任
After <u>resigning</u>, she must return her laptop.

退任後、彼女は、パソコンを返却しなければならない。

453 retirement [ritáɪərmənt] — 退職
The enterprise must not demote, reduce salary for, or refuse to pay <u>retirement</u> allowance for a whistleblower.

事業者は、公益通報をしたことを理由として、当該公益通報者に対して、降格、減給又は**退職**金の不支給をしてはならない。

454 representative director — 代表取締役
The <u>representative director</u> led the company through a successful merger.

代表取締役は、合併を成功に導いた。

455 arrest [ərést] — 逮捕
The <u>arrest</u> of the CFO sent shockwaves through the financial markets.

CFOの**逮捕**は、金融市場に衝撃を与えた。

456 agency [éɪdʒənsi] — 代理
Article 115 of the Civil Code provides the right to rescind of counterparty of unauthorized <u>agency</u>.

民法第115条は、無権**代理**の相手方の取消権を定めている。

457	**right to represent**	①代理権、②代表権
	She was an officer who has the <u>right to represent</u> the corporation.	彼女は、当該事業者の**代表権**を有する者であった。
458	**agent** [éɪdʒənt]	①代理者、②代理人（任意代理）
	An <u>agent</u> was appointed to handle the sale of the assets.	資産の売却を担当する**代理人**が任命された。
459	**proxy** [prá:ksi]	①会社法の議決権行使代理人、②代理委任状
	The <u>proxy</u> vote was crucial to the decision's outcome.	**代理委任状**による投票は、決定の結果を左右する重要なものだった。
460	**representative** [rèprəzéntətɪv]	①代理人、②代表者 ※法定代理人も含む言葉
	If a <u>representative</u> of a foreign juridical person fails to complete a registration provided for in this Article, the representative is punished by a civil fine of not more than 500,000 yen.	外国法人の**代表者**が、この条に規定する登記を怠ったときは、50万円以下の過料に処する。
461	**;provided, however, that ...**	ただし… ※「；」は「，」でも差しつかえない。
	Either husband or wife may at any time during marriage rescind a contract between husband and wife<u>; provided, however, that</u> this may not harm the rights of a third party.	夫婦間でした契約は、婚姻中、いつでも、夫婦の一方からこれを取り消すことができる。**ただし**、第三者の権利を害することはできない。
462	**proviso** [prəváɪzə]	ただし書
	The nullity of a manifestation of intention under the provisions of the <u>proviso</u> to the preceding paragraph may not be duly asserted against a third party in good faith.	前項**ただし書**の規定による意思表示の無効は、善意の第三者に対抗することができない。
463	**immediately** [ɪmíːdiətli]	直ちに
	A stock company must <u>immediately</u> notify persons who have submitted applications of the matter changed.	株式会社は、**直ちに**、当該変更があった事項を申込みをした者に通知しなければならない。
464	**evacuation** [ɪvækjəwéɪʃən]	明渡し
	The unit owner is likely to suffer extreme difficulty in their daily life as a result of <u>evacuation</u>.	その区分所有者は、**明渡し**により、生活上著しい困難を受ける可能性がある。

RANK 1

RANK 1

465 security [sɪkjúrəti]
An obligor may demand that a right of retention be terminated by providing a reasonable <u>security</u>.

担保
債務者は、相当の**担保**を供して、留置権の消滅を請求することができる。

466 warranty [wɔ́:rənti]
With respect to gifts with burden, the donor provides the same <u>warranty</u> as that of a seller, to the extent of that burden.

担保責任
負担付贈与については、贈与者は、その負担の限度において、売主と同じく**担保責任**を負う。

467 without delay
A person that has effected a deposit must notify the obligee of the deposit <u>without delay</u>.

遅滞なく
供託をした者は、**遅滞なく**、債権者に供託の通知をしなければならない。

468 district court
Each <u>district court</u> is composed of an appropriate number of judges and assistant judges.

地方裁判所
各**地方裁判所**は、相応な員数の判事及び判事補でこれを構成する。

469 duty of care
Directors owe a <u>duty of care</u> to their shareholders.

注意義務
取締役は、株主に対して、(善管)**注意義務**を負う。

470 suspend [səspénd]
We decided to <u>suspend</u> production to address quality concerns.

中止する
品質上の懸念に対処するため、当社は、生産を一時**中止する**ことにした。

471 imprisonment [ìmprízənmənt]
The judge sentenced him to two years of <u>imprisonment</u>.

懲役
裁判官は、2年の**懲役**刑を言い渡した。

472 disciplinary action
<u>Disciplinary action</u> will be considered following the investigation.

懲戒
調査後、**懲戒**処分が検討される。

473 copyright [ká:piràɪt]
The <u>copyright</u> for the novel belongs to the author.

著作権
小説の**著作権**は、著者にある。

474 copyright holder
The <u>copyright holder</u> decided to license the work for adaptation.

著作権者
著作権者は、この作品を映画化するためにライセンスを供与することを決定した。

475	**author** [ɔ́:θər] "<u>Author</u>" means a person who creates a work.	**著作者** 「**著作者**」とは、著作物を創作する者をいう。
476	**work(s)** [wərk] The <u>works</u> of the Constitution and other laws and regulations are not subject to the rights under the Copyright Act.	**著作物** ※通例はworks（複数形）を用いる。 憲法その他の法令に該当する**著作物**は、著作権法の権利の目的となることができない。
477	**wage** [wéɪdʒ] <u>Wage</u> negotiations between the union and management are ongoing.	**賃金** 労使間の**賃金**交渉は継続中である。
478	**right of lease** The tenant enjoys a <u>right of lease</u> under local law.	**賃借権** 借主は現地法に基づく**賃借権**を享受している。
479	**currency** [kə́:rənsi] <u>Currency</u> fluctuations have impacted our international sales.	①**通貨**、②**為替** **為替**変動は海外売上高に影響を与えている。
480	**loss ordinarily incurred from (by)** The <u>loss ordinarily incurred from</u> the delay was significant.	**通常生ずべき損失** 遅延によって**通常生ずべき損失**は大きかった。
481	**collude** [kəlú:d] The penalty shall apply to a person who <u>colludes</u> for the purpose of acquiring a wrongful gain.	①**通謀する（民事など）**、②**談合する** 罰則は、不正な利益を得る目的で**談合した**者に適用される。
482	**interpreter** [ìntə́:rprətər] If the court has a person who is not proficient in Japanese make a statement, it must have an <u>interpreter</u> interpret said statement.	**通訳人・翻訳人** 日本語に通じない者に陳述をさせる場合には、**通訳人**に通訳をさせなければならない。
483	**articles of incorporation** Amendments to the <u>articles of incorporation</u> were approved at the shareholders' meeting.	**定款** ※実務上、AOIと省略されることがある。 株主総会では、**定款**の変更が承認された。
484	**definition** [dèfəníʃən] The <u>definition</u> of "confidential information" includes client data.	**定義** 「機密情報」の**定義**には、顧客データも含まれる。

RANK 1

485	**suspension** [səspénʃən]	停止
	The CEO's <u>suspension</u> was announced amid the investigation.	CEOの職務**停止**は、調査の最中に発表された。
486	**annual general meeting**	（株式会社以外の）定時総会
	The <u>annual general meeting</u> will be held virtually this year.	**定時総会**は、今年、バーチャルで開催される。
487	**annual shareholders meeting**	（株式会社の）定時総会
	The <u>annual shareholders meeting</u> is scheduled for next quarter.	（株式会社の）**定時総会**は、来期に予定されている。
488	**conflict** [ká:nflıkt]	①抵触、②国家間の紛争、③競合
	There was <u>conflict</u> among special statutory liens against the same immovables.	同一の不動産について、特別の先取特権が互いに**競合**した。
489	**mortgage** [mɔ́:rgədʒ]	抵当権
	The <u>mortgage</u> on the property will be fully paid off by next year.	この物件の**抵当権**について、来年までに完済する予定だ。
490	**mortgagor** [mɔ̀rgədʒɔ́r]	抵当権設定者
	The <u>mortgagor</u> agreed to a revised repayment schedule.	**抵当権設定者**は、返済スケジュールの見直しに同意した。
491	**mortgaged real property**	抵当不動産
	The <u>mortgaged real property</u> is located in a prime downtown location.	**抵当不動産**は、繁華街の一等地にある。
492	**lawful** [lɔ́:fəl]	適法な（末尾⓭参照）
	The contract is <u>lawful</u> under the current legislation.	この契約は、現行法において**適法**なものである。
493	**legal** [líːgəl]	適法な（末尾⓭参照）
	The transaction was conducted in a <u>legal</u> manner.	取引は、**適法**な方法で行われた。
494	**valid** [vǽlɪd]	①適法な（末尾⓭参照）、②効力を有する
	The agreement is considered <u>valid</u> by all parties involved.	この合意は、関係者全員によって**適法**（有効）とみなされる。

#	Term	Japanese
495	**exemption** [ɪgzémpʃən] An <u>exemption</u> was made for small businesses under the new tax law.	**適用除外** 新しい税法では、中小企業に対する**適用除外**が設けられた。
496	**revocation** [rèvəkéɪʃən] The <u>revocation</u> of the license was a significant setback.	**撤回** 許可の**撤回**は、大きな後退だった。
497	**procedure** [prəsíʤɚr] <u>Procedure</u> in civil litigation is governed by the provisions of the Code of Civil Procedure.	**手続** 民事訴訟に関する**手続**については、民事訴訟法の定めるところによる。
498	**sublessee** [sʌ̀blesíː] The <u>sublessee</u> is responsible for monthly utility payments.	**転借人** **転借人**は、毎月の光熱費の支払義務を負う。
499	**sublease** [sʌ́blìːs] A <u>sublease</u> agreement was signed for the office space.	**転貸** オフィススペースの**転貸**契約が締結された。
500	**sublessor** [sʌ̀blesɔ́ː] The <u>sublessor</u> must ensure the property is in good condition for the sublessee.	**転貸人** **転貸人**は、転借人のために物件を良好な状態に保たなければならない。
501	**relevant** [réləvənt] The <u>relevant</u> clause is essential to our discussion on property rights.	**当該** **当該**条項は、財産権に関する議論に重要である。
502	**registration** [rèʤɪstréɪʃən] <u>Registration</u> of the new office was completed last week.	**登記** 先週、新しいオフィスの**登記**が完了した。
503	**certificate of registered information** A <u>certificate of registered information</u> is required for the transaction.	**登記事項証明書** 取引には、**登記事項証明書**が必要である。
504	**registry office** If a foreign juridical person relocates its office within the jurisdictional district of the same <u>registry office</u>, it is sufficient to register the relocation.	**登記所** 外国法人が同一の**登記所**の管轄区域内において事務所を移転したときは、その移転を登記すれば足りる。

RANK 1

505	**movables** [múːvəbl] Things other than immovables are <u>movables</u>.	**動産** 不動産以外の物は、すべて**動産**とする。
506	**party** [páːrti] Each <u>party</u> must sign the contract for it to be valid.	**当事者** 契約を有効にするためには、各**当事者**が契約書に署名しなければならない。
507	**defense of simultaneous performance** The <u>defense of simultaneous performance</u> applies in this case.	**同時履行の抗弁** この場合、**同時履行の抗弁**が適用される。
508	**arrival** [əráɪvəl] The <u>arrival</u> of the document is expected by Friday.	**到達** 書類の**到達**は、金曜日を予定している。
509	**poll** [póʊl] The national government must develop facilities for <u>polling</u> stations and take other necessary measures so that persons with disabilities are able to smoothly vote.	**投票（例：障害者基本法）** 国は、障害者が円滑に投票できるようにするため、**投票**所の施設の整備その他必要な施策を講じなければならない。
510	**vote** [vóʊt] The directors at incorporation are to be elected in the order of the <u>votes</u> obtained by respective candidates.	**投票** **投票**の最多数を得た者から順次設立時取締役に選任されたものとする。
511	**plead** [plíːd] The defendant will <u>plead</u> not guilty.	**答弁** 被告は無罪を**答弁**する。
512	**(written) answer** [ǽnsər] The <u>answer</u> to the complaint must be filed promptly.	**答弁書** 訴状に対する**答弁書**は、速やかに提出しなければならない。
513	**(certified) copy** [kápi] A <u>certified copy</u> of the registration is necessary for the process.	**謄本** 手続きには登記の**謄本**が必要である。

514	**transcript** [trǽnskrìpt] This does not apply if a party may request the issuance of a <u>transcript</u> of the document pursuant to law or regulation.	謄本 当事者が法令により文書の**謄本**の交付を求めることができる場合は、この限りでない。
515	**if** [íf] <u>If</u> the conditions are met, the contract shall become effective.	とき（末尾㉕参照） 条件が満たされた**とき**、契約は効力を生じるものとする。
516	**when** [wén] If the person making a juridical act did not have mental capacity <u>when</u> manifesting the relevant intention, the juridical act is void.	とき（末尾㉕参照） 法律行為の当事者が意思表示をした時に意思能力を有しなかった**とき**は、その法律行為は、無効とする。
517	**independence** [ìndɪpéndəns] As for <u>independence</u> on exercising authority, a chairperson and commissioners of the commission exercise their official authority independently.	独立性（例：個人情報保護法第133条） 職権行使の**独立性**に関して、委員会の委員長及び委員は、独立してその職権を行う。
518	**landowner** [lǽndòʊnər] The <u>landowner</u> decided to sell a portion of the property.	土地の所有者 **土地の所有者**は、土地の一部を売却することを決めた。
519	**patent** [pǽtənt] The term "<u>patented</u> invention" as used in this Act means an invention for which a patent has been granted.	特許 この法律で「**特許**発明」とは、特許を受けている発明をいう。
520	**patent right** In an action involving a <u>patent right</u>, the action is under the exclusive jurisdiction of the court.	特許権 **特許権**に関する訴えについて、その訴えは、裁判所の管轄に専属する。
521	**patentee** [pèɪtəntíː] The <u>patentee</u> may enforce their rights against infringements.	特許権者 **特許権者**は、侵害行為に対して権利を行使できる。
522	**notification** [nòʊtəfəkéɪʃən] Marriage shall take effect upon <u>notification</u> pursuant to the Family Registration Act.	届出 婚姻は、戸籍法の定める**届出**によって、その効力を生ずる。

RANK 1

#	Term	Translation
523	**rescission** [rɪsíʒən] As for the effect of a <u>rescission</u>, the act that has been rescinded is deemed void ab initio.	**取消し** <u>取消し</u>の効果に関して、取り消された行為は、初めから無効であったものとみなす。
524	**right to rescind** The buyer has a <u>right to rescind</u> the purchase within 14 days.	**取消権** 買主は、14日以内に購入の<u>取消権</u>を有する。
525	**withdrawal** [wɪðdrɔ́ːəl] The <u>withdrawal</u> of an action after conducted oral arguments on the merits, is invalid without the consent of the adverse party.	**取下げ** 訴えの<u>取下げ</u>は、口頭弁論をした後にあっては、相手方の同意を得なければ、その効力を生じない。
526	**director** [dəréktər] The <u>directors</u> execute the operations of the stock company, unless otherwise provided in the articles of incorporation.	**取締役** <u>取締役</u>は、定款に別段の定めがある場合を除き、株式会社の業務を執行する。
527	**board of directors** <u>Board of directors</u> is composed of all directors.	**取締役会** <u>取締役会</u>は、すべての取締役で組織する。
528	**terms and conditions (of transaction)** The <u>terms and conditions of the transaction</u> were agreed upon by both parties.	**取引条件（T＆C）** <u>取引条件</u>は、両者によって合意された。
529	**Cabinet Office Order** The <u>Cabinet Office Order</u> regulates administrative matters.	**内閣府令** <u>内閣府令</u>は、行政事項を規定するものである。
530	**limited to** If a child has died, a father or mother may still give affiliation, <u>limited to</u> the case where that child had a lineal descendant.	**に限り（限る）** 父又は母は、死亡した子でも、その直系卑属があるとき<u>に限り</u>、認知することができる。
531	**in lieu of** Written consent was made <u>in lieu of</u> physical board meeting.	**に代わる** 取締役会の実開催<u>に代わる</u>書面決議が、実施された。
532	**the Act on [○○]** [ǽkt] Professor Shishido is well-versed in <u>the Act on</u> the Protection of Personal Information.	**○○に関する法律・○○法** 宍戸教授は、個人情報の保護<u>に関する法律</u>に精通している。

533	**under** [ʌ́ndər]	に満たない（年齢の場合）
	An act of a person <u>under</u> 14 years of age is not punishable.	14歳**に満たない**者の行為は、罰しない。
534	**based on**	に基づく
	The obligor may duly assert a defense <u>based on</u> the contract against a third party that benefits from the contract.	債務者は、契約**に基づく**抗弁をもって、その契約の利益を受ける第三者に対抗することができる。
535	**voluntarily** [vàːləntérəli]	任意に
	The prescription is renewed if the possessor discontinues the possession <u>voluntarily</u>.	時効は、占有者が**任意に**その占有を中止したときは、中断する。
536	**term of office**	任期
	A financial auditor's <u>term of office</u> continues until the conclusion of the annual shareholders meeting for the last business year which ends within one year from the time of their election.	会計監査人の**任期**は、選任後1年以内に終了する事業年度のうち最終のものに関する定時株主総会の終結の時までとする。
537	**certification** [sə̀ːrtəfəkéɪʃən]	①認証、②証明（公的機関による証明）
	<u>Certification</u> was granted by the accrediting body.	認定機関から**認証**を受けた。
538	**fall under any of**	のいずれかに該当する
	His action does not <u>fall under any of</u> the prohibited acts.	彼の行為は、禁止行為**のいずれかに該当する**ものでない。
539	**spouse** [spáʊs]	配偶者
	The <u>spouse</u> has a right to a portion of the estate.	**配偶者**は、遺産の一部に対する権利を有する。
540	**dividend** [dívɪdènd]	配当（会社の利益の処分）
	The <u>dividend</u> was distributed to shareholders last quarter.	**配当**は、前四半期に株主に分配された。
541	**purchase and sale**	売買
	An option contract for a <u>purchase and sale</u> made by one party becomes effective when the other party manifests the intention to complete the purchase and sale.	**売買**の一方の予約は、相手方が売買を完結する意思を表示した時から、売買の効力を生ずる。

RANK 1

542	**staffing** [stǽfɪŋ] The English term "<u>staffing</u> agency worker" does not appear to be in common use at present.	**派遣** 「<u>派遣</u>労働者」という英語の表記は、現在一般的には使われていないようだ。
543	**bankruptcy** [bǽŋkrəpsi] If the party ordering work receives an order commencing <u>bankruptcy</u> proceeding, the contractor may cancel the contract.	**破産** 注文者が<u>破産</u>手続開始の決定を受けたときは、請負人は、契約の解除をすることができる。
544	**fine** [fáɪn] The representative is punished by a <u>fine</u> of not more than 500,000 yen.	**罰金** 代表者は、50万円以下の<u>罰金</u>に処せられる。
545	**be subject to a fine** The individual <u>was subject to a fine</u> for repeated parking violations.	**罰金刑を科す** その個人は、駐車違反の繰り返しにより<u>罰金刑を科された</u>。
546	**issue** [íʃu] The new <u>issue</u> of shares was announced today.	**発行** 新株<u>発行</u>は、本日発表された。
547	**issue price** The <u>issue price</u> of the stock was set at 1,000 yen.	**発行価額** 株式の<u>発行価額</u>は、1,000円に設定された。
548	**total number of authorized shares** The <u>total number of authorized shares</u> was increased.	**発行可能株式総数** <u>発行可能株式総数</u>が増加された。
549	**issuer** [íʃuər] The <u>issuer</u> of the bonds will pay interest annually.	**発行者** 債券の<u>発行者</u>は、毎年利息を支払う。
550	**issued shares** The <u>issued shares</u> represent a portion of the company's equity.	**発行済株式** <u>発行済株式</u>は、会社の資本の一部である。
551	**paid money** The <u>paid money</u> for the shares totals 1 million yen.	**払込金** 株式の<u>払込金</u>は、合計100万円である。

552	**amount to be paid in** The <u>amount to be paid in</u> was outlined in the subscription agreement.	払込金額（会社法で用いられる払込金額） <u>払込金額</u>は、引受契約書に記載されている。
553	**refund** [rɪfʌ́nd] Only the assignee is entitled to request the <u>refund</u> of the money deposited.	①還付、②払戻し 供託をした金銭は、譲受人に限り、<u>還付</u>を請求することができる。
554	**judgment** [dʒʌ́dʒmənt] The <u>judgment</u> in the case was delivered by the court.	判決（末尾㉖参照） この事件の<u>判決</u>は、裁判所から言い渡された。
555	**judgment of conviction** The <u>judgment of conviction</u> was appealed by the defendant.	判決（末尾㉖参照） （有罪）<u>判決</u>は、被告により控訴された。
556	**sentence** [séntəns] The <u>sentence</u> was deemed too harsh by many.	①宣告する、②判決（末尾㉖参照） この<u>判決</u>は、多くの人々から厳しすぎると判断された。
557	**crime** [kráɪm] The <u>crime</u> involved financial fraud on a large scale.	犯罪 この<u>犯罪</u>は、大規模な金融詐欺に関与していた。
558	**precedent** [présidənt] The Supreme Court may rule to accept as the final appellate court, a case in which a prior instance judgment reflects a determination that conflicts with supreme court <u>precedent</u>.	判例 最高裁判所は、原判決に最高裁判所の<u>判例</u>と相反する判断がある事件について、決定で、上告審として事件を受理することができる。
559	**judicial precedent** A court clerk assists the judges in researching laws, regulations as well as <u>judicial precedent</u>, in relation to the cases of the court.	判例 裁判所書記官は、裁判所の事件に関し、裁判官の行なう法令の調査及び<u>判例</u>の調査を補助する。
560	**victim** [víktəm] The <u>victim</u> was awarded compensation.	被害者（末尾⑨参照） <u>被害者</u>には、賠償金が支払われた。

RANK 1

RANK 1

561	**subscription** [səbskrípʃən]	引受け
	The amount to be paid in was particularly favorable to subscribers for the shares for subscription.	払込金額が募集株式を**引き受け**る者に特に有利な金額であった。
562	**guarantor** [gə̀rəntɔ́:r]	①債務の引受人（末尾㉗参照）、②保証人
	The guarantor agreed to back the loan.	**保証人**は、融資を保証することに同意した。
563	**subscriber** [səbskráɪbər]	引受人（末尾㉗参照）
	Subscribers for shares for subscription must pay in the entire amount to be paid in for the shares for subscription for which the subscribers respectively subscribed.	募集株式の**引受人**は、それぞれの募集株式の払込金額の全額を払い込まなければならない。
564	**non-resident** [nɑnrézədənt]	非居住者
	A non-resident is defined in the Foreign Exchange and Foreign Trade Act.	**非居住者**は、外国為替及び外国貿易法に定義される。
565	**accused** [əkjú:zd]	被告人
	The accused denies all charges.	**被告人**は、すべての容疑を否認している。
566	**defendant** [dɪféndənt]	①被告、②被告人
	The defendant will present their case next week.	**被告**は、来週、弁論を行なう。
567	**person** [pə́:rsən]	①者、②人
	A person who has been sentenced to the death penalty is detained in a jail until their execution.	死刑の言渡しを受けた**者**は、その執行に至るまで刑事施設に拘置する。
568	**form** [fɔ́:rm]	ひな形
	The application form must be filled out completely.	申請の**ひな形**は、完全に記入されていなければならない。
569	**secrecy** [síkrəsi]	秘密
	In all elections, secrecy of the ballot shall not be violated.	すべて選挙における投票の**秘密**は、これを侵してはならない。

570	**secret** [síkrət] A <u>secret</u> meeting may be held where a majority of two-thirds or more of those members present passes a resolution therefor.	秘密 出席議員の3分の2以上の多数で議決したときは、**秘密**会を開くことができる。
571	**duty of confidentiality** Employees have a <u>duty of confidentiality</u> towards company data.	秘密保持義務 従業員には、会社のデータに対する**秘密保持義務**がある。
572	**cost** [kɔ́:st] The project's <u>cost</u> exceeded initial estimates.	費用 プロジェクト**費用**は、当初の見積もりを上回った。
573	**expense** [ɪkspéns] Each co-owner pays the <u>expenses</u> of management and bears burdens regarding the property in co-ownership, in proportion to each co-owner's interest.	費用 各共有者は、その持分に応じ、管理の**費用**を支払い、その他共有物に関する負担を負う。
574	**manifestation** [mæ̀nəfestéɪʃən] His actions were a clear <u>manifestation</u> of intent to resign.	表示 彼の行動は、明らかに辞任の意思**表示**だった。
575	**representation** [rèprəzentéɪʃən] Act against Unjustifiable Premiums and Misleading <u>Representations</u> was revised.	表示 不当景品類及び不当**表示**防止法が改正された。
576	**force majeure** The contract was voided due to a <u>force majeure</u> event.	不可抗力 契約は、**不可抗力**により無効となった。
577	**unfair** [ənféɪr] The practice was deemed <u>unfair</u> by the regulatory body.	不正な（末尾㉘参照） この慣行は、監督機関によって、**不正**とみなされた。
578	**unlawful** [ənlɔ́:fəl] Their actions were found to be <u>unlawful</u> in court.	不正な（末尾㉘参照） 彼らの行為は、法廷で**不正**（違法）とされた。
579	**wrongful** [rɔ́:ŋfəl] The company's <u>wrongful</u> termination lawsuit was settled out of court.	不正な（末尾㉘参照） 同社の**不正な**解雇に対する訴訟は、法廷外で和解した。

RANK 1

#	英語	日本語
580	**bear** [bér] The party agrees to <u>bear</u> the costs of repair.	**負担する** 当事者は、修理費用を**負担する**ことに同意する。
581	**incur** [ìnkə́:r] The firm will <u>incur</u> significant expenses for the recall.	**負担する** 会社は、リコールのために多額の費用を**負担する**。
582	**right in rem** She holds a <u>right in rem</u> against the property.	**物権** 彼女は、その不動産に対して、**物権**を有している。
583	**real property** The <u>real property</u> is located in a prime commercial area.	**不動産** この**不動産**は、一等地の商業地域に位置している。
584	**tort** [tɔ́:rt] The lawsuit was filed due to a <u>tort</u> claim.	**不法行為** この訴訟は、**不法行為**に基づくものである。
585	**tortfeasor** [ˈtɔrtˈfizər] The <u>tortfeasor</u> was ordered to pay damages.	**不法行為者** **不法行為者**は、損害賠償の支払いを命じられた。
586	**dispute** [dɪspjúːt] The <u>dispute</u> was resolved through mediation.	**紛争** **紛争**は、調停によって解決された。
587	**dispute resolution organization** The case was referred to a <u>dispute resolution organization</u>.	**紛争解決機関** この件は、**紛争解決機関**に付託された。
588	**Part** [pɑ́rt] The matter is set out in <u>Part</u> II of the Act.	**編** この件については、法の第2**編**が規定している。
589	**attorney (at law)** [ətɔ́ətɔ́:rni] The <u>attorney (at law)</u> advised on the legal strategy.	**弁護士** **弁護士**は、法的戦略について助言した。
590	**defense counsel** A <u>defense counsel</u> must be appointed from among attorneys.	**弁護人（例：刑事訴訟法第31条）** **弁護人**は、弁護士の中からこれを選任しなければならない。

591	**due date**	**弁済期**
	The loan's <u>due date</u> is approaching.	ローンの**弁済期**が迫っている。
592	**time of performance**	**弁済期**
	The <u>time of performance</u> is stipulated in the contract.	**弁済期**は、契約で定められている。
593	**oral argument**	**弁論**
	The judge listened to the <u>oral argument</u> before making a decision.	裁判官は、判決を下す前に**弁論**に耳を傾けた。
594	**Act** [ǽkt]	**法**
	When identifying the Japanese law for foreign clients, you should state, for example, "<u>Act</u> No. 25 of 1948" regarding the Financial Instruments and Exchange Act.	外国のクライアントに対しては、日本法を特定する場合には、例えば、金融商品取引法（1948年**法**第25号）と記載すべきである。
595	**Code** [kóud]	**法**
	The Civil <u>Code</u> may override a contract clause.	民**法**は契約の条項に優先することがある。
596	**law** [lɔ́ː]	**法**
	Japanese <u>law</u> requires specific procedures for contract formation.	日本**法**では、契約成立のための具体的な手続きを定めている。
597	**right to defense**	**防御権**
	Everyone has the <u>right to defense</u> in a legal proceeding.	誰もが法的手続において**防御権**を持っている。
598	**compensation** [kɑ̀ːmpənséɪʃən]	①**報酬**、②**補償**
	<u>Compensation</u> was awarded for the damages suffered.	被った損害に対する**補償**が、認められた。
599	**reward** [rɪwɔ́ːrd]	**報酬**
	An object acquired as <u>reward</u> for a criminal act may be confiscated.	犯罪行為の**報酬**として得た物は、没収することができる。
600	**corporation** [kɔ̀ːrpəréɪʃən]	**法人**
	The <u>corporation</u> was registered under national laws.	**法人**は、国内法に基づいて登録された。

#	英語	日本語
601	**juridical person**	法人
	A <u>juridical person</u> can own property and enter contracts.	<u>法人</u>は、財産を所有し、契約を結ぶことができる。
602	**court** [kɔ́ːrt]	①法廷、②裁判所
	The <u>court</u> decided in favor of the plaintiff.	<u>裁判所</u>は、原告を支持する判決を下した。
603	**laws and regulations**	法令
	All operations comply with <u>laws and regulations</u>.	すべての業務は、<u>法令</u>を遵守している。
604	**guarantee** [gə̀rəntíː]	保証
	The <u>guarantee</u> covers defects for two years.	瑕疵の<u>保証</u>期間は、2年間である。
605	**guarantee contract**	保証契約
	The <u>guarantee contract</u> specifies conditions for liability.	<u>保証契約</u>には、責任に関する条件が明記されている。
606	**guarantee obligation**	保証債務
	He fulfilled his <u>guarantee obligation</u> without delay.	彼は、遅滞なく<u>保証債務</u>を履行した。
607	**incorporator** [inkɔ́ːpərèitər]	発起人（会社の場合）
	The <u>incorporator</u> signed the articles of incorporation.	<u>発起人</u>が、定款に署名した。
608	**merits** [mérəts]	本案
	If the defendant presents an oral argument on the <u>merits</u> of the case without entering the affirmative defense that the Japanese courts lack jurisdiction, the courts have jurisdiction.	被告が日本の裁判所が管轄権を有しない旨の抗弁を提出しないで<u>本案</u>について弁論をしたときは、裁判所は、管轄権を有する。
609	**judgment on the merits**	本案判決
	The <u>judgment on the merits</u> was issued yesterday.	<u>本案判決</u>は、昨日出された。
610	**head office**	本店
	The company's <u>head office</u> is located in Tottori Prefecture.	<u>本店</u>は、鳥取県にある。
611	**main clause**	本文
	The <u>main clause</u> of Article 5 specifies the delivery terms.	第5条<u>本文</u>には、納品条件が明記されている。

612	**less than**	未満
	The damages were less than JPY 50,000.	損害賠償額は、5万円**未満**だった。
613	**civil suit**	民事訴訟
	A civil suit was filed for breach of contract.	契約違反を理由に、**民事訴訟**が提起された。
614	**without negligence**	無過失
	A person that commences the possession of movables peacefully and openly by a transactional act acquires the rights that are exercised with respect to the movables immediately if the person possesses it in good faith and without negligence.	取引行為によって、平穏に、かつ、公然と動産の占有を始めた者は、善意であり、かつ、**無過失**のときは、即時にその動産について行使する権利を取得する。
615	**void** [vɔ́ɪd]	無効な
	If the person making a juridical act did not have mental capacity when manifesting the relevant intention, the juridical act is void.	法律行為の当事者が意思表示をした時に意思能力を有しなかったときは、その法律行為は、**無効**とする。
616	**license** [láɪsəns]	①免許、②許可
	The license was approved by the regulatory body.	この**許可**は、監督機関によって承認された。
617	**exemptions** [ɪgzémpʃənz]	免責
	Certain exemptions apply to liabilities caused by small businesses.	中小企業により生じた責任には、一定の**免責**がある。
618	**offer** [ɔ́:fər]	申込み
	The offer was accepted by the seller.	この**申込み**は、売主により承諾された。
619	**offeror** [ɔ́fərər]	申込者
	The offeror withdrew the proposal last minute.	**申込者**は直前になって提案を取り下げた。
620	**motion** [móʊʃən]	申立て
	A motion to challenge may be filed with the court in charge of the case.	受訴裁判所に対して、忌避の**申立て**ができる。
621	**purpose** [pə́:rpəs]	目的
	The purpose of the meeting is to elect a new director.	会議の**目的**は、新理事を選出することである。

RANK 1

622	**object** [ɑ́:bdʒekt]	The term "things" as used in the Civil Code means tangible <u>objects</u>.	物 民法において「物」とは、有体**物**をいう。
623	**officer** [ɔ́:fəsər]	The company's <u>officer</u> was appointed yesterday.	役員 昨日、同社の**役員**が任命された。
624	**general conditions**	If a preparer of the standard form contract is to amend the standard form contract, the preparer must make the details of the amended standard <u>general conditions</u> known by the Internet.	約款 定型約款準備者は、定型約款の変更をするときは、変更後の定型**約款**の内容をインターネットにより周知しなければならない。
625	**securities** [sɪkjɔ́rətiz]	The <u>securities</u> were issued at market value.	有価証券 その**有価証券**は、時価で発行された。
626	**guilty** [gílti]	Before conducting an examination, the court must inform a witness of the fact that they may refuse to give testimony that may risk themselves to a <u>guilty</u> verdict.	有罪 証人に対しては、尋問前に、**有罪**判決を受けるおそれのある証言を拒むことができる旨を告げなければならない。
627	**assignee** [əsàiní]	The <u>assignee</u> received the rights to the patent.	譲受人 **譲受人**は、特許の権利を得た。
628	**transferee** [trænsfərí:]	The <u>transferee</u> is now responsible for the obligations.	譲受人 **譲受人**は、現在、債務の責任を負っている。
629	**foresee** [fɔrsí]	The outcome was difficult to <u>foresee</u> due to market volatility.	予見する 市場のボラティリティのため、結果を**予見する**ことは、困難であった。
630	**budget** [bʌ́dʒɪt]	The project's <u>budget</u> was approved by the board.	予算 プロジェクトの**予算**は、取締役会で承認された。
631	**conflict of interests**	The director disclosed a <u>conflict of interests</u>.	利益相反 その取締役は、**利益相反**を開示した。

#	Term	Japanese
632	**performance** [pərfɔ́:rməns] The <u>performance</u> of the contract was completed on time.	**履行** 契約の<u>履行</u>は、予定通りに完了した。
633	**place of performance** The <u>place of performance</u> is the buyer's premises.	**履行地** <u>履行地</u>は、買主の所在地である。
634	**interest** [íntrəst] The creditor charged <u>interest</u> on the late payments.	**①利子・利息、②持分** 債権者は、支払いの遅延分の<u>利息</u>を請求した。
635	**prove** [prú:v] The claimant failed to <u>prove</u> the damages.	**立証する** 請求者は、損害の<u>立証する</u>ことに失敗した。
636	**Cabinet Order** The new <u>Cabinet Order</u> updated the regulations.	**令（法形式が政令の場合）** 新たな<u>政令</u>は、規制を更新した。
637	**warrant** [wɔ́:rənt] No person shall be apprehended except upon <u>warrant</u> issued by a competent judicial officer which specifies the offense with which the person is charged the offense being committed.	**令状** 何人も、権限を有する司法官憲が発し、かつ、理由となっている犯罪を明示する<u>令状</u>によらなければ、逮捕されない。
638	**jointly and severally** The debts were guaranteed <u>jointly and severally</u>.	**連帯して** 債務は、<u>連帯して</u>保証された。
639	**labor contract** The <u>labor contract</u> specifies the terms of employment.	**労働契約** <u>労働契約</u>は、雇用期間を規定する。
640	**settlement** [sétəlmənt] A <u>settlement</u> becomes effective when the parties to a dispute promise to settle the dispute through reciprocal concessions.	**和解** <u>和解</u>は、当事者が互いに譲歩をしてその間に存する争いをやめることを約することによって、その効力を生ずる。
641	**not exceeding** The amount <u>not exceeding</u> half of the amount of the contribution may not be recorded as stated capital.	**を超えない** 払込みに係る額の2分の1<u>を超えない</u>額は、資本金として計上しないことができる。

RANK 1

642	**exceeding** [ɪksídɪŋ]	を超える
	An act <u>exceeding</u> the limits of self-defense may lead to the punishment being reduced the offender in light of the circumstances.	防衛の程度**を超えた**行為は、情状により、その刑を減軽することができる。
643	**except** [ɪksépt]	を除くほか・を除き
	<u>Except</u> as otherwise provided, the court may examine any person as a witness.	裁判所は、特別の定めがある場合**を除き**、何人でも証人として尋問することができる。

法律英単語® Ⅰ 2100
RANK2

#	英語	日本語
644	**adverse party**	相手方（末尾❶参照）
	The <u>adverse party</u> declined the settlement offer.	<u>相手方</u>は、和解案を拒否した。
645	**counterparty** [káʊntərpɑ̀ːrti]	相手方（末尾❶参照）
	The <u>counterparty</u> breached the contract.	<u>相手方</u>が、契約に違反した。
646	**opponent** [əpóʊnənt]	相手方（末尾❶参照）
	When requesting examination of a witness, the public prosecutor must give the <u>opponent</u> an opportunity to learn of the name and address of that person in advance.	検察官が証人の尋問を請求するについては、あらかじめ、<u>相手方</u>に対し、その氏名及び住居を知る機会を与えなければならない。
647	**in bad faith**	悪意で（末尾❷参照）
	If officers have acted <u>in bad faith</u> or with gross negligence in performing their duties, relevant officers are liable to a third party for damages arising as a result thereof.	役員がその職務を行うについて**悪意**又は重大な過失があったときは、当該役員は、これによって第三者に生じた損害を賠償する責任を負う。
648	**maliciously** [məlíʃɪsli]	悪意で（末尾❷参照）
	Actions were taken <u>maliciously</u> to harm the business.	<u>悪意</u>をもって事業に損害を与える行為が行われた。
649	**eviction** [ɪvíkʃən]	明渡し（強制的な）
	The tenant faced <u>eviction</u> due to unpaid rent.	賃借人は、家賃未払いによる<u>明渡</u>に直面していた。
650	**vacation** [veɪkéɪʃən]	明渡し（自主的）
	The tenant offered a <u>vacation</u> before the landlord contacted him.	賃借人は、賃貸人が連絡する前に、（自主的な）<u>明渡し</u>を申し出た。
651	**mediation** [mìdiéɪʃən]	①あっせん、②調停
	<u>Mediation</u> under the Civil Conciliation Act is recommended in this case.	本件では、民事調停法による<u>調停</u>が推奨される。
652	**be appointed from among**	（ある範疇の者を役職に）選定する
	The committee members of each committee <u>are appointed from among</u> the directors by a resolution at the board of directors meeting.	各委員会の委員は、取締役の中から、取締役会の決議によって<u>選定する</u>。
653	**serve as**	（特定の者を役職に）選定する
	She will <u>serve as</u> the committee's chairperson.	彼女は、委員会の会長に<u>選定</u>される。

654	**pronouncement** [prənáʊnsmənt] Trial records must be completed promptly after each trial date, and at the latest, by the time of <u>pronouncement</u> of the judgment.	言渡し・宣告 公判調書は、各公判期日後速やかに、遅くとも判決を<u>宣告</u>するまでにこれを整理しなければならない。
655	**rendering** [réndərɪŋ] The presiding judge must designate a court date for <u>rendering</u> the judgment within one month from the date when the oral arguments are concluded.	言渡し（民事の場合） 裁判長は、口頭弁論を終結する日から一月以内の間において判決<u>言渡し</u>をする期日を指定しなければならない。
656	**written opinion** His <u>written opinion</u> clarified the legal standing.	意見書 彼の<u>意見書</u>は、法的立場を明確にした。
657	**estate** [ɪstéɪt] The <u>estate</u> includes both real and personal property.	遺産 <u>遺産</u>は、不動産及び動産の両方を含む。
658	**division of estate** The <u>division of estate</u> was contested by the heirs.	遺産の分割 <u>遺産の分割</u>は、相続人によって争われた。
659	**entrustor** The <u>entrustor</u> relies on the agent's discretion.	委託者（末尾❸参照） <u>委託者</u>は、代理人の裁量に依存する。
660	**consign** [kənsáɪn] We will <u>consign</u> these goods for overseas shipping.	（商品の販売を）委託する 当社は、海外発送を<u>委託する</u>。
661	**lump sum payment** If an insured person has become unemployed, a special <u>lump sum payment</u> is to be made.	一時金 被保険者が失業した場合には、特例<u>一時金</u>を支給する。
662	**general successor** The <u>general successor</u> inherits all assets and liabilities.	一般承継人 <u>一般承継人</u>は、すべての資産及び負債を承継する。
663	**business accounting standards generally accepted as fair and appropriate** The firm follows <u>business accounting standards generally accepted as fair and appropriate</u>.	一般に公正妥当と認められる企業会計の基準 当社は、<u>一般に公正妥当と認められる企業会計の基準</u>に従っている。

RANK 2

#	英語	日本語
664	**relocation** [rìlóʊkéɪʃən] The company's <u>relocation</u> to a larger office was announced.	**（主たる事務所の）移転** より広いオフィスへの会社の**移転**が、発表された。
665	**removal** [rɪmúːvəl] A person who <u>removes</u> a detained or confined person in accordance with the laws and regulations from authorities is punished by imprisonment for not less than 3 months but not more than 5 years.	**（人・物の場所的な）移転・奪取** ※例文は動詞のremoveを用いた。 法令により拘禁された者を**奪取**した者は、3月以上5年以下の懲役に処する。
666	**mandate** [mǽndèɪt] An agent appointed by <u>mandate</u> may not appoint a subagent unless the authorization of the principal is obtained.	**委任（民法上の委任契約）** **委任**による代理人は、本人の許諾を得たときでなければ、復代理人を選任することができない。
667	**privately appointed agent** A <u>privately appointed agent</u> handled the sensitive transaction.	**委任による代理人** **委任による代理人**が、機密性の高い取引を担当した。
668	**by filing an action** The dispute was escalated <u>by filing an action</u> in court.	**訴えによって** 争いは、法廷での**訴えによって**、エスカレートした。
669	**sales volume** Last quarter's <u>sales volume</u> exceeded projections.	**売上高** 前四半期の**売上高**は、予想を上回った。
670	**secondary distribution** The term "<u>secondary distribution</u> of securities" includes offers to sell already-issued securities.	**売出し** 「有価証券の**売出し**」とは、既に発行された有価証券の売付けの申込みを含む。
671	**investment report** A financial instruments business operator must periodically prepare an <u>investment report</u> for invested assets.	**運用報告書** 金融商品取引業者は、運用財産について、定期に**運用報告書**を作成しなければならない。
672	**permanent resident** She is a <u>permanent resident</u>.	**永住者** 彼女は、**永住者**である。
673	**enterprise for profit** No official may they personally operate any <u>enterprise for profit</u>.	**営利企業** 職員は、自ら**営利企業**を営んではならない。

674	**business for profit**	営利事業
	The "trade association" does not include any organization whose principal purpose is to run and is actually running a commercial, industrial, financial or any other <u>business for profit</u>.	「事業者団体」には、商業、工業、金融業その他の**営利事業**を営むことを主たる目的とする団体を含まない。
675	**gross income**	益金
	<u>Gross income</u> for the year was reported during the meeting.	会議では、年間の**益金**が報告された。
676	**invocation** [ìnvəkéɪʃən]	援用
	<u>Invocation</u> of prescription was overlooked by the attorney.	弁護士が時効の**援用**を見落とした。
677	**reference** [réfərəns]	援用
	<u>Reference</u> to the court case supports the argument.	裁判例を**援用**することで、その主張は裏付けられる。
678	**seized article**	押収物
	The <u>seized article</u> was entered as evidence.	**押収物**は、証拠として提出された。
679	**jurisdiction by appearance**	応訴管轄
	<u>Jurisdiction by appearance</u> was established when the defendant responded.	**応訴管轄**は、被告が答弁した時点で成立した。
680	**day corresponding to...**	〜に応当する日
	If the period is not calculated from the beginning of a month, the period expires on the day preceding the <u>day corresponding to</u> the first day of the calculation in the final month.	月の始から期間を起算しないときは、その期間は、最後の月においてその起算日に**応当する日**の前日に満了する。
681	**public policy**	公の秩序又は善良の風俗
	A juridical act that is against <u>public policy</u> is void.	**公の秩序又は善良の風俗**に反する法律行為は、無効とする。
682	**likelihood** [láɪklihòd]	おそれ
	If the buyer is likely to lose the rights that the buyer has bought, the buyer may refuse to pay the price in proportion to the degree of that <u>likelihood</u>.	買主がその買い受けた権利を失う**おそれ**があるときは、買主は、その危険の程度に応じて、代金の支払を拒むことができる。

RANK 2

683	**risk** [rísk]	おそれ
	If the court may not be convened without defense counsel, and there is the <u>risk</u> that the defense counsel will not appear at court, the court may appoint defense counsel ex officio.	弁護人がなければ開廷することができない場合において、弁護人が出頭しない**おそれ**があるときは、裁判所は、職権で弁護人を付することができる。
684	**threat** [θrét]	①おそれ、②加害 ※主要な法律で「おそれ」について、threatを用いている例は乏しい。
	A person who kidnaps another person through the use of force or enticement for the purpose of <u>threat</u> to the life or body is punished by imprisonment for not less than 1 year but not more than 10 years.	身体に対する**加害**の目的で、人を略取し、又は誘拐した者は、1年以上10年以下の懲役に処する。
685	**financial audit report**	会計監査報告書
	The <u>financial audit report</u> had no discrepancies.	**会計監査報告書**に、不一致はなかった。
686	**accounting advisor**	会計参与
	The <u>accounting advisor</u> recommended more stringent controls.	**会計参与**は、より厳格な管理を推奨した。
687	**foreign company**	外国会社
	The <u>foreign company</u> established a local branch.	**外国会社**は、現地に支店を設立した。
688	**calling** [kɔ́ːlɪŋ]	①（債権の）回収、②招集
	Shareholders having consecutively for the preceding six months or more, not less than three hundredths (3/100) of the votes of all shareholders may demand the directors that they <u>call</u> the shareholders meeting.	総株主の議決権の100分の3以上の議決権を6ヶ月前から引き続き有する株主は、取締役に対し、株主総会の**招集**を請求することができる。
689	**cancellation** [kæ̀nsəléɪʃən]	①解除、②株式・新株予約権の消却
	The <u>cancellation</u> of the contract was a mutual decision.	契約**解除**は双方合意の上だった。
690	**condition subsequent**	解除条件
	The agreement includes a <u>condition subsequent</u>.	この合意には、**解除条件**が含まれている。

691	**harm** [hάːrm]	害する
	The transferor company transfers business, with the knowledge that it <u>harms</u> creditors of the obligations that are not succeeded by the transferee company.	譲渡会社は、譲受会社に承継されない債務の債権者を**害する**ことを知って、事業を譲渡した。
692	**prejudice** [prédʒədɪs]	①害する、②予断
	The project might <u>prejudice</u> our legal defense.	このプロジェクトは、私たちの法的防御を**害する**可能性がある。
693	**improvement measure**	改善措置
	The company decided to take <u>improvement measures</u> promptly.	当該会社は、速やかに**改善措置**を講ずることを決定した。
694	**order for improvement**	改善命令
	The regulator issued an <u>order for improvement</u> to the factory.	規制当局は、工場に対して、**改善命令**を出した。
695	**appraisal rights**	買取請求権
	Shareholders exercised their <u>appraisal rights</u> during the merger.	株主は、合併に際して、**買取請求権**を行使した。
696	**avoid** [əvɔ́ɪd]	回避する
	Steps were taken to <u>avoid</u> contractual penalties.	契約上の違約金を**回避する**ための措置が講じられた。
697	**irreparable damage**	回復することができない損害
	For the purpose of the application of the relevant provisions to a company with company auditor(s), "substantial detriment" in that paragraph is read as "<u>irreparable damage</u>".	監査役設置会社における当該適用については、同項中「著しい損害」とあるのは、「**回復することができない損害**」とする。
698	**alteration** [ɔ̀ːltəréɪʃən]	①改変・変更、②変造
	<u>Alteration</u> of the deliverable requires approval.	納品物の**変更**には、承認が必要である。
699	**registered mail**	書留郵便
	If a document is sent by <u>registered mail</u>, the document is deemed to have been served at the time it is sent.	書類を**書留郵便**に付して発送した場合には、その発送の時に、送達があったものとみなす。
700	**tax return**	確定申告
	He filed his <u>tax return</u> before the March deadline.	彼は、3月の期限前に**確定申告**をおこなった。

RANK 2

RANK 2

701 action for declaratory judgment
An <u>action for declaratory judgment</u> clarifies legal rights.

確認の訴え
<u>確認の訴え</u>は、法的権利を明確にするものである。

702 warranty against defects
The product comes with a <u>warranty against defects</u> for one year.

瑕疵担保責任
製品には、1年間の<u>瑕疵担保責任</u>が付いている。

703 fruits
[frúːts]
Products obtained from the intended use of a thing are its natural <u>fruits</u>. Money and other things that may be obtained in exchange for the use of any thing are civil <u>fruits</u>.

果実
物の用法に従い収取する産出物を天然<u>果実</u>とする。また、物の使用の対価として受けるべき金銭その他の物を法定<u>果実</u>とする。

704 loan trust
The <u>loan trust</u> agreement was finalized yesterday.

貸付信託
昨日、<u>貸付信託</u>契約がまとまった。

705 administrative monetary penalty
The company faced an <u>administrative monetary penalty</u> for non-compliance.

課徴金
同社は、法令違反により<u>課徴金</u>を受けた。

706 merged company
The <u>merged company</u> announced its new leadership team.

合併会社
<u>合併会社</u>は、新しいリーダーシップチームを発表した。

707 family court
The <u>family court</u> handled the adoption proceedings.

家庭裁判所
養子縁組の手続きは、<u>家庭裁判所</u>が行った。

708 share certificate-issuing company
The <u>share certificate-issuing company</u> updated its shareholder records.

株券発行会社
<u>株券発行会社</u>が、株主名簿を更新した。

709 share transfer
<u>Share transfer</u> procedures were completed smoothly.

株式移転
<u>株式移転</u>の手続きは、滞りなく完了した。

710 exercise of appraisal rights
Investors considered the <u>exercise of appraisal rights</u> during the merger.

株式買取請求権
投資家は合併の際に、<u>株式買取請求権</u>の行使を検討した。

711 share exchange
The <u>share exchange</u> was part of the strategic partnership.

株式交換
<u>株式交換</u>は、戦略的パートナーシップの一環であった。

712 share split
A <u>share split</u> was announced to increase liquidity.

株式分割
流動性を高めるために、<u>株式分割</u>が発表された。

713	**consolidation of shares**	**株式併合**
	The <u>consolidation of shares</u> was aimed at enhancing value.	**株式併合**は、価値の向上を目的としていた。
714	**allotment of share without contribution**	**株式無償割当て**
	The startup benefited from a regulatory update on an <u>allotment of share without contribution</u>.	新興企業は、**株式無償割当て**に関する法改正の恩恵を受けた。
715	**reference documents for shareholders meeting**	**株主総会参考書類**
	<u>Reference documents for shareholders meeting</u> were distributed electronically.	**株主総会参考書類**が電子配布された。
716	**shareholder register administrator**	**株主名簿管理人**
	The <u>shareholder register administrator</u> updated the list.	**株主名簿管理人**が、名簿を更新した。
717	**member state**	**加盟国**
	The <u>member state</u> agreed to new environmental regulations.	**加盟国**は、新たな環境規制に同意した。
718	**borrowings** [bɑ́ːrəɪŋz]	**借入金**
	<u>Borrowings</u> were increased to fund expansion.	事業拡大のために、**借入金**を増額した。
719	**provisional attachment**	**仮差押え（末尾㉙参照）**
	The court ordered a <u>provisional attachment</u> on the assets.	裁判所は、資産の**仮差押え**を命じた。
720	**provisional garnishment**	**仮差押え（末尾㉙参照）**
	<u>Provisional garnishment</u> secured the creditor's claim.	**仮差押え**は、債権者の債権を確保した。
721	**provisional seizure**	**仮差押え（末尾㉙参照）**
	<u>Provisional seizure</u> of property was authorized by the court.	財産の**仮差押え**は、裁判所によって許可された。
722	**provisional execution**	**仮執行**
	<u>Provisional execution</u> allowed immediate enforcement of the judgment.	**仮執行**は、判決の即時執行を可能にした。
723	**provisional disposition**	**仮処分**
	The judge granted a <u>provisional disposition</u> to protect the employee.	裁判官は、従業員を保護するために**仮処分**を認めた。

RANK 2

RANK 2

724 provisional registration — 仮登記
The court, upon a petition of a person entitled to register regarding a <u>provisional registration</u>, may make a disposition to order a provisional registration.
裁判所は、<u>仮登記</u>の登記権利者の申立てにより、仮登記を命ずる処分をすることができる。

725 provisional payment — 仮納付
<u>Provisional payment</u> is provided in the Road Traffic Act.
<u>仮納付</u>は、道路交通法に定めがある。

726 provisional payment figured by estimate — 仮払
<u>Provisional payment figured by estimate</u> was calculated by the court.
<u>仮払</u>の額が、裁判所により計算された。

727 civil fine — 過料
The court imposed a <u>civil fine</u>.
裁判所は、<u>過料</u>を科した。

728 petty fine — 科料
A person is subject to a criminal fine or <u>petty fine</u> of not more than 20,000 yen.
違反した者は、2万円以下の罰金又は<u>科料</u>に処する。

729 lack of jurisdiction — 管轄違い
The court acknowledged a <u>lack of jurisdiction</u> over the case.
裁判所は、<u>管轄違い</u>を認めた。

730 related company — 関係会社
The startup became a <u>related company</u> through investment.
スタートアップは、投資によって、<u>関係会社</u>となった。

731 recommendation [rèkəməndéɪʃən] — 勧告
The person that has received that <u>recommendation</u> failed to comply with it.
<u>勧告</u>を受けた当該人物は、勧告に従わなかった。

732 audit committee member — 監査委員
The <u>audit committee member</u> reviewed the financial statements.
<u>監査委員</u>は、財務諸表を確認した。

733 trustee in bankruptcy [trÀstíː] — 破産管財人
The <u>trustee in bankruptcy</u> managed the asset distribution.
<u>破産管財人</u>が、資産分配を管理した。

734 company with audit and supervisory committee — 監査等委員会設置会社
The <u>company with audit and supervisory committee</u> is well reputed.
その<u>監査等委員会設置会社</u>は、良い評判である。

735	**audit report** The <u>audit report</u> highlighted areas for financial improvement.	**監査報告** <u>監査報告</u>では、財務面での改善点が強調された。
736	**company with board of company auditors** The <u>company with board of company auditors</u> ensures compliance.	**監査役会設置会社** <u>監査役会設置会社</u>は、コンプライアンスを確保する。
737	**company with company auditor(s)** The <u>company with company auditor(s)</u> is seeking better governance.	**監査役設置会社** その<u>監査役設置会社</u>は、より良いガバナンスを求めている。
738	**monitoring** [mά:nətərɪŋ] The provisions prescribed concerning working hours do not apply to a worker engaged in <u>monitoring</u>, for which the employer has obtained permission from the relevant government agency.	**監視** 労働時間に関する規定は、<u>監視</u>に従事する者で、使用者が行政官庁の許可を受けた労働者については適用しない。
739	**accounting title** The CFO discussed the <u>accounting title</u> changes.	**勘定科目** CFOは、<u>勘定科目</u>の変更について議論した。
740	**customs** [kʌ́stəmz] <u>Customs</u> imposed by the new U.S. president significantly affect import costs.	**①関税、②税関** 新しい米国大統領により課された<u>関税</u>は、輸入コストに大きく影響する。
741	**indirect compulsory execution** <u>Indirect compulsory execution</u> is a legal enforcement mechanism.	**間接強制** <u>間接強制</u>は、法的な強制執行の仕組みである。
742	**supervisor** [sú:pərvàɪzər] If any act constituting the cause of registration is avoided, a <u>supervisor</u> must apply for a registration of avoidance.	**監督委員** 登記の原因である行為が否認されたときは、<u>監督委員</u>は、否認の登記を申請しなければならない。
743	**custodian** [kəstóʊdiən] The court, at the request of the performer, must designate the depository and appoint a <u>custodian</u> of the thing to be deposited.	**保管者** 裁判所は、弁済者の請求により、供託所の指定及び供託物の<u>保管者</u>の選任をしなければならない。

RANK 2

#	英語	日本語
744	**proposal** [prəpóuzəl]	議案
	The board considered a <u>proposal</u> for acquisition.	取締役会は、買収の**議案**を検討した。
745	**assembly** [əsémbli]	（国や独立した州レベルでの）議会
	The <u>assembly</u> passed the resolution unanimously.	**議会**は、全会一致で可決した。
746	**after the passage of a period (of time)**	期間の経過後
	Benefits increase <u>after the passage of a period</u> of employment.	雇用の**期間の経過後**、給付は増加する。
747	**fixed-term labor contract**	期間の定めのある労働契約
	The <u>fixed-term labor contract</u> expires next month.	**期間の定めのある労働契約**は、来月で満了する。
748	**expiration of a period (of time)**	期間の満了
	<u>Expiration of a period</u> triggers automatic renewal of the contract.	**期間の満了**により、契約は自動更新される。
749	**foundation** [faʊndéɪʃən]	基金
	The <u>foundation</u> supports educational initiatives worldwide.	その**基金**は、世界中の教育活動を支援している。
750	**voting form**	議決権行使書面
	Shareholders received a <u>voting form</u> for the upcoming general meeting.	株主は、次の総会の**議決権行使書面**を受け取った。
751	**share with restricted voting right**	議決権制限株式
	The <u>share with restricted voting right</u> offers limited influence.	**議決権制限株式**は、影響力を限定的にする。
752	**time limit**	期限
	The <u>time limit</u> for submissions is tomorrow at noon.	提出の**期限**は、明日の正午までである。
753	**deemed** [díːmd]	擬制
	The document was <u>deemed</u> valid by the law.	この文書は、法律によって有効と**擬制**された。
754	**counterfeit** [káʊntərfɪt]	偽造
	The suspect <u>counterfeited</u> a document.	被疑者は、文書を**偽造**した。

RANK 2

755	**forgery** [fɔ́ːrdʒəri]	偽造
	A person who has <u>forged</u>, altered, destroyed, or concealed a will may not become an heir.	遺言書を**偽造**し、変造し、破棄し、又は隠匿した者は、相続人となることができない。
756	**discontinuance** [dìskəntínjuəns]	休止（それ以上継続させない停止）
	<u>Discontinuance</u> of the business was announced due to low demand.	需要の低迷により、事業の**休止**が発表された。
757	**absorption-type merger**	吸収合併
	The <u>absorption-type merger</u> consolidated two leading firms.	**吸収合併**により、大手2社が統合された。
758	**absorption-type company split**	吸収分割
	An <u>absorption-type company split</u> facilitated the strategic realignment.	**吸収分割**により、戦略的再編が促進された。
759	**right to indemnification**	求償権（末尾⓫参照）
	The guarantor has a <u>right to indemnification</u> from the principal obligor for the amount of property expended.	保証人は、主たる債務者に対し、支出した財産の額の**求償権**を有する。
760	**salary income**	給与所得
	<u>Salary income</u> is subject to taxes.	**給与所得**には、税が課される。
761	**consultation** [kɑ̀ːnsəltéɪʃən]	（専門家との）協議
	<u>Consultation</u> with a legal expert clarified the new regulations.	法律の専門家と**協議**したところ、新しい規制が明確になった。
762	**divorce by agreement**	協議上の離婚
	They opted for <u>divorce by agreement</u>, simplifying the process.	彼らは、**協議上の離婚**を選択し、手続きを簡略化した。
763	**abetment** [əbétmənt]	教唆
	<u>Abetment</u> in the homicide led to his arrest.	殺人罪の**教唆**により、彼は逮捕された。
764	**administrative case litigation**	行政事件訴訟
	The <u>administrative case litigation</u> challenged the new regulation.	**行政事件訴訟**では、新しい規制が争われた。
765	**administrative authority**	行政庁
	The <u>administrative authority</u> issued new guidelines for compliance.	**行政庁**は、コンプライアンスに関する新しいガイドラインを発表した。

766	**administrative procedure** The <u>administrative procedure</u> ensures fairness in government actions.	<u>行政手続</u> <u>行政手続</u>は、政府の行動の公正さを保証するものである。
767	**administrative appeal** An <u>administrative appeal</u> can contest a decision before going to court.	<u>行政不服審査</u> <u>行政不服審査</u>は、裁判を起こす前に決定を争うことができる。
768	**competitive position** Maintaining a <u>competitive position</u> requires constant innovation.	<u>競争上の地位</u> <u>競争上の地位</u>を維持するには、絶え間ないイノベーションが必要だ。
769	**deposit with an official depository** The principal obligor may be released from the obligation for reimbursement by making a <u>deposit with an official depository</u>.	<u>供託</u> 主たる債務者は、<u>供託</u>をして、その償還の義務を免れることができる。
770	**money deposit with an official depositary** A <u>money deposit with an official depositary</u> offers security.	<u>供託金</u> <u>供託金</u>は、担保を提供する。
771	**official depository** A performer may deposit the subject matter of the performance with an <u>official depository</u> for the benefit of the obligee.	<u>供託、供託所</u> 弁済者は、債権者のために弁済の目的物を<u>供託</u>することができる。
772	**in the course of trade** Providing accommodation <u>in the course of trade</u> are subject to registration.	<u>業として（反復・継続して）</u> 宿泊の<u>業として</u>の提供は、登録を要する。
773	**on a regular basis** The term "the Money Lending Business" includes the business of loaning money <u>on a regular basis</u>.	<u>業として（営利目的をもって）</u> 「貸金業」とは、金銭の貸付けで<u>業として</u>行うものを含む。
774	**accomplice** [əkɑ́:mpləs] The <u>accomplice</u> was also charged in the robbery.	<u>共犯（共犯である者）</u> <u>共犯</u>者も、強盗で起訴された。
775	**execution of business** Article 590 (<u>execution of business</u>) of the Company Act sets out that a member executes the business of the membership company.	<u>業務執行</u> 会社法第590条（<u>業務執行</u>）は、社員は、持分会社の業務を執行することを定める。
776	**executive** [ɪgzékjətɪv] The <u>executive</u> outlined the vision for the next fiscal year.	<u>業務執行者（会社法の場合）</u> <u>業務執行者</u>は、来期のビジョンを説明した。

777	**person who executes (the) business** The <u>person who executes the business</u> oversees daily operations.	**業務執行者** **業務執行者**は、日々の業務を監督する。
778	**executive director** A committee member of the audit committee may not concurrently act as an executive officer or <u>executive director</u> of a company with a nominating committee.	**業務執行取締役** 監査委員会の委員は、指名委員会設置会社の執行役又は**業務執行取締役**を兼ねることができない。
779	**co-ownership** If there are two or more heirs, the inherited property shall belong to those heirs in <u>co-ownership</u>.	**共有** 相続人が数人あるときは、相続財産は、その**共有**に属する。
780	**co-owners** The <u>co-owners</u> agreed to renovate the shared facilities.	**共有者** **共有者**は、共有施設の改修に同意した。
781	**give** [gív] When a public employee, agreeing to perform an act in response to a request, is involved in a bribe in connection with the employee's duty to be <u>given</u> to a third party, imprisonment for not more than 5 years is imposed.	**供与** 公務員が、その職務に関し、請託を受けて、第三者に賄賂を**供与**させたときは、5年以下の懲役に処する。
782	**force** [fɔ́ːrs] No person is conducted to a police station by <u>force</u>, against his or her will unless this is based on the provisions of an act concerning criminal proceedings.	①**強要**、②**連行** (be conducted to X by force) 何人も、刑事訴訟に関する法律の規定によらない限り、その意に反して警察署に**連行**されることはない。
783	**false manifestation of intention** His <u>false manifestation of intention</u> led her misunderstand the value of the estate.	**虚偽表示** 彼の**虚偽表示**は、不動産の価値について彼女を誤信せしめた。
784	**recording medium** The <u>recording medium</u> contained critical data for the investigation.	**記録媒体** **記録媒体**には、捜査のための重要なデータが含まれていた。
785	**necessity** [nəsésəti] Pursuant to Article 37 (<u>necessity</u>) of the Penal Code, the act is not punishable.	**緊急避難** 刑法第37条（**緊急避難**）に基づくと、当該行為は、処罰されない。
786	**monetary claim** The company exercised a <u>monetary claim</u> against the debtor.	**金銭債権** 同社は、債務者に対する**金銭債権**を行使した。

RANK 2

787	**monetary debt**	金銭債務
	Settling the <u>monetary debt</u> improved the credit rating.	その<u>金銭債務</u>を弁済したことで、信用度は向上した。
788	**money and goods**	金品
	The charity distributes <u>money and goods</u> to those in need.	このチャリティーは、困っている人々に<u>金品</u>を配るものである。
789	**financial instruments**	金融商品
	<u>Financial instruments</u> are a key part of our investment strategy.	<u>金融商品</u>は、当社の投資戦略の重要な一部である。
790	**financial instruments business**	金融商品取引業
	The firm operates as a <u>financial instruments business</u> under Japanese laws.	同社は、日本法のもとで<u>金融商品取引業</u>を営んでいる。
791	**financial instruments exchange**	金融商品取引所
	Trades on the <u>financial instruments exchange</u> were temporarily halted.	<u>金融商品取引所</u>での取引は、一時的に停止された。
792	**complaint processing**	苦情処理
	<u>Complaint processing</u> becomes mandatory for platform operators under the new law.	<u>苦情処理</u>は、新法により、プラットフォーム事業者に義務付けられた。
793	**national government**	国（地方公共団体と比較する場合）
	The <u>national government</u> advised local governments.	<u>国</u>は、地方公共団体に対して助言した。
794	**the State**	国（例：国の利害に関係のある訴訟についての法務大臣の権限等に関する法律）
	The Minister of Justice represents the State with regard to suits in which <u>the State</u> is a party.	<u>国</u>を当事者とする訴訟については、法務大臣が、国を代表する。
795	**partner** [pá:rtnər]	組合員
	Each <u>partner</u> contributes unique skills to the business.	各<u>組合員</u>は、それぞれ独自の技能で事業に貢献している。
796	**carry forward**	繰越し
	Losses were <u>carried forward</u> into the next fiscal year.	損失は、翌年度に<u>繰越された</u>。
797	**transitional measure**	経過措置
	<u>Transitional measure</u> allowed for a smoother policy implementation.	<u>経過措置</u>により、よりスムーズな政策実施が可能となった。

798	**publication** [pʌ̀blɪkéɪʃən]	**掲載**
	Publication of the notice is expected next month.	告知の**掲載**は、来月に予定されている。
799	**criminal prosecution**	**刑事訴追**
	Criminal prosecution was initiated following the investigation.	捜査の結果、**刑事訴追**が開始された。
800	**auction applicant**	**競売申立人**
	The auction applicant submit a legally-required document.	**競売申立人**は、決定の書類を提出した。
801	**premiums** [príməmz]	**景品類**
	The term "Premiums" as used in this Act means any article, money, or other source of economic gain given as a means of inducing customers, by an entrepreneur to another party, in connection with a transaction involving goods or services which the entrepreneur supplies.	この法律で「**景品類**」とは、顧客を誘引するための手段として、事業者が自己の供給する商品又は役務の取引に付随して相手方に提供する物品、金銭その他の経済上の利益をいう。
802	**(person) with a special interest in a resolution**	**決議について特別の利害関係を有する者**
	A person with a special interest in a resolution attended the meeting.	決議について特別の利害関係を有する者が、会議に出席した。
803	**accounting period**	**決算期**
	The accounting period ends on December 31st each year.	**決算期**は、毎年12月31日締めである。
804	**statement of accounts**	**決算報告**
	The statement of accounts was reviewed during the annual audit.	**決算報告**は、年次監査で見直された。
805	**order** [ɔ́ːrdər]	**（裁判形式の）決定**
	The court may order on a ruling that the case be subject to an inter-trial arrangement proceeding.	裁判所は、**決定**で、事件を期日間整理手続に付することができる。
806	**written ruling**	**決定書**
	A written ruling was disclosed by the court on the application.	この申立てに関して、裁判所から**決定書**が開示された。
807	**suspicion** [səspíʃən]	**嫌疑**
	The arrest was made on suspicion of embezzlement.	逮捕の**嫌疑**は、横領であった。

RANK 2

808	**title** [táɪtəl]	①権原、②本権
	If a possessor in good faith is defeated in an action on the <u>title</u> (that legally supports the possession), that possessor is deemed to be a possessor in bad faith as from the time when the action is filed.	善意の占有者が<u>本権</u>の訴えにおいて敗訴したときは、その訴えの提起の時から悪意の占有者とみなす。
809	**standing to sue**	原告適格
	Only parties with <u>standing to sue</u> can initiate a lawsuit.	訴えを提起することができるのは、<u>原告適格</u>を有する当事者のみである。
810	**audit** [ɔ́ːdɪt]	会計検査
	The <u>audit</u> of the financial statements uncovered discrepancies.	財務諸表の<u>会計監査</u>により、矛盾が発見された。
811	**actual delivery**	現実の引渡し
	<u>Actual delivery</u> of the goods satisfied the contract terms.	商品の<u>現実の引渡し</u>は、契約条件を満たしていた。
812	**restoration** [rèstəréɪʃən]	原状回復
	<u>Restoration</u> of the building will begin in the spring.	建物の<u>原状回復</u>は、春から始まる。
813	**actual enrichment**	現に受けている利益(現存利益)
	It is sufficient for the other party to return the <u>actual enrichment</u> that the relevant party enjoys.	相手方は、その<u>現に受けている利益</u>を償還すれば足りる。
814	**contribution in kind**	現物出資
	A <u>contribution in kind</u> was made to the startup.	スタートアップに対する<u>現物出資</u>が行われた。
815	**register** [rédʒɪstər]	原簿
	A stock company must, without delay after the day share options are issued, prepare a share option <u>register</u>.	株式会社は、新株予約権を発行した日以後遅滞なく、新株予約権<u>原簿</u>を作成ししなければならない。
816	**(legal) capacity (to hold rights)**	権利能力
	The group has limited <u>legal capacity to hold rights</u>.	その集団は、限られた<u>権利能力</u>を有する。
817	**requirements for perfection of change in rights**	権利変動の対抗要件
	<u>Requirements for perfection of change in rights</u> were met.	<u>権利変動の対抗要件</u>は、充足された。

818	**have an exclusive right**	**権利を専有する**
	The holder of an exclusive right to use will **have an exclusive right** to use a registered trademark in connection with the designated goods or designated services to the extent provided by the agreement under which the right is granted.	専用使用権者は、設定行為で定めた範囲内において、指定商品又は指定役務について登録商標の使用をする**権利を専有する**。
819	**place of the act**	**行為地**
	The law punishes an act that constitutes any crimes under the laws and regulations of the **place of the act**.	当該法律は、**行為地**の法令により罪にあたるものが含まれる。
820	**(legal) capacity (to act)** [kəpǽsəti]	**行為能力**
	Adults possess full **legal capacity to act**.	成人は完全な、**行為能力**を有する。
821	**writ of physical escort**	**勾引状**
	A **writ of physical escort** was issued to ensure appearance in court.	出廷を確実にするため、**勾引状**が発行された。
822	**whistleblowing**	**公益通報**
	Whistleblowing policies protect employees who report misconduct.	**公益通報**規程は、不正行為を報告した従業員を保護する。
823	**whistleblower** [wísəlblòuər]	**公益通報者**
	The **whistleblower** was granted anonymity.	**公益通報者**は、匿名を認められた。
824	**performing** [pərfɔ́ːmiŋ]	**実演**
	"**Performing**" means giving a dramatic performance of, dancing, giving a musical performance of, singing, delivering, declaiming, or by any other means giving a performance of a work.	「**実演**」とは、著作物を、演劇的に演じ、舞い、演奏し、歌い、口演し、朗詠し、又はその他の方法により演ずることをいう。
825	**public charges**	**公課**
	The amount of money to be allocated to distribution will be deducted from the tax or **public charges** imposed on the immovable property.	配当に充てるべき金銭は、不動産に対して課される租税その他の**公課**を控除したものとする。
826	**novation** [nouvéiʃən]	**更改**
	Novation of the contract requires agreement from all parties.	契約の**更改**は、全当事者の合意を要する。

RANK 2

827	**public company** A <u>public company</u> must disclose financial information.	**公開会社** <u>公開会社</u>は、財務情報を開示しなければならない。
828	**tender offer (bid)** The <u>tender offer bid</u> for the company was publicly announced.	**公開買付け（TOB）** 同社に対する<u>公開買付け</u>が、公示された。
829	**permanent establishment** The corporation established a <u>permanent establishment</u> overseas.	**恒久的施設（PE）** 法人は、海外に<u>恒久的施設</u>を設立した。
830	**public facility** The new <u>public facility</u> will include a library and community center.	**公共施設** 新しい<u>公共施設</u>には、図書館及びコミュニティセンターが含まれる。
831	**industrial property right** The company holds an <u>industrial property right</u> for the new design.	**工業所有権** 同社は、新しいデザインの<u>工業所有権</u>を保有している。
832	**public safety** If the supervisory government agency has stated the opinion that submission of said document would cause a risk that the document will hinder maintenance of <u>public safety</u>, the court may not, in general, order the person in possession of the document to submit the document.	**公共の安全** 監督官庁が当該文書の提出により、<u>公共の安全</u>の維持に支障を及ぼすおそれがある旨の意見を述べたときは、裁判所は、文書の所持者に対し、原則として提出を命ずることができない。
833	**detention** [dɪténʃən] The suspect was taken into <u>detention</u> pending further investigation.	**勾留** 被疑者は<u>勾留</u>され、今後の捜査が待たれる。
834	**appeal from/against a ruling** An <u>appeal from a ruling</u> was filed with the higher court.	**抗告** 決定に対する<u>抗告</u>が、高等裁判所に提出された。
835	**public notice** <u>Public notice</u> of the business transfer was posted in the newspaper.	**公告** 事業譲渡の<u>公告</u>は、新聞に掲載された。
836	**limited partnership company** The <u>limited partnership company</u> is a popular business structure.	**合資会社** <u>合資会社</u>は、一般的な事業形態である。
837	**public notification** <u>Public notification</u> is required for certain legal processes.	**公示催告** 特定の法的手続においては、<u>公示催告</u>が義務付けられている。

838	**service by publication**	公示送達
	Service by publication is used when parties cannot be directly contacted.	公示送達は、当事者に直接連絡できない場合に利用される。
839	**notary** [nóʊtəri]	公証人（末尾㉚参照）
	The notary authenticated the signatures on the agreement.	公証人は、契約書の署名を認証した。
840	**reassessment** [riəsésmənt]	更正（税務）
	"Reassessment" includes reassessment pursuant to the provisions of Article 24 of the Act on General Rules for National Taxes.	「更正」とは、国税通則法第24条の規定による更正を含む。
841	**reorganization** [rìɔrgənəzéɪʃən]	更生（会社）
	Reorganization of the subsidiary aims to improve efficiency.	子会社の更生は、効率化を目指す。
842	**notarial instrument**	公正証書（末尾㉞参照）
	The notarial instrument confirmed the agreement legally.	公正証書は、この合意を法的に確認するものである。
843	**fair trade**	公正取引
	These regulations ensure fair trade among businesses.	これらの規制は、企業間の公正取引を確保する。
844	**impartial** [impáːrʃəl]	公正な
	Decisions were made by an impartial arbitrator.	決定は、公平な仲裁人によって下された。
845	**fair practice**	公正な慣行
	Fair practice in advertising is regulated.	広告の公正な慣行は、規制されている。
846	**fair competition**	公正な競争
	Fair competition is crucial for a healthy market.	公正な競争は、健全な市場にとって重要である。
847	**employees pension insurance**	厚生年金
	Employees' pension insurance provides retirement benefits.	厚生年金は、退職給付を提供する。

RANK 2

848	**in public**	公然と
	A person who defames another person by making allegations <u>in public</u>, regardless of whether such facts are true or false, is punished by imprisonment or imprisonment without work for not more than 3 years or a fine of not more than 500,000 yen.	**公然と**事実を摘示し、人の名誉を毀損した者は、その事実の有無にかかわらず、3年以下の懲役若しくは禁錮又は50万円以下の罰金に処する。
849	**binding** [báɪndɪŋ]	拘束（力）
	The contract is <u>binding</u> upon signature by both parties.	契約は、両当事者の署名によって**拘束力**を持つ。
850	**court of second instance**	控訴裁判所・控訴審
	The case was elevated to the <u>court of second instance</u>.	裁判は、**控訴審**に持ち越された。
851	**statement of reasons for appeal**	控訴趣意書
	The <u>statement of reasons for appeal</u> was meticulously prepared.	**控訴趣意書**は、綿密に作成されていた。
852	**petition for appeal**	控訴状
	The <u>petition for appeal</u> must be submitted by the deadline.	**控訴状**は、期限までに提出しなければならない。
853	**appellant** [əpélɪnt]	①控訴人、②抗告人
	The <u>appellant</u> argues for a reevaluation of the evidence.	**控訴人**は、証拠の再評価を主張する。
854	**robber** [rá:bər]	強盗
	The <u>robber</u> was apprehended shortly after the incident.	**強盗**は、事件直後に逮捕された。
855	**robbery** [rá:bəri]	強盗（罪名）
	The <u>robbery</u> investigation is ongoing, with leads being followed.	**強盗**の捜査は継続中で、手がかりを追っている。
856	**limited liability company**	合同会社
	"Company" means any stock company, general partnership company, limited partnership company or <u>limited liability company</u>.	「会社」とは、株式会社、合名会社、合資会社又は**合同会社**をいう。
857	**certified public accountant**	公認会計士
	The <u>certified public accountant</u> reviewed the financial statements.	**公認会計士**が、財務諸表をレビューした。

858	**trial preparation**	公判準備
	With regard to a statement made by a person other than the accused during <u>trial preparation</u> and which contains the statement of the accused, the provisions of Article 322 of Code of Criminal Procedure shall apply mutatis mutandis to it.	被告人以外の者の**公判準備**における供述で被告人の供述をその内容とするものについては、刑事訴訟法第322条の規定を準用する。
859	**pretrial conference procedure**	公判前整理手続
	The <u>pretrial conference procedure</u> aims to streamline the trial.	**公判前整理手続**は、裁判を合理化することを目的としている。
860	**delivery** [dɪlívəri]	①**物の給付**、②**交付**、③**弁済**、④**現実の物の引渡し**
	If the obligor has completed the acts necessary to <u>deliver</u> the thing, that thing thenceforth constitutes the subject matter of the claim.	債務者が**物の給付**をするのに必要な行為を完了したときは、以後その物を債権の目的物とする。
861	**issuance** [íʃuəns]	免許・命令の交付
	The <u>issuance</u> of the license takes a week.	**免許の交付**は、1週間を要する。
862	**personal service**	交付送達
	Pursuant to Article 102-2 (principle of <u>personal service</u>) of the Civil Procedure Act, except as otherwise provided, a service of documents is effected through the delivery of the document with which a person is to be served, to the person on whom it is to be served.	民事訴訟法第102条の2（**交付送達**の原則）によれば、書類の送達は、特別の定めがある場合を除き、送達を受けるべき者に送達すべき書類を交付してする。
863	**joint venture**	合弁企業（JV）
	The <u>joint venture</u> will explore new market opportunities.	**合弁企業**は新たな市場機会を模索する。
864	**general partnership company**	合名会社
	A Company must use in its trade name the words "Kabushiki-Kaisha", "Gomei-Kaisha", "Goushi-Kaisha" or "Goudou-Kaisha" respectively for stock company, <u>general partnership company</u>, limited partnership company or limited liability company.	会社は、株式会社、**合名会社**、合資会社又は合同会社の種類に従い、それぞれその商号中に株式会社、合名会社、合資会社又は合同会社という文字を用いなければならない。
865	**validity** [vəlídəti]	効力
	The <u>validity</u> of the contract is under dispute.	契約の**効力**が、争われている。

RANK 2

#	Term	Translation
866	**accusation** [ækjəzéɪʃən] The <u>accusation</u> was serious, prompting immediate police investigation.	告発 <u>告発</u>は深刻で、直ちに警察の捜査が行われた。
867	**sole proprietor** As a <u>sole proprietor</u>, the business decisions rest solely with her.	個人事業者 <u>個人事業者</u>であるため、ビジネス上の決断は彼女一人に委ねられている。
868	**shares of different classes** <u>Shares of different classes</u> offer varying rights and dividends.	異なる種類の株式 <u>異なる種類の株式</u>は、さまざまな権利と配当を提供する。
869	**administrative determination** The <u>administrative determination</u> was challenged by the affected party.	裁決 この<u>裁決</u>は、影響を受けた当事者によって争われた。
870	**meeting of creditors** The <u>meeting of creditors</u> will be held at a conference center.	債権者集会 <u>債権者集会</u>は、会議場で開催される。
871	**creditor's (obligee's) right of subrogation** Pursuant to Article 423 (requirements for <u>creditor's right of subrogation</u>) of the Civil Act, an obligee may exercise the right of the obligor when it is necessary to do so in order to preserve the obligee's own claim.	債権者代位権 民法第423条（<u>債権者代位権</u>の要件）によれば、債権者は、自己の債権を保全するため必要があるときは、債務者に属する権利を行使することができる。
872	**common interests of the creditors** Protecting the <u>common interests of the creditors</u> was essential.	債権者の一般の利益 <u>債権者の一般の利益</u>を守ることは、不可欠であった。
873	**list of holders of dischargeable claims** The <u>list of holders of dischargeable claims</u> was distributed to the lawyers.	債権者名簿 <u>債権者名簿</u>が、弁護士に対して、配布された。
874	**act that would harm creditors** Any <u>act that would harm creditors</u> is strictly prohibited.	債権者を害する行為 <u>債権者を害する行為</u>は、固く禁じられている。
875	**equitable distribution** <u>Equitable distribution</u> ensures fair treatment of children.	財産分与 <u>財産分与</u>は、子の公平な扱いを保証する。
876	**inventory of assets** The <u>inventory of assets</u> was completed.	財産目録 <u>財産目録</u>が完成した。

RANK 2

877	**most recent business year** Financial reports for the <u>most recent business year</u> were analyzed.	**最終事業年度（会社法）** **最終事業年度**の財務報告書が、分析された。
878	**re-examination** The <u>re-examination</u> of evidence could lead to new insights.	**再尋問** 証拠を**再尋問**することで、新たな洞察が得られるかもしれない。
879	**(proposed) rehabilitation plan** The <u>proposed rehabilitation plan</u> offers a pathway to solvency.	**再生計画** **再生計画**案は、支払への道筋を示すものである。
880	**rehabilitation debtor** The <u>rehabilitation debtor</u> is working closely with financial advisors.	**再生債務者** **再生債務者**はファイナンシャルアドバイザーと緊密に連携している。
881	**rehabilitation proceedings** <u>Rehabilitation proceedings</u> aim to restore the company's financial health.	**再生手続** **再生手続**は、会社の財務的健全性を回復することを目的としている。
882	**detailed regulations** <u>Detailed regulations</u> govern the court process.	**細則** **細則**は、法廷の手続を規定している。
883	**ruling** [rúːlɪŋ] A <u>ruling</u> on the matter is expected soon.	**裁定** この件に関する**裁定**は、近日中に出る予定だ。
884	**be in office** The elected official will <u>be in office</u> for a four-year term.	**在任する** 選出された役員の**在任する**期間（任期）は4年である。
885	**court clerk** The <u>court clerk</u> meticulously recorded the trial proceedings.	**裁判所書記官** **裁判所書記官**は裁判の経過を丹念に記録した。
886	**reduction or release of debts** The <u>reduction or release of debts</u> can offer a fresh start.	**債務の減免** **債務の減免**は、再出発のきっかけとなる。
887	**title of obligation** Compulsory execution shall be carried out based on the <u>title of obligation</u>.	**債務名義** 強制執行は、**債務名義**により行う。
888	**statutory lien** A <u>statutory lien</u> provides security to the creditor.	**先取特権** **先取特権**は、当該債権者に担保を提供する。

RANK 2

889	**seizure-prohibition**	**差押禁止**
	The court ordered a <u>seizure-prohibition</u> to protect assets.	裁判所は、資産保全のために<u>**差押禁止**</u>を命じた。
890	**attaching creditor**	**差押債権者**
	The <u>attaching creditor</u> refused to meet the debtor.	<u>**差押債権者**</u>は、債務者との面談を拒絶した。
891	**negotiable (debt) instrument payable to order**	**指図証券（債権）** ※民法改正により証券的債権の規定が削除された。
	Assignment of a <u>negotiable instrument payable to order</u> does not become effective unless the instrument is indorsed and delivered to the assignee.	<u>**指図証券**</u>の譲渡は、その証券に譲渡の裏書をして譲受人に交付しなければ、その効力を生じない。
892	**remand** [rɪmǽnd]	**差戻し**
	If the court of second instance reverses a judgment in the first instance that has dismissed the action without prejudice as unlawful, it shall <u>remand</u> the case to the court of first instance.	控訴裁判所は、訴えを不適法として却下した第一審判決を取り消す場合には、事件を第一審裁判所に<u>**差し戻**</u>さなければならない。
893	**discriminatory treatment**	**差別的取扱い**
	<u>Discriminatory treatment</u> of employees is strictly prohibited.	従業員に対する<u>**差別的取扱い**</u>は、固く禁じられている。
894	**participation** [pərtìsəpéɪʃən]	**参加**
	If a liquidating stock company regards it as necessary in preparing a draft agreement, it may seek the <u>participation</u> of the creditors.	清算株式会社は、協定案の作成に当たり必要があると認めるときは、債権者の<u>**参加**</u>を求めることができる。
895	**grounds** [gráʊndz]	①**敷地**、②**原因**、③**事由**
	The authority to represent by mandate ceases to exist, other than on the <u>grounds</u> set forth in the respective items of the preceding paragraph, upon the termination of the mandate.	委任による代理権は、前項各号に掲げる<u>**事由**</u>のほか、委任の終了によって消滅する。
896	**site** [sáɪt]	**敷地**
	The term "Building Lot" means land used as a building <u>site</u>.	「宅地」とは、建物の<u>**敷地**</u>に供せられる土地をいう。

897	**magnetic form**	磁気的方式
	Articles of incorporation may be prepared in the form of an electronic or magnetic record (meaning a record created in electronic form, magnetic form, or any other form that cannot be perceived by the human senses).	定款は、電磁的記録(電子的方式、**磁気的方式**その他人の知覚によっては認識することができない方式で作られる記録をいう。)をもって作成することができる。
898	**business transfer**	事業の譲渡
	In cases where business transfer is to be effected, dissenting shareholders may demand that the stock company effecting the business transfer purchase, at a fair price, the shares that they hold.	**事業の譲渡**をする場合には、反対株主は、事業譲渡をする株式会社に対し、自己の有する株式を公正な価格で買い取ることを請求することができる。
899	**transfer of business**	事業の譲渡
	Transfer of business involves complex legal considerations.	**事業の譲渡**には、複雑な法的考慮事項が伴う。
900	**acquisition of a business**	事業の譲受け
	The acquisition of a business was finalized last month.	先月、**事業の譲受け**が決まった。
901	**private right**	私権
	Private right enforcement varies significantly from public law.	**私権**の行使は、公法とは大きく異なる。
902	**treasury share**	自己株式
	The company decided to buy back treasury shares.	同社は、**自己株式**の取得を決定した。
903	**equity capital**	自己資本
	Equity capital increased following the recent share issuance.	最近の株式発行により、**自己資本**が増加した。
904	**expenditure** [ɪkspéndətʃər]	支出
	The project's expenditures exceeded initial budget forecasts.	プロジェクトの**支出**は、当初の予算の予測を上回った。
905	**pledge** [pléʤ]	①質権、②誓約
	A thing that cannot be transferred to another person may not be made the subject of a pledge.	**質権**は、譲り渡すことができない物をその目的とすることができない。
906	**pledgee** [pleʤíː]	質権者
	A pledgee has the right to possess a thing received from an obligor as security for their claims.	**質権者**は、その債権の担保として債務者から受け取った物を占有する権利を有する。

RANK 2

907	**pledgor** [pledʒɔ́ː]	**質権設定者**
	A pledgee may not allow a <u>pledgor</u> to possess the thing pledged on behalf of the pledgee.	質権者は、**質権設定者**に、自己に代わって質物の占有をさせることができない。
908	**municipality** [mjùːnɪsəpǽləti]	**市町村**
	The <u>municipality</u> approved the new public park projects.	**市町村**は、新しい公営公園の計画を承認した。
909	**certificate of execution**	**執行文**
	Execution of a provisional remedy is to be implemented based on an authenticated copy of the order for the provisional remedy with a <u>certificate of execution</u> attached thereto.	保全執行は、**執行文**の付された保全命令の正本に基づいて実施する。
910	**executive officer**	**執行役**
	The <u>executive officer</u> announced a strategic shift.	**執行役**は、戦略転換を発表した。
911	**suspended execution of the sentence**	**執行猶予**
	<u>Suspended execution of the sentence</u> offers a conditional reprieve.	**執行猶予**は、条件付きで猶予を与えるものである。
912	**private monopolization**	**私的独占**
	<u>Private monopolization</u> is prohibited under antitrust laws.	**私的独占**は、独占禁止法で禁止されている。
913	**manager** [mǽnədʒər]	**支配人**
	A company may appoint <u>managers</u> and have them carry out its business at its head office or branch office.	会社は、**支配人**を選任し、その本店又は支店において、その事業を行わせることができる。
914	**place for payment**	**支払地**
	The contract specifies the <u>place for payment</u>.	契約書には、**支払地**が明記されている。
915	**delay in payment**	**支払遅延**
	A <u>delay in payment</u> may incur additional charges.	**支払遅延**の場合、追加の手数料が発生する場合がある。
916	**ability to pay**	**支払能力**
	The company's <u>ability to pay</u> is under scrutiny by analysts.	同社の**支払能力**は、アナリストによって精査されている。
917	**quarterly securities report**	**四半期報告書**
	The <u>quarterly securities report</u> was abolished to some extent.	**四半期報告書**は、一定程度廃止された。

918	**private placement**		**私募**
	A bank is considering **private placements** of securities.		銀行は、有価証券の**私募**を検討している。
919	**amount of stated capital**		**資本金の額**
	The **amount of stated capital** is disclosed in the company's website.		**資本金の額**は、会社のウェブサイトに開示されている。
920	**capital reserve**		**資本準備金**
	Capital reserve is one of the metrics in financial health.		**資本準備金**は、財務の健全性の指標の1つである。
921	**nominating committee**		**指名委員会**
	The **nominating committee** proposed new board candidates.		**指名委員会**は、新取締役候補者を提案した。
922	**company with nominating committee, etc.**		**指名委員会等設置会社**
	The **company with nominating committee, etc.**, upholds governance standards.		**指名委員会等設置会社**は、ガバナンス基準を堅持している。
923	**nominative claim**		**指名債権**
	After the day on which the monetary claims record ceases to be effective, electronically recorded monetary claims continue to exist as **nominative claims** with the contents of the electronically recorded monetary claims which were recorded in the record.		電子記録債権は、債権記録がその効力を失った日以後は、当該債権記録に記録された電子記録債権の内容をその権利の内容とする**指名債権**として存続するものとする。
924	**general meeting (of members)**		**社員総会**
	The **general meeting (of members)** is scheduled for June.		**社員総会**は、6月に予定されている。
925	**release** [rilíːs]		①**免除**、②**釈放**
	Release from contractual obligations requires mutual consent.		契約上の義務の**免除**には双方の同意が必要である。
926	**authority to ask for clarification**		**釈明権**
	The Rules on Hearings by the Fair Trade Commission provides the chief hearing officer's **authority to ask for clarification**.		公正取引委員会の審判に関する規則は、審判長の**釈明権**を定める。
927	**bond administrator**		**社債管理者**
	Bond administrators must perform the administration of bonds in a fair and sincere manner on behalf of the bondholders.		**社債管理者**は、社債権者のために、公平かつ誠実に社債の管理を行わなければならない。

RANK 2

928 bondholder
[báːndhòʊldər]

Bond administrators must manage the bonds with due care of a prudent manager to the <u>bondholders</u>.

社債権者

社債管理者は、**社債権者**に対し、善良な管理者の注意をもって社債の管理を行わなければならない。

929 bondholders meeting

The court may dismiss a bond administrator in response to a petition by a <u>bondholders meeting</u> if there are other justifiable grounds.

社債権者集会

裁判所は、正当な理由があるときは、**社債権者集会**の申立てにより、当該社債管理者を解任することができる。

930 final order

When the timing is right for making a judicial decision in a non-contentious case, the court will make a <u>final order</u>.

終局決定（非訟事件訴訟法）

裁判所は、非訟事件が裁判をするのに熟したときは、**終局決定**をする。

931 final judgment

An objection against the <u>final judgment</u> on an action on small claim may be made to the court that has made the judgment, within an unextendable period of two weeks from the day on which a judgment document is served.

終局判決

少額訴訟の**終局判決**に対しては、判決書の送達を受けた日から2週間の不変期間内に、その判決をした裁判所に異議を申し立てることができる。

932 secondary
[sékəndèri]

The guarantee obligation includes interest, penalty and compensation for loss or damage in connection with the principal obligation, and all other charges <u>secondary</u> to that obligation.

従たる

保証債務は、主たる債務に関する利息、違約金、損害賠償その他その債務に**従たる**すべてのものを包含する。

933 focused examination of witnesses and parties

<u>Focused examination of witnesses and parties</u> streamlines trials.

集中証拠調べ

集中証拠調べは、裁判を効率化する。

934 public inspection

<u>Public inspection</u> of documents ensures transparency.

縦覧

文書の**縦覧**は、透明性を確保する。

935 beneficial interest

A person designated by the clause of the terms of trust as the person who is to be a beneficiary automatically acquires a <u>beneficial interest</u>.

受益権

信託行為の定めにより受益者となるべき者として指定された者は、当然に**受益権**を取得する。

936	**beneficiary** [bènəfíʃièri] The term "beneficiary" as used in this Act means a person who holds a beneficial interest in a trust.	受益者 この法律において「受益者」とは、受益権を有する者をいう。
937	**bailee** [bèilí:] The bailee is responsible for the safekeeping of the goods.	受寄者 受寄者は、商品の保管に責任を負う。
938	**delegation of powers** Delegation of powers is critical in large organizations.	授権 授権は、大きな組織では非常に重要である。
939	**direct examination** Direct examination is the first phase of witness testimony.	主尋問 主尋問は、証人尋問の第一段階である。
940	**consignee** [kànsainí] The consignee receives the shipped goods.	①（委託販売における）受託者、②荷受人 荷受人は、出荷された商品を受け取る。
941	**entrustee** The entrustee managed assets on behalf of another.	（その他の事務における）受託者 受託者は、他人に代わって資産を管理した。
942	**trustee** [trʌ́stí] The term "trustee" means a person who is under the obligation to administer of property that comes under trust property.	受託者 「受託者」とは、信託財産に属する財産の管理をすべき義務を負う者をいう。
943	**principal debtor** The principal debtor bears the primary obligation for debt.	主たる債務者（金銭債務の場合） 主たる債務者は、債務の一時的な返済義務を負う。
944	**principal obligor** The principal obligor acknowledged the performance of the contract.	主たる債務者（金銭債務以外の一般債務の場合） 主たる債務者が、契約の履行を確認した。
945	**capital investor** A capital investor provides funds for business growth.	出資者 出資者は、事業成長のために資金を提供する。
946	**equity investor** An equity investor takes a stake in the company.	出資者 出資者は、会社に出資する。

RANK 2

947	**return of contribution**	出資の払戻し
	Return of contribution occurs upon dissolution of the entity.	出資の払戻しは、事業体の解散時に行われる。
948	**statute of limitations for filing an action**	出訴期間
	The statute of limitations for filing an action is five years.	出訴期間は、5年である。
949	**appearance** [əpíərəns]	出頭
	The special inquiry officer may order the appearance of witnesses, put them under oath and seek testimony.	特別審理官は、証人の出頭を命じて、宣誓をさせ、証言を求めることができる。
950	**share subject to call**	取得条項付株式
	The share subject to call gives the company a repurchase right.	取得条項付株式は、会社に買戻しの権利を与える。
951	**share option subject to call**	取得条項付新株予約権
	Employees were offered a share option subject to call as part of their compensation package.	従業員には、報酬パッケージの一部として、取得条項付新株予約権が提供された。
952	**share with put option**	取得請求権付株式
	A share with put option allows investors to sell back to the company.	取得請求権付株式は、投資家が会社に売り戻すことを可能にする。
953	**delegatee** [dèligətí:]	受任者（末尾㉛参照）
	The delegatee efficiently managed the delegated tasks.	受任者は、委任された仕事を効率的に管理した。
954	**mandatary** [mǽndətèri]	受任者（末尾㉛参照）
	The mandatary is authorized to act on behalf of another.	受任者は、他者に代わって行動する権限を有する。
955	**major shareholder**	主要株主
	If a major shareholder becomes the specified major shareholder of the financial instruments business operator, it must notify the Prime Minister of this without delay, pursuant to the provisions of Cabinet Office Order.	主要株主は、金融商品取引業者の特定主要株主となったときは、内閣府令で定めるところにより、遅滞なく、その旨を内閣総理大臣に届け出なければならない。
956	**obligee's delay in acceptance**	受領遅滞
	The contract faced obligee's delay in acceptance, complicating matters.	この契約は、債権者の受領遅滞に直面し、問題を複雑にした。

957	**company with class shares**	**種類株式発行会社**
	"Company with Class Shares" means any stock company which issues two or more classes of shares with different features as to the matter including, but not limited to, the dividend of surplus.	**種類株式発行会社**とは、剰余金の配当その他の事項について内容の異なる二以上の種類の株式を発行する株式会社をいう。
958	**general meeting of class shareholders**	**種類株主総会**
	The general meeting of class shareholders discussed unique rights.	**種類株主総会**では、独自の権利について話し合われた。
959	**a class of shares**	**種類の株式**
	A company with class shares may provide in the articles of incorporation that, as a feature of a class of shares, a resolution at the general meeting of class shareholders is not required.	種類株式発行会社は、**種類の株式**の内容として、種類株主総会の決議を要しない旨を定款で定めることができる。
960	**order** [ɔ́ːrdər]	**順位**
	If more than one mortgage is created with respect to the same immovables, the order of priority of those mortgages follows the chronological order of their registration.	同一の不動産について数個の抵当権が設定されたときは、その抵当権の**順位**は、登記の前後による。
961	**reserve** [rɪzə́ːrv]	**準備金**
	The amount not recorded as stated capital must be recorded as capital reserves.	資本金として計上しないこととした額は、資本**準備金**として計上しなければならない。
962	**preliminary oral arguments**	**準備的口頭弁論**
	Preliminary oral arguments clarified the case's scope.	**準備的口頭弁論**では、この訴訟の範囲が明確にされた。
963	**inquiry** [ínkwəri]	**照会**
	The inquiry into the matter is ongoing.	この件に関する**照会**は、進行中である。
964	**redemption** [rɪdémpʃən]	①**株式・社債の償還**、②**買戻し**
	The right to claim the redemption of bonds will be extinguished by prescription if not exercised for ten years from the time that this right can be exercised.	**社債の償還**請求権は、これを行使することができる時から10年間行使しないときは、時効によって消滅する。
965	**upper instance court**	**上級審**
	The upper instance court reviewed the appeal thoroughly.	**上級審**は、この訴えを徹底的に検討した。

RANK 2

966	**assumption** [əsʌ́mpʃən]	①債務の承継、②債務引受
	An additional obligor resulting from the <u>assumption</u> of obligation not releasing an obligor assumes, jointly and severally with the initial obligor, an obligation of the same content as the obligation assumed by the initial obligor to the obligee.	併存的**債務引受**の引受人は、債務者と連帯して、債務者が債権者に対して負担する債務と同一の内容の債務を負担する。
967	**testify** [téstəfaɪ]	証言（する）
	Witnesses are scheduled to <u>testify</u> next week.	来週、証人の**証言**が予定されている。
968	**commercial act(s)**	商行為
	The term "ship" means a ship that is used in a voyage at sea for the purpose of conducting a <u>commercial act</u>.	「船舶」とは、**商行為**をする目的で航海の用に供する船舶をいう。
969	**collection of evidence**	証拠収集
	The <u>collection of evidence</u> is crucial for building the case.	**証拠収集**は、立件のために極めて重要である。
970	**description of evidence**	証拠説明書
	The <u>description of evidence</u> detailed its relevance.	**証拠説明書**には、その関連性が詳述されている。
971	**offer of evidence**	証拠の申出
	The prosecution made an <u>offer of evidence</u> to strengthen their case.	検察側は立証を強化するために、**証拠の申出**をした。
972	**category of evidence**	証拠の類型
	The defense counsel must promptly disclose the evidence which he or she has requested to be examined to the public prosecutor according to each <u>category of evidence</u>.	弁護人は、取調べを請求した証拠については、速やかに、検察官に対し、**証拠の類型**に応じ、開示をしなければならない。
973	**preservation of evidence**	証拠保全
	<u>Preservation of evidence</u> is crucial for the trial's integrity.	**証拠保全**は、裁判の完全性のために極めて重要である。
974	**convocation notice**	招集通知
	The <u>convocation notice</u> was sent to all relevant parties.	**招集通知**は、関係者全員に送られた。

975	**circumstances** [sə́ːrkəmstænsəz]	情状
	When a person has been sentenced to imprisonment or imprisonment without work for not more than 3 years or a fine of not more than 500,000 yen, the execution of the entire sentence may be suspended in light of <u>circumstances</u> for a period of not less than 1 year but not more than 5 years from the day on which the sentence becomes final and binding.	3年以下の懲役若しくは禁錮又は50万円以下の罰金の言渡しを受けたときは、**情状**により、裁判が確定した日から1年以上5年以下の期間、その刑の全部の執行を猶予することができる。
976	**petition** [pətíʃən]	上申
	The persons listed below may, ex officio, <u>petition</u> for a special pardon or commutation of a sentence with respect to a specific person.	次に掲げる者は、職権で、特赦又は特定の者に対する減刑の**上申**をすることができる。
977	**loan for use**	使用貸借
	If the parties specify a period of a <u>loan for use</u>, the loan for use is terminated upon the expiration of the period.	当事者が**使用貸借**の期間を定めたときは、使用貸借は、その期間が満了することによって終了する。
978	**capital gain**	譲渡所得
	Real estate sales generated significant <u>capital gain</u>.	不動産売却は、多額の**譲渡所得**をもたらした。
979	**consumer** [kənsúːmər]	消費者
	<u>Consumer</u> rights are protected by law.	**消費者**の権利は、法律によって保護されている。
980	**consumer contract**	消費者契約
	The term "<u>consumer contract</u>" means a contract entered into by and between a consumer and a business operator.	「**消費者契約**」とは、消費者と事業者との間で締結される契約をいう。
981	**loan (for consumption)** [lóun]	消費貸借
	The <u>loan (for consumption)</u> agreement specifies the interest rate.	**消費貸借**契約書には、金利が明記されている。
982	**trademark registration**	商標登録
	<u>Trademark registration</u> protects the brand's identity.	**商標登録**は、ブランドのアイデンティティを保護する。
983	**access to information**	情報公開
	<u>Access to information</u> is a key right.	**情報公開**は、重要な権利である。

RANK 2

984	**extract** [ékstrækt]	**抄本**
	The parties to a case may file a request to copy the non-electronic or magnetic case records, or to issue an authenticated copy, transcript or **extract** of the electronic or magnetic case records.	当事者は、非電磁的訴訟記録の謄写又はその正本、謄本若しくは**抄本**の交付を請求することができる。
985	**facts to be proved**	**①立証趣旨、②証明予定事実**
	In a pretrial arrangement proceeding, disclosure of the **facts to be proved**, the particulars to be examined and other particulars relating to the evidence requested may be taken.	公判前整理手続において、請求に係る証拠について、その**立証趣旨**、尋問事項等を明らかにさせることができる。
986	**probative value (of evidence)**	**証明力**
	The **probative value (of evidence)** can sway the trial's outcome.	証拠の**証明力**は、裁判の結果を左右する。
987	**extinction** [ɪkstíŋkʃən]	**消滅（末尾㉑参照）**
	Extinction of a claim can occur over time.	請求権の**消滅**は、時間の経過とともに起こりうる。
988	**extinguishment** [ɪkstíŋgwɪʃmənt]	**消滅（末尾㉑参照）**
	Extinguishment of debt frees the debtor from obligation.	債務の**消滅**は、債務者を義務から解放する。
989	**disappearing company**	**消滅会社**
	The **disappearing company** was absorbed through a merger.	**消滅会社**は、合併によって吸収された。
990	**extinctive prescription**	**消滅時効**
	Extinctive prescription limits the time to bring forward a claim.	**消滅時効**は、請求権を行使できる期間を制限する。
991	**convention** [kənvénʃən]	**条約**
	The **convention** set new standards for international trade.	この**条約**は、国際貿易の新しい基準を定めた。
992	**treaty** [tríti]	**条約**
	The **treaty** enhanced cooperation between the countries.	この**条約**により、両国間の協力関係が強化された。

993	**surplus** [sə́ːrpləs]	**剰余金**
	A stock company may distribute dividends of <u>surplus</u> to its shareholders.	株式会社は、その株主に対し、**剰余金**の配当をすることができる。
994	**appropriation of surplus**	**剰余金の処分**
	The board discussed the <u>appropriation of surplus</u> funds.	取締役会は、**剰余金の処分**について討議した。
995	**dividend of surplus**	**剰余金の配当**
	A <u>dividend of surplus</u> was declared this fiscal year.	今期は、**剰余金の配当**が宣言された。
996	**commission** [kəmíʃən]	①嘱託（裁判の嘱託手続）、②委託料金（コミッション）
	A court clerk is to <u>commission</u> the registration of a provisional seizure.	仮差押えの登記は、裁判所書記官が**嘱託**する。
997	**employee invention**	**職務発明**
	The <u>employee invention</u> is patented under the company's name.	**職務発明**は、会社名で特許が取得される。
998	**direct control (over things)**	①直接に支配する、（②所持） ※②の「所持」の意味でdirect controlが用いられる条文は見当たらなかった。
	The relationship of <u>direct control</u> means any relationships between one person and another person whereby the relevant other person falls under the category of corporation listed in the following.	**直接に支配する**関係とは、一方の者と他方の者との間に当該他方の者が次に掲げる法人に該当する関係がある場合における当該関係をいう。
999	**holder** [hóʊldər]	**所持者**
	The <u>holder</u> of the document presented it as evidence.	その書類の**所持者**が、証拠として提出した。
1000	**possessor** [pəzésər]	①所持人、②占有者
	The <u>possessor</u> of the property maintained it well.	不動産の**占有者**は、適切に管理をしていた。
1001	**documentary evidence**	**書証**
	<u>Documentary evidence</u> was crucial for the case's outcome.	**書証**は、この裁判の結果を左右する重要なものであった。
1002	**examination of evidence by court's own authority**	**職権証拠調べ**
	The <u>examination of evidence by court's own authority</u> is thorough.	裁判所の**職権証拠調べ**は、徹底している。

RANK 2

RANK 2

1003 matters to be examined upon court's own authority (by the court sua sponte) — 職権調査事項

The provisions of the preceding two Articles do not apply to <u>matters to be examined by the court sua sponte</u>.

前二条の規定は、裁判所が**職権調査事項**には、適用しない。

1004 first day — 初日

When a period is provided for in days, weeks, months, or years, the <u>first day</u> of the period is not included in the computation.

日、週、月又は年によって期間を定めたときは、期間の**初日**は、算入しない。

1005 consider [kənsídər] — 思料する

The court may, when it is necessary, seize articles of evidence or articles which it is <u>considered</u> should be confiscated.

裁判所は、必要があるときは、証拠物又は没収すべき物と**思料する**ものを差し押えることができる。

1006 known creditor — 知れている債権者

If creditors of a stock company may state their objections, relevant stock company must give public notice of the matters set forth below in the official gazette and must give notices inviting objections separately to each <u>known creditor</u>, if any.

株式会社の債権者が異議を述べることができる場合には、当該株式会社は、次に掲げる事項を官報に公告し、かつ、**知れている債権者**には、各別にこれを催告しなければならない。

1007 moral right — 人格権

An author's <u>moral right</u> to their work is protected by law.

著作者**人格権**は、法律によって保護されている。

1008 share option holder — 新株予約権者

The <u>share option holder</u> awaits market improvement.

新株予約権者は、市況の改善を待っている。

1009 bond with share option — 新株予約権付社債

A <u>bond with share option</u> offers investment flexibility.

新株予約権付社債は、投資の柔軟性を提供する。

1010 allotment of share option without contribution — 新株予約権無償割当て

<u>Allotment of share option without contribution</u> benefits key employees.

新株予約権無償割当ては、主要な従業員に給付される。

1011 novelty [ná:vəlti] — 新規性

<u>Novelty</u> is a key criterion for patent applications.

新規性は、特許出願の重要な基準である。

#	Term	Japanese
1012	**person who has parental authority**	親権者
	The <u>person who has parental authority</u> may consent to the medical procedure.	<u>親権者</u>は、医療行為に同意できる。
1013	**date for scheduling conference**	進行協議期日
	The <u>date for scheduling conference</u> was agreed upon by both parties.	<u>進行協議期日</u>について、両者の合意が得られた。
1014	**conviction** [kənvíkʃən]	心証（末尾㉒参照）
	If the Fair Trade Commission is <u>convinced</u>, after an investigation conducted pursuant to the procedures provided in Chapter XII, that a criminal offense has taken place, it must file an accusation with the Prosecutor General.	公正取引委員会は、第12章に規定する手続による調査により犯則の<u>心証</u>を得たときは、検事総長に告発しなければならない。
1015	**authentic** [əθéntɪk]	真正な
	The e-signature was verified as <u>authentic</u> by experts.	この電子署名は、専門家によって<u>真正な</u>署名であることが確認された。
1016	**consolidation-type merger**	新設合併
	A <u>consolidation-type merger</u> unites companies into a single entity.	<u>新設合併</u>は、企業を1つの事業体に統合するものである。
1017	**incorporation-type company split**	新設分割
	The <u>incorporation-type company split</u> created specialized subsidiaries.	<u>新設分割</u>により、専門の子会社が設立された。
1018	**trust** [trʌ́st]	信託
	A <u>trust</u> manages assets for beneficiaries.	<u>信託</u>は、受益者のために資産を管理する。
1019	**trust agreement**	信託契約
	The <u>trust agreement</u> outlines the trustee's duties.	<u>信託契約</u>には、受託者の義務の概要が記載されている。
1020	**diagnosis** [dàɪəɡnóʊsəs]	診断
	The doctor's <u>diagnosis</u> was confirmed by a second opinion.	医師の<u>診断</u>は、セカンドオピニオンで確認された。
1021	**medical certificate**	診断書
	A <u>medical certificate</u> is required for extended sick leave.	長期病気休暇には、<u>診断書</u>が必要である。
1022	**letter of credit**	信用状
	A <u>letter of credit</u> facilitates international trade.	<u>信用状</u>は、国際貿易を促進する。

RANK 2

#	Term	Japanese
1023	**tax credit**	**税額控除**
	A credit under paragraphs (1) through (3) is referred to as a foreign **tax credit**.	第1項から第3項までの規定による控除は、外国**税額控除**という。
1024	**addition of claim**	**請求の追加**
	Addition of claim can occur during ongoing litigation.	**請求の追加**は、進行中の訴訟において発生する可能性がある。
1025	**liquidation** [líkwɪdéɪʃən]	**清算**
	Liquidation proceedings dissolve the company.	**清算**手続は、会社を解散させる。
1026	**product liability**	**製造物責任**
	Product liability holds manufacturers accountable for harm.	**製造物責任**は、製造業者に損害賠償責任を負わせるものである。
1027	**enactment** [enǽktmənt]	**制定**
	The **enactment** of the law was a significant achievement.	この法律の**制定**は、大きな成果だった。
1028	**establishment** [ɪstǽblɪʃmənt]	**制定**
	The **establishment** of the new local ordinance was well-received.	新しい条例の**制定**は、好評だった。
1029	**self-defense** [sèlfdɪféns]	**正当防衛**
	Self-defense is a justified response to imminent harm.	**正当防衛**は、差し迫った危害に対する正当な対応である。
1030	**the life or (and) person**	**生命又は身体**
	The **life or (and) person** is protected by various laws.	**生命又は身体**は、様々な法律によって保護されている。
1031	**agreement limiting liability**	**責任限定契約**
	An **agreement limiting liability** must be carefully scrutinized.	**責任限定契約**は、慎重に精査されなければならない。
1032	**theft** [θéft]	**窃盗**
	Theft is a punishable offense.	**窃盗**は、処罰の対象となる犯罪である。

1033	**exclusive jurisdiction**	**専属管轄**
	An action about the existence or absence of an intellectual property right that arises through a registration establishing that intellectual property right is under the <u>exclusive jurisdiction</u> of the Japanese courts if that registration was made in Japan.	知的財産権のうち設定の登録により発生するものの存否に関する訴えの管轄権は、その登録が日本においてされたものであるときは、日本の裁判所の**専属管轄**である。
1034	**constructive transfer with retention of possession**	**占有改定**
	Article 183 (<u>constructive transfer with retention of possession</u>) of Civil Act provides that, if an agent manifests the intention to thenceforward possess a thing under the agent's own possession on behalf of the principal, the principal thereby acquires the possessory rights.	民法第183条（**占有改定**）は、代理人が自己の占有物を以後本人のために占有する意思を表示したときは、本人は、これによって占有権を取得することを規定する。
1035	**count** [káʊnt]	**訴因**
	Each <u>count</u> in the indictment was discussed separately.	起訴状の各**訴因**は、別々に議論された。
1036	**investigation** [ìnvèstəgéɪʃən]	**捜査**
	The <u>investigation</u> into the matter is ongoing.	この件に関する**捜査**は、継続中である。
1037	**heir** [ér]	**相続人**
	The <u>heir</u> inherits according to the will.	**相続人**は、遺言に従って相続する。
1038	**suit** [súːt]	**訴訟・訴え**
	The <u>suit</u> challenges the contract's fairness.	この**訴訟**は、契約の公正さを争うものである。
1039	**capacity to sue or be sued**	**訴訟能力**
	<u>Capacity to sue or be sued</u> is a fundamental factor to be examined.	**訴訟能力**は、検討すべき基本的要素である。
1040	**prima facie showing**	**疎明**
	<u>Prima facie showings</u> shall be made using evidence that can be examined immediately.	**疎明**は、即時に取り調べることができる証拠によってしなければならない。
1041	**profit and loss statement**	**損益計算書**
	The <u>profit and loss statement</u> reveals financial performance.	**損益計算書**は、財務実績を明らかにする。

RANK 2

1042	**surviving company**	存続会社
	The <u>surviving company</u> continues operations after the merger.	<u>存続会社</u>は、合併後も事業を継続する。
1043	**subrogation** [sʌ̀brəgéiʃən]	代位
	If performance by <u>subrogation</u> occurs with respect to one part of a claim, the subrogee, with the consent of the obligee, may exercise the rights of the subrogee together with the obligee in proportion to the value of the subrogee's performance.	債権の一部について<u>代位</u>弁済があったときは、代位者は、債権者の同意を得て、その弁済をした価額に応じて、債権者とともにその権利を行使することができる。
1044	**large company**	大会社
	In general, a <u>large company</u> must have a board of company auditors and a financial auditor.	原則として、<u>大会社</u>は、監査役会及び会計監査人を置かなければならない。
1045	**duly assert against**	対抗する
	An obligor may <u>duly assert against</u> the assignee any event that has taken place with regard to the assignor by the time of completion of the perfection.	債務者は、対抗要件具備時までに譲渡人に対して生じた事由をもって譲受人に<u>対抗する</u>ことができる。
1046	**can be asserted against**	対抗することができる
	If the obligee exercises the subrogor's right, the other party may duly assert against the obligee any defense that <u>can be asserted against</u> the obligor.	債権者が被代位権利を行使したときは、相手方は、債務者に対して主張することができる抗弁をもって、債権者に<u>対抗することができる</u>。
1047	**requirement for perfection**	対抗要件
	<u>Requirement for perfection</u> involves registration.	<u>対抗要件</u>には、登記が含まれる。
1048	**requirement to duly assert against third parties**	対抗要件
	<u>Requirement to duly assert against third parties</u> involves legal notification.	<u>対抗要件</u>には、法定の通知が含まれる。
1049	**third party debtor**	第三債務者
	<u>Third party debtor</u> obligations are overlooked in the case.	<u>第三債務者</u>の義務は、訴訟で見落された。

1050	**third party obligor**		**第三債務者**
	If a <u>third party obligor</u> of a claim that has been attached performs the obligation to that third party's own obligee, the attaching obligee is entitled to request the third party obligor to perform the obligation de novo to the extent of the damage sustained by the attaching obligee.		差押えを受けた債権の**第三債務者**が自己の債権者に弁済をしたときは、差押債権者は、その受けた損害の限度において更に弁済をすべき旨を第三債務者に請求することができる。
1051	**balance sheet**		**貸借対照表**
	The <u>balance sheet</u> offers a snapshot of financial health.		**貸借対照表**は、財務の健全性を示すスナップショットである。
1052	**representative executive officer**		**代表執行役**
	The <u>representative executive officer</u> leads the corporation.		**代表執行役**が、会社を率いる。
1053	**representative liquidator**		**代表清算人**
	A <u>representative liquidator</u> manages dissolution processes.		**代表清算人**が、解散手続を管理する。
1054	**accord and satisfaction**		**代物弁済**
	<u>Accord and satisfaction</u> resolve disputes of non-performance through agreement.		**代物弁済**は、合意によって債務不履行の紛争を解決する。
1055	**substitute performance**		**代物弁済**
	<u>Substitute performance</u> fulfills contractual obligations differently.		**代物弁済**は、契約上の義務を異なる形で履行する。
1056	**possession through agent**		**代理占有**
	<u>Possession through agent</u> extends control indirectly.		**代理占有**は、間接的に占有を拡大する。
1057	**share unit number**		**単元株式数**
	<u>Share unit number</u> was specified by the Tokyo Stock Exchange.		**単元株式数**が、東京証券取引所により指定された。
1058	**share less than one unit**		**単元未満株式**
	Owning a <u>share less than one unit</u> is possible in some systems.		**単元未満株式**を所有することは、システムによっては可能である。
1059	**holder of share less than one (share) unit**		**単元未満株主**
	The <u>holder of share less than one (share) unit</u> does not have specific rights.		**単元未満株主**は、特定の権利を有しない。
1060	**collateral** [kəlǽtərəl]		**担保**
	<u>Collateral</u> secures a loan or obligation.		**担保**は、ローンや債務を担保する。

RANK 2

RANK 2

1061 security right 担保権
A <u>security right</u> protects the lender's interests.
<u>担保権</u>は、貸主の利益を保護するものである。

1062 secured real property auction 担保不動産競売
<u>Secured real property auction</u> liquidates assets to satisfy debts.
<u>担保不動産競売</u>は、債務を満たすために資産を競売する。

1063 delay [dɪléɪ] 遅延
<u>Delay</u> in performance can lead to breach of contract.
履行の<u>遅延</u>は、契約違反につながる可能性がある。

1064 delay damages 遅延損害金
<u>Delay damages</u> compensate for late performance.
<u>遅延損害金</u>は、履行遅滞を補償するものである。

1065 delayed interest 遅延利息
<u>Delayed interest</u> accumulates on overdue payments.
<u>遅延利息</u>は、延滞した支払いに累積される。

1066 local government 地方公共団体
<u>Local government</u> manages community resources and services.
<u>地方公共団体</u>は、地域の資源及びサービスを管理する。

1067 local public employee 地方公務員
<u>Local public employee</u> serves the municipal administration.
<u>地方公務員</u>は、自治体行政に仕える。

1068 brokerage [bróʊkərɪdʒ] ①仲介・仲立ち、②媒介
<u>Brokerage</u> facilitates transactions between buyers and sellers.
<u>仲介</u>は、買主と売主の間の取引を促進する。

1069 intermediation [ìntərmìːdiéɪʃən] ①仲介、②媒介
<u>Intermediation</u> connects parties in financial transactions.
<u>仲介</u>は、金融取引の当事者を結びつける。

1070 arbitration [ɑ̀ːrbɪtréɪʃən] 仲裁
The dispute was resolved through <u>arbitration</u>.
紛争は、<u>仲裁</u>によって解決された。

1071 arbitration agreement 仲裁合意
Except as otherwise provided for in laws and regulations, an <u>arbitration agreement</u> is effective only when its subject is a civil dispute which can be settled between the parties.
<u>仲裁合意</u>は、法令に別段の定めがある場合を除き、当事者が和解をすることができる民事上の紛争を対象とする場合に限り、その効力を有する。

1072	**place of arbitration**	**仲裁地**
	The <u>place of arbitration</u> was set in a neutral location.	<u>仲裁地</u>は、中立の場所に設定された。
1073	**arbitral tribunal**	**仲裁廷**
	The rules of an arbitration procedure which the <u>arbitral tribunal</u> should observe are as provided by the agreement of the parties.	<u>仲裁廷</u>が従うべき仲裁手続の準則は、当事者が合意により定めるところによる。
1074	**arbitration procedure**	**仲裁手続**
	The <u>arbitration procedure</u> was outlined in the agreement.	<u>仲裁手続</u>は、契約書にまとめられている。
1075	**arbitrator** [ά:rbɪtrèɪtər]	**仲裁人**
	The number of <u>arbitrators</u> are as prescribed by the agreement of the parties.	<u>仲裁人</u>の数は、当事者が合意により定めるところによる。
1076	**suspension order**	**中止命令**
	A <u>suspension order</u> halted proceedings temporarily.	<u>中止命令</u>により、手続きは、一時的に停止された。
1077	**books and documents**	**帳簿書類**
	<u>Books and documents</u> were reviewed as evidence.	証拠となる<u>帳簿書類</u>が、審査された。
1078	**moral right of author**	**著作者人格権**
	The author's <u>moral right of author</u> was upheld by the court.	その著者の<u>著作者人格権</u>は、裁判所によって認められた。
1079	**reserve fund**	**積立金**
	The <u>reserve fund</u> covered unexpected expenses.	<u>積立金</u>は、予期せぬ出費をカバーした。
1080	**condition precedent**	**停止条件**
	Fulfillment of <u>condition precedent</u> allowed the contract to activate.	<u>停止条件</u>が満たされたことで、契約は有効になった。
1081	**period for submission**	**提出期間（末尾㉜参照）**
	The <u>period for submission</u> of documents was established.	書類の<u>提出期間</u>が、設けられた。
1082	**period for advancement**	**提出期間（末尾㉜参照）**
	<u>Period for advancement</u> of arguments was allocated.	主張の<u>提出期間</u>が、割り当てられた。
1083	**period for production**	**提出期間（末尾㉜参照）**
	<u>Period for production</u> of evidences was critical.	証拠の<u>提出期間</u>は、重要であった。

RANK 2

1084	**proceedings** [prəsídɪŋz] Legal **proceedings** commenced on the set date.	**手続** 決められた期日に、法的**手続**が開始された。
1085	**order commencing ... (proceedings)** An **order commencing proceedings** was issued by the tribunal.	**手続開始の決定** 審理の**手続開始の決定**が出された。
1086	**re-pledge** Assets were re-pledged in a **re-pledge** agreement.	**転質** 資産は再担保権（**転質**）設定契約により再担保権が設定された。
1087	**subpledge** A **subpledge** was created as additional security.	**転質** 追加担保として、**転質**が設定された。
1088	**pledge on movable property** A **pledge on movable property** secured the loan.	**動産質** **動産質**が、ローンを担保した。
1089	**inquiry to opponent** **Inquiry to opponent** sought clarification on disputed issues.	**当事者照会** **当事者照会**では、争点について明確化を求めた。
1090	**special provision** A **special provision** was included for unique circumstances.	**特約** 特殊な事情がある場合は、**特約**が設けられた。
1091	**patent application** The **patent application** described an innovative solution.	**特許出願** **特許出願**には革新的なソリューションが記載されていた。
1092	**claims** [kléɪmz] **Claims** defined the scope of the patent protection.	**特許請求の範囲** **特許請求の範囲**は、特許の保護範囲を規定した。
1093	**patented invention** The **patented invention** revolutionized the market.	**特許発明** この**特許発明**は、市場に革命をもたらした。
1094	**right to grant of patent** The inventor received the **right to grant of patent**.	**特許を受ける権利** 発明者は、**特許を受ける権利**を得た。
1095	**prefecture** [príːfəktʃər] The **prefecture** implemented new environmental guidelines.	**都道府県** **都道府県**は、新しい環境ガイドラインを実施した。

1096	**prefectural governor**	都道府県知事
	The prefectural governor initiated community improvement projects.	都道府県知事は、地域改善プロジェクトを開始した。
1097	**rescission right**	取消権
	Parties negotiated the rescission right in the contract.	両当事者は契約の中で取消権について交渉した。
1098	**company with board of directors**	取締役会設置会社
	The company with board of directors followed corporate governance best practices.	取締役会設置会社は、コーポレートガバナンスのベストプラクティスに従った。
1099	**domestic corporation**	内国法人
	A domestic corporation expanded its operations nationally.	内国法人は、全国的に事業を拡大した。
1100	**remain in force**	なおその効力を有する
	The regulation will remain in force.	この規則は、なおその効力を有する。
1101	**discretionary provision**	任意規定
	A discretionary provision allowed flexibility in implementation.	任意規定によって、柔軟な実施が可能となった。
1102	**acknowledgment** [æknáːlɪdʒmənt]	①認諾、②承認
	If a right is acknowledged, a new period of prescription commences to run at the time of the acknowledgment.	時効は、権利の承認があったときは、その承認の時から新たにその進行を始める。
1103	**cognizance (acknowledgment of a claim)** [káːɡnəzəns]	認諾
	When a court clerk creates an electronic statement of an acknowledgment of a claim (cognizance) and enters it in a file, that entry has the same effect as a final and binding judgment.	裁判所書記官が、請求の認諾について電子調書を作成し、これをファイルに記録したときは、その記録は、確定判決と同一の効力を有する。
1104	**approval or disapproval**	認否
	A written answer must contain the answer to the object of claim, and contain approval or disapproval of the factual circumstances stated in the complaint.	答弁書には、請求の趣旨に対する答弁を記載するほか、訴状に記載された事実に対する認否を記載しなければならない。
1105	**revolving mortgage**	根抵当権
	A revolving mortgage facilitated ongoing financing needs.	根抵当権は、継続的な資金需要を促進した。

RANK 2

RANK 2

1106 revolving guarantee — 根保証
The agreement included a **revolving guarantee**.
この契約には、**根保証**も含まれていた。

1107 pension [pénʃən] — 年金
The new **pension** plan was introduced to employees.
新しい**年金**制度が、従業員に導入された。

1108 cease and desist order — 排除命令
A **cease and desist order** was issued to stop the infringement.
侵害行為の**排除命令**が、発出された。

1109 liquidating distribution — 配当（民事執行・配当手続）
The court, according to a distribution list, must implement **liquidating distribution** to security interest holders.
裁判所は、配当表に基づいて、担保権者に対する**配当**を実施しなければならない。

1110 breach of duty of loyalty — 背任
An investigation into the **breach of duty of loyalty** was launched.
背任に関する調査が、開始された。

1111 total number of authorized shares in a class — 発行可能種類株式総数
The **total number of authorized shares in a class** was increased to accommodate growth.
発行可能種類株式総数は、成長に対応するために増加された。

1112 invention [ìnvénʃən] — 発明
The **invention** was patented, revolutionizing the industry.
この**発明**は、特許を取得し、業界に革命をもたらした。

1113 inventor [ìnvéntər] — 発明者
The **inventor** was awarded a patent for their innovative design.
発明者は、その革新的なデザインで特許を取得した。

1114 paid-in amount — 払込金額
The **paid-in amount** reflects the investment made by shareholders.
払込金額は、株主による投資を反映している。

1115 semiannual securities report — 半期報告書
The **semiannual securities report** provides insights into the company's financial health.
半期報告書は、会社の財務の健全性に関する洞察を提供する。

1116 criminal [krímənəl] — 犯罪人
The **criminal** was apprehended after a thorough investigation.
徹底的な捜査の結果、**犯罪人**が逮捕された。

#	英語	日本語
1117	**offender** [əféndər] The <u>offender</u> received a sentence based on the severity of their actions.	犯罪人 **犯罪人**は、その行為の重大性に応じた量刑を受けた。
1118	**counterclaim** [káʊntərklèɪm] The <u>counterclaim</u> challenged the allegations made in the original lawsuit.	反訴 **反訴**は、本訴で主張された内容を争うものであった。
1119	**dissenting shareholder** A <u>dissenting shareholder</u> expressed concerns over the proposed merger.	反対株主 **反対株主**は、合併案に懸念を表明した。
1120	**injured party** The <u>injured party</u> sought compensation for damages incurred.	被害者(末尾❾参照) **被害者**は、発生した損害の賠償を求めた。
1121	**underwriting** [ʌ́ndərràɪtɪŋ] The term "the <u>underwriting</u> of securities" includes secondary distribution or private placement of securities.	引受け 「有価証券の**引受け**」とは、有価証券の売出し又は私募を含む。
1122	**subscription price** The <u>subscription price</u> was set after evaluating market conditions.	引受価額 **引受価額**は、市場環境を評価した上で設定された。
1123	**underwriter** [ʌ́ndərràɪtər] Notwithstanding the provisions of other Acts, a financial instruments business operator may become an <u>underwriter</u>.	引受人(末尾㉗参照) 金融商品取引業者は、他の法律の規定にかかわらず、**引受人**となることができる。
1124	**alleged facts of crime** The <u>alleged facts of crime</u> were detailed in the police report.	被疑事実 犯罪の**被疑事実**は、警察の報告書に詳しく書かれている。
1125	**suspect** [səspékt] The <u>suspect</u> denied any involvement in the incident.	被疑者 **被疑者**は、事件への関与を否定している。
1126	**transfer** [trænsfə́ːr] The <u>transfer</u> of possessory rights is effected by the delivery of the thing possessed.	①引渡し、②譲渡 占有権の**譲渡**は、占有物の引渡しによってする。

1127	**model** [mɑ́:dəl]	ひな形
	The <u>model</u> served as a basis for developing further business tie-up.	この**ひな形**は、さらなる業務提携のための基礎となった。
1128	**template** [témplət]	ひな形
	A <u>template</u> was used to ensure consistency in documentation.	文書の一貫性を確保するため、**ひな形**が使用された。
1129	**right of avoidance**	否認権（倒産法上の否認）
	The exercise of a <u>right of avoidance</u> is not to be precluded even when an act to be avoided is accompanied by an enforceable title of obligation.	**否認権**は、否認しようとする行為について執行力のある債務名義があるときでも、行使することを妨げない。
1130	**apparent representative director**	表見代表取締役
	The <u>apparent representative director</u> deceived the corporation.	**表見代表取締役**は、会社を欺罔した。
1131	**indication** [ìndəkéɪʃən]	表示
	The following matters must be entered in a record of oral argument: <u>indication</u> of the case; names of the judges and the court clerk; names of public prosecutors in attendance and so on.	口頭弁論の調書には、事件の**表示**、裁判官及び裁判所書記官の氏名、立ち会った検察官の氏名などを記載しなければならない。
1132	**subagent** [sʌbéɪdʒənt]	復代理人
	A <u>subagent</u> was appointed to assist in the transaction.	取引を支援するために、**復代理人**が任命された。
1133	**inaction** [ìnækʃən]	不作為
	<u>Inaction</u> on the part of the management led to further non-compliance.	経営陣の**不作為**が、さらなる法令違反を引き起こした。
1134	**unauthorized** [ənɔ́:θəràɪzd]	不正な
	<u>Unauthorized</u> access to the facility is under investigation.	施設への**不正な**アクセスは、調査中である。
1135	**annex** [ǽnəks]	附属書
	The <u>annex</u> detailed additional terms not covered in the master agreement.	**附属書**には、基本契約でカバーされていない追加条項が詳述されていた。

RANK 2

1136	**incidental**	附帯の
	[ìnsɪdéntəl]	
	Incidental costs were accounted for in the project budget.	附帯の費用は、プロジェクト予算に計上された。
1137	**general venue**	普通裁判籍
	The general venue for the lawsuit was determined based on jurisdiction.	訴訟の普通裁判籍は、裁判管轄に基づいて決定された。
1138	**appeal**	不服申立て
	[əpíːl]	
	An appeal was filed against the court decision.	決定に対して、不服申立てが提起された。
1139	**adverse disposition**	不利益処分
	The order was considered an adverse disposition.	この処分は、不利益処分とみなされた。
1140	**disadvantageous fact**	不利益な事実
	A written statement including a disadvantageous fact made by the accused may be used as evidence, when the statement is made under circumstances that afford special credibility.	被告人が作成した不利益な事実を含む供述書は、その供述が特に信用すべき情況の下にされたものであるときに限り、これを証拠とすることができる。
1141	**split company**	分割会社
	The split company resulted from a strategic restructuring.	分割会社は、戦略的再編成の結果生まれた。
1142	**divisible obligation**	分割債務
	The court recognized that the obligation is divisible obligation.	裁判所は、当該債務が分割債務であることを認めた。
1143	**installment payments**	分割払い
	Installment payments were agreed upon to facilitate the purchase.	購入を容易にするために分割払いが合意された。
1144	**order to submit a document**	文書提出命令
	An order to submit a document was issued by the court.	裁判所から、文書提出命令が発出された。
1145	**distribution**	分配
	[dìstrəbjúːʃən]	
	If there are no provisions in the articles of incorporation with respect to the proportions of the distribution of residual assets, the proportions are prescribed in accordance with the value of each member's contribution.	残余財産の分配の割合について定款の定めがないときは、その割合は、各社員の出資の価額に応じて定める。

RANK 2

1146	**consolidation** [kənsɑ́:lədéɪʃən] The <u>consolidation</u> of shares was likely to violate laws and regulations.	**併合** 株式の**併合**は、法令に違反するおそれがあった。
1147	**prohibition of payments** The plaintiff seeks a <u>prohibition of payments</u>.	**弁済の禁止** 原告は、**弁済の禁止**を求めている。
1148	**preparatory proceedings** <u>Preparatory proceedings</u> helped clarify the case's complexities.	**弁論準備手続** **弁論準備手続**は、事件の複雑さを明らかにするのに役立った。
1149	**record of preparatory proceedings** The <u>record of preparatory proceedings</u> was kept.	**弁論準備手続調書** **弁論準備手続調書**は、保管された。
1150	**waiver** [wéɪvər] A <u>waiver</u> of rights was signed by the parties involved.	**放棄** 権利**放棄**書は、当事者によって署名された。
1151	**remuneration** [rɪmjù:nəréɪʃən] <u>Remuneration</u> for the board members was discussed by the board.	**報酬（役員報酬等の場合）** 役員**報酬**は、取締役会で審議された。
1152	**compensation committee** Each nominating committee, audit committee, and <u>compensation committee</u> are composed of three or more committee members.	**報酬委員会** 指名委員会、監査委員会又は**報酬委員会**の各委員会は、委員3人以上で組織する。
1153	**statutory interest** <u>Statutory interest</u> accrues on overdue payments.	**法定利息** 延滞金には、**法定利息**が発生する。
1154	**statutory interest rate** The <u>statutory interest rate</u> was adjusted in response to economic conditions.	**法定利率** **法定利率**は、経済状況に応じて調整された。
1155	**... is in violation of the applicable laws and regulations or the articles of incorporation** The action <u>is in violation of the applicable laws and regulations or the articles of incorporation</u>.	**法令又は定款に違反する場合** その行為は、**法令又は定款に違反する場合**に該当する。

1156	**hold** [hóʊld]	保管する
	When a public prosecutor comes to <u>hold</u> new evidence, the public prosecutor must promptly deliver to the defense counsel a list of the new evidence the public prosecutor comes to hold.	検察官は、証拠を新たに**保管する**に至ったときは、速やかに、弁護人に対し、当該新たに保管するに至った証拠の一覧表の交付をしなければならない。
1157	**store** [stɔ́ːr]	保管する
	Retailers <u>store</u> customer data for convenience and analysis.	小売業者は、利便性と分析のために顧客データを**保管する**。
1158	**insurance** [ɪnʃʊ́rəns]	保険
	<u>Insurance</u> provides a safety net against unforeseen losses.	**保険**は、不測の損失に対するセーフティネットを提供する。
1159	**bail** [béɪl]	保釈（金）
	The court set <u>bail</u> at an amount reflective of the charges.	裁判所は、**保釈金**を罪に見合った額に設定した。
1160	**share for subscription**	募集株式
	<u>Share for subscription</u> offers investors a chance to invest in new shares.	**募集株式**は、投資家に新株への投資機会を提供する。
1161	**share option for subscription**	募集新株予約権
	A <u>share option for subscription</u> gives the holder the right to buy shares in the future.	**募集新株予約権**は、保有者に将来株式を購入する権利を与える。
1162	**(security) deposit** [dɪpázɪt]	保証金
	A <u>(security) deposit</u> is required for renting property.	物件を借りる際には、**保証金**が必要である。
1163	**assistant** [əsístənt]	補助人
	A person subject to a decision for commencement of assistance becomes a person under assistance, and an <u>assistant</u> is appointed for that person.	補助開始の審判を受けた者は、被補助人とし、これに**補助人**を付する。
1164	**registered domicile**	本籍
	The <u>registered domicile</u> affects jurisdiction and legal proceedings.	**本籍**は、裁判管轄及び法的手続に影響する。

RANK 2

1165	**definitive registration**	**本登記**
	When there is any third party who has an interest in the definitive registration, an application for a **definitive registration** based on a provisional registration relating to ownership may be filed only when the third party gives consent.	所有権に関する仮登記に基づく**本登記**は、登記上の利害関係を有する第三者がある場合には、当該第三者の承諾があるときに限り、申請することができる。
1166	**identity verification**	**本人確認**
	Identity verification is a crucial step in online transactions.	オンライン取引において、**本人確認**は重要なステップである。
1167	**attempt** [ətémpt]	**未遂**
	An **attempt** is punishable only when specifically so provided in the Article concerned.	**未遂**を罰する場合は、各本条で定める。
1168	**minor** [máɪnər]	**未成年者**
	A **minor** cannot enter into contracts without parental consent under the T&C.	利用規約のもと、**未成年者**は、親の同意なしに契約を結ぶことはできない。
1169	**acquittal** [əkwítəl]	**無罪**
	When there is a notification of a judicial decision of **acquittal**, dismissal by a bar to prosecution, absolute discharge, suspended execution of a sentence in whole, dismissal of prosecution, a fine or a petty fine, the detention warrant loses its effect.	**無罪**、免訴、刑の免除、刑の全部の執行猶予、公訴棄却、罰金又は科料の裁判の告知があったときは、勾留状は、その効力を失う。
1170	**not guilty**	**無罪**
	The jury in the foreign court found the defendant **not guilty** of the charges.	外国の裁判所の陪審員は、被告を**無罪**とした。
1171	**gratuitously** [ɡrətú:ətəsli]	**無償で**
	The donation was made **gratuitously**, without expecting anything in return.	見返りを期待せず、**無償で**寄付された。
1172	**defamation** [dèfəméɪʃən]	**名誉毀損**
	The lawsuit for **defamation** was initiated after false statements were made.	**名誉棄損**の訴訟は、虚偽の発言がなされた後に開始された。
1173	**exemption** [ɪɡzémpʃən]	**免除**
	The **exemption** was granted based on environmental conservation efforts.	この**免除**は、環境保護への取り組みに基づいて認められた。

1174	**movant** [múːvənt]	申立人
	The <u>movant</u> requested a postponement of the trial date.	<u>申立人</u>は、公判期日の延期を要求した。
1175	**petitioner** [pətíʃənər]	申立人
	When a <u>petitioner</u> does not correct defects, the presiding judge must dismiss the written petition by an order.	<u>申立人</u>が不備を補正しないときは、裁判長は、命令で、申立書を却下しなければならない。
1176	**objective** [əbdʒéktɪv]	目的
	"Broadcasting" means the transmission to the public of wireless communications with the <u>objective</u> of allowing the public to simultaneously receive transmissions with the same content.	「放送」とは、公衆送信のうち、公衆によって同一の内容の送信が同時に受信されることを<u>目的</u>として行う無線通信の送信をいう。
1177	**holding company**	持株会社
	The <u>holding company</u> oversees several technology startups.	<u>持株会社</u>は、複数のテクノロジー新興企業を統括している。
1178	**equity** [ékwəti]	持分
	A member cannot transfer all or part of the member's own <u>equity</u> (interests) to others without the approval of all other members.	社員は、他の社員の全員の承諾がなければ、その<u>持分</u>の全部又は一部を他人に譲渡することができない。
1179	**equity interest**	持分
	Our <u>equity interest</u> in the joint venture is substantial.	ジョイントベンチャーに対する当社の<u>持分</u>は相当なものである。
1180	**membership company**	持分会社
	Article 590 of the Company Act sets out that a member executes the business of the <u>membership company</u>, unless otherwise provided for in the articles of incorporation.	会社法第590条は、社員は、定款に別段の定めがある場合を除き、<u>持分会社</u>の業務を執行することを定める。
1181	**unavoidably** [ʌ̀nəvɔ́ɪdəbli]	やむを得ない（得ず）
	When found <u>unavoidably</u> necessary, the road management body may, use the land belonging to other persons temporarily to the extent necessary.	道路管理者は、<u>やむを得ない</u>必要があるときは、その必要な限度において、他人の土地を一時使用することができる。
1182	**compelling reason**	やむを得ない事由
	An agent appointed by mandate may not appoint a subagent unless there is a <u>compelling reason</u> to do so.	委任による代理人は、<u>やむを得ない事由</u>があるときでなければ、復代理人を選任することができない。

RANK 2

1183	**unavoidable grounds**	やむを得ない事由
	If there are any <u>unavoidable grounds</u>, any member may withdraw at any time.	各社員は、**やむを得ない事由**があるときは、いつでも退社することができる。
1184	**preferred share**	優先株式
	<u>Preferred shares</u> offer dividends before common stocks.	**優先株式**は、普通株より先に配当金を受け取ることができる。
1185	**preferred equity investment**	優先出資
	There is an act called Act on <u>Preferred Equity Investment</u> by Cooperative Structured Financial Institution.	協同組織金融機関の**優先出資**に関する法律と題された法律がある。
1186	**transferee company**	譲受会社
	The <u>transferee company</u> acquired all assets and liabilities.	**譲受会社**は、すべての資産及び負債を取得した。
1187	**outline** [áʊtlàɪn]	要旨（概要）
	The project <u>outline</u> was approved by the board.	プロジェクトの**要旨（概要）**は、取締役会で承認された。
1188	**deposit** [dəpάːzɪt]	①預金、②預託
	A <u>deposit</u> is required to secure the booking.	予約の確保には、**預託**が必要である。
1189	**appropriation of profit**	利益の処分
	<u>Appropriation of profit</u> focuses on future investments and dividends.	**利益の処分**は、将来の投資及び配当に焦点を当てる。
1190	**interested party**	利害関係人
	An <u>interested party</u> filed a complaint regarding the proposed development.	**利害関係人**が、開発計画に関して苦情を申し立てた。
1191	**interested person**	利害関係人
	If the court finds it necessary, it may, in response to a petition by <u>interested persons</u>, appoint a person who is to temporarily perform the duties of an officer.	裁判所は、必要があると認めるときは、**利害関係人**の申立てにより、一時役員の職務を行うべき者を選任することができる。
1192	**delay in performance**	履行遅滞
	<u>Delay in performance</u> may result in contractual penalties.	**履行遅滞**の場合、契約上の違約金が発生する可能性がある。
1193	**impossibility of performance**	履行不能
	<u>Impossibility of performance</u> can void a contract under specific circumstances under the local law.	**履行不能**は、その現地法のもとでは、特定の状況下で契約を無効にすることができる。

1194	**divorce** [dɪvɔ́ːrs] <u>Divorce</u> proceedings are handled with confidentiality.	離婚 離婚手続は、守秘義務をもって取り扱われる。
1195	**retention** [riténʃən] Articles which the accused has left behind may be <u>retained</u>.	領置 ＊例文ではretain（動詞） 被告人が遺留した物は、これを<u>領置</u>することができる。
1196	**authorization to exploit** The copyright owner may grant another person <u>authorization to exploit</u> the work.	利用の許諾 著作権者は、他人に対し、その著作物の<u>利用の許諾</u>を行える。
1197	**dual criminal liability provision** The <u>dual criminal liability provision</u> affects both individuals and corporations.	両罰規定 <u>両罰規定</u>は、個人及び法人の両方に影響する。
1198	**labor union** The <u>labor union</u> negotiated for better working conditions.	労働組合 <u>労働組合</u>は、労働条件の改善を求めて交渉した。
1199	**employee** [emplɔ́ɪi] An <u>employee</u> was recognized for outstanding contributions to the project.	①労働者、②被用者 プロジェクトに多大な貢献をした<u>被用者</u>が、表彰された。
1200	**bribe** [bráɪb] Offering a <u>bribe</u> constitutes a criminal act under anti-corruption laws.	賄賂 <u>賄賂</u>の提供は、腐敗防止法のもとで、犯罪行為にあたる。

法律英単語® Ⅰ 2100
RANK3

1201	**sentencing (sentence)** [séntənsɪŋ] The suspended execution of a <u>sentence</u> must be rendered by a judgment at the same time as rendition of the punishment.	**言渡し（刑事の場合）** 刑の執行猶予は、刑の**言渡し**と同時に、判決でその言渡しをしなければならない。
1202	**company with committees** The <u>company with committees</u> ensures compliance through internal governance.	**委員会設置会社** **委員会設置会社**は、内部統制を通じてコンプライアンスを確保する。
1203	**hereinafter the same applies in this ...** <u>Hereinafter, the same applies in this</u> section.	**以下この…において同じ** **以下この**項**において同じ**。
1204	**opposition** [ɑ̀ːpəzíʃən] The procedure was suspended until a decision on an <u>opposition</u> to a granted patent has become final and binding.	**異議** 特許**異議**の申立てについての決定が確定するまで、その手続は、中止された。
1205	**filing of an objection** The attorney recommended <u>filing of an objection</u> to the court's preliminary ruling.	**異議の申立て** 弁護士は、裁判所の決定に対して**異議の申立て**を勧めた。
1206	**executor** [ɪgzékjətər] The <u>executor</u> is legally responsible for administering the estate per the testator's wishes.	**遺言執行者** **遺言執行者**は、遺言者の意思に従って遺産を管理する法的責任を負う。
1207	**testator** [tésteɪtər] The <u>testator</u>'s estate plan includes specific instructions for asset distribution.	**遺言者** **遺言者**の遺産分割計画には、資産分配に関する具体的な指示が含まれている。
1208	**delegation** [dèləgéɪʃən] The <u>delegation</u> of authority was formalized in a written agreement.	**（信託法等における）権限の委託** **権限の委託**は、書面の契約により行われた。
1209	**delegating party** The <u>delegating party</u> retains ultimate responsibility for the actions taken.	**委託者（末尾❸参照）** **委託者**は、取られた行動に対する最終的な責任を負う。
1210	**settlor** [sétlər] The <u>settlor</u> of the trust has stipulated terms for asset management.	**委託者（末尾❸参照）** 信託の**委託者**（設定者）は、資産管理に関する条件を定めた。

1211	**general incorporated association**	一般社団法人
	The <u>general incorporated association</u> must adhere to its founding principles.	<u>一般社団法人</u>は、設立の理念を遵守しなければならない。
1212	**general statutory lien**	一般の先取特権
	A <u>general statutory lien</u> gives a creditor a security interest by law.	<u>一般の先取特権</u>は、法律により債権者に担保権を与える。
1213	**deception or other wrongful act**	偽りその他不正の行為
	Engaging in <u>deception or other wrongful acts</u> voids the contract.	<u>偽りその他不正の行為</u>に関与した場合、契約は無効となる。
1214	**deception or other wrongful means**	偽りその他不正の手段
	The court found the defendant guilty of using <u>deception or other wrongful means</u>.	裁判所は、<u>偽りその他不正の手段</u>を用いた被告を有罪とした。
1215	**contravention** [kɑ̀:ntrəvénʃən]	違反
	<u>Contravention</u> of the regulations resulted in severe penalties for the corporation.	規制に<u>違反</u>した場合、企業には厳しい罰則が課される。
1216	**legally reserved portion (statutory reserved share)**	遺留分 ※民法の英訳には「legally reserved portion」が用いられている
	Heirs other than siblings shall receive an amount set out by the law as <u>legally reserved portion</u>.	兄弟姉妹以外の相続人は、<u>遺留分</u>として、法律に定める割合の額を受ける。
1217	**force** [fɔ́:rs]	威力
	A person who obstructs the business of another person by <u>force</u> is dealt with in the same manner as prescribed under the preceding Article.	<u>威力</u>を用いて人の業務を妨害した者も、前条の例による。
1218	**bring to (physical escort)**	①引致、②勾引 ※刑事訴訟法の英訳には「(being) brought to...」が用いられている
	The subpoenaed accused must be released within twenty-four hours from the time of being <u>brought to</u> the court.	勾引した被告人は、裁判所に<u>引致</u>した時から24時間以内にこれを釈放しなければならない。
1219	**concealment (conceal)** [kənsíːlmənt]	隠匿（する）
	A person who <u>conceals</u> a letter of another person is punished by imprisonment or imprisonment for not more than 6 months, a fine of not more than 100,000 yen or a petty fine.	他人の信書を<u>隠匿した</u>者は、6月以下の懲役若しくは禁錮又は10万円以下の罰金若しくは科料に処する。

RANK 3

1220	**enable the escape (to escape)** A person who <u>enables the escape</u> of another person who has either committed a crime punishable with a fine or a severer punishment is punished by imprisonment for not more than 3 years or a fine of not more than 300,000 yen.	隠避させる 罰金以上の刑に当たる罪を犯した者を**隠避させた**者は、3年以下の懲役又は30万円以下の罰金に処する。
1221	**destruction** [dɪstrʌ́kʃən] A person who damages a corpse is punished by imprisonment for not more than 3 years (<u>destruction</u> of corpses).	①隠滅、②損壊 死体を損壊した者は、3年以下の懲役に処する（死体**損壊**罪）。
1222	**surname** [sə́ːrnèɪm] A husband and wife shall adopt the <u>surname</u> of the husband or wife in accordance with that which is decided at the time of marriage.	氏 夫婦は、婚姻の際に定めるところに従い、夫又は妻の**氏**を称する。
1223	**amendment of claim** The <u>amendment of claim</u> expanded the lawsuit's scope significantly.	訴えの変更 **訴えの変更**は、訴訟の範囲を大幅に拡大した。
1224	**selling** [sélɪŋ] The term "financial instruments business" may include secondary distribution of securities or solicitation for <u>selling</u> only for professional investors.	売付け 金融商品取引業には、有価証券の売出し又は特定投資家向け**売付け**勧誘が含まれる。
1225	**shares subject to a cash-out** <u>Shares subject to a cash-out</u> were offered a buyout option in the merger.	売渡株式 **売渡株式**は、合併に際してバイアウトのオプションが提供された。
1226	**shareholder subject to a cash-out** The <u>shareholder subject to a cash-out</u> contested the valuation.	売渡株主 **売渡株主**は、評価額を争った。
1227	**shareholder, etc. subject to a cash-out** <u>Shareholder, etc. subject to a cash-out</u> were notified via official communication.	売渡株主等 **売渡株主等**には、公式の連絡を通じて通知した。
1228	**management committee** The <u>management committee</u> reviewed compliance with corporate governance standards.	運営委員会 **運営委員会**は、コーポレートガバナンス基準の遵守を検討した。

RANK 3

1229	**operation committee**	運営委員会
	An inspector must not concurrently hold the position of the president, director, member of the <u>operation committee</u>.	監事は、理事長、理事、**運営委員会**の委員を兼ねてはならない。
1230	**transportation** [trænspərtéɪʃən]	運送
	<u>Transportation</u> contracts are subject to the local ordinance.	**運送**契約は、条例の対象となる。
1231	**freight (charge)** [fréit]	運送賃
	The <u>freight charge</u> was determined based on negotiated carrier rates.	**運送賃**は、交渉した運送会社の運賃に基づいて決定された。
1232	**freight forwarder**	運送取扱人
	A <u>freight forwarder</u> facilitated international shipping arrangements.	**運送取扱人**が、国際輸送の手配をした。
1233	**carrier** [kǽriər]	運送人
	The <u>carrier</u>'s liability for the cargo is defined by the bill of lading.	貨物に対する**運送人**の責任は、船荷証券によって定められている。
1234	**cargo** [káːrgòʊ]	運送品
	The <u>cargo</u> was insured against loss and damage during transit.	**運送品**は、輸送中の損失及び損害に対して保険がかけられていた。
1235	**management (utilization)** [jùːtələzéɪʃən]	運用
	The term "financial instruments business" may include the <u>management</u> of property contributed by a person as an investment in securities based on investment decisions that are grounded in an analysis of the values of financial instruments.	金融商品取引業には、金融商品の価値の分析に基づく投資判断に基づいて、有価証券に対する投資として、拠出を受けた財産の**運用**を行うことが含まれる。
1236	**operating fund**	運用資金
	The <u>operating fund</u> was allocated for essential business operations.	**運用資金**は、必要不可欠な事業運営のために割り当てられた。
1237	**business report**	事業報告
	The <u>business report</u> detailed financial performance over the fiscal year.	**事業報告**には、会計年度の業績が詳細に記されていた。
1238	**permanent residence**	永住
	<u>Permanent residence</u> applications in that country are processed by immigration services.	その国の**永住**権の申請は、移民局で処理される。

RANK 3

#	Term	Japanese
1239	**health** [hélθ] A person who pollutes drinking water with poisonous materials or any other substance harming human <u>health</u> is punished by imprisonment for not more than 3 years.	①衛生、②健康 人の飲料に供する浄水に毒物その他人の<u>健康</u>を害すべき物を混入した者は、3年以下の懲役に処する。
1240	**sanitation** [sæ̀nətéɪʃən] <u>Sanitation</u> measures were implemented to meet public health standards.	衛生 公衆衛生基準を満たすための<u>衛生</u>対策が、実施された。
1241	**remote place** Delivery services to <u>remote places</u> may incur additional charges.	遠隔の地 <u>遠隔の地</u>への配送には、追加料金がかかる場合がある。
1242	**assistance, support** [əsístəns] The term "companion <u>support</u>" as used in this Act means the provision of services to persons or children with disabilities who experience severe difficulty with mobility due to a visual impairment.	援護 この法律において「同行<u>援護</u>」とは、視覚障害により、移動に著しい困難を有する障害者等につき、移動の援護その他の便宜を供与することをいう。
1243	**citation (cite)** [saɪtéɪʃən] A document, photograph, audio tape, video tape or any other object that is found to be appropriate by the court may be <u>cited</u> in a record of oral argument, and be attached to the case record as part of that record of oral argument.	①援用、②引用（…する） 口頭弁論の調書には、書面、写真、録音テープ、ビデオテープその他裁判所において適当と認めるものを<u>引用</u>し、訴訟記録に添付して調書の一部とすることができる。
1244	**corresponding day** If the period is not calculated from the beginning of a year, the period expires on the day preceding the day <u>corresponding</u> to the first <u>day</u> of the calculation in the final year.	応当する日 年の始から期間を起算しないときは、その期間は、最後の年においてその起算日に<u>応当する日</u>の前日に満了する。
1245	**company with financial auditor(s)** "Company with Financial Auditor(s)" means any stock company which has financial auditor(s), or any stock company which is required to have financial auditor(s) under the provisions of the Company Act.	会計監査人設置会社 「<u>会計監査人設置会社</u>」とは、会計監査人を置く株式会社又は会社法の規定により会計監査人を置かなければならない株式会社をいう。

RANK 3

1246	**company with accounting advisor(s)**	**会計参与設置会社**
	If it is necessary for the purpose of performing duties of an accounting advisor, an accounting advisor may request reports on accounting from a subsidiary company of the <u>company with accounting advisor(s)</u>.	会計参与は、その職務を行うため必要があるときは、**会計参与設置会社**の子会社に対して会計に関する報告を求めることができる。
1247	**admonition** [ǽdməníʃən]	**戒告**
	There are four types of disciplinary action against attorneys, as follows: (i) <u>admonition</u>; (ii) suspension for not more than two years; (iii) order to withdraw from the bar association in which the attorney holds a membership; or (iv) disbarment.	弁護士に対する懲戒は4つあり、(i) **戒告**、(ii) 2年以内の業務の停止、(iii) 退会命令又は (iv) 除名である。
1248	**alien registration**	**外国人登録**
	<u>Alien registration</u> is required under Japanese laws.	**外国人登録**が、日本法上義務付けられている。
1249	**dispersion (disperse)** [dɪspə́ːrʒən]	**解散（する）**
	When a crowd refuses to disperse after being ordered three times or more to <u>disperse</u> by a public employee with authority, the ringleader is punished by imprisonment or imprisonment without work for not more than 3 years.	権限のある公務員から解散の命令を3回以上受けたにもかかわらず、多衆が、なお**解散**しなかったときは、首謀者は3年以下の懲役又は禁錮に処する。
1250	**request for disclosure**	**開示請求**
	The <u>request for disclosure</u> was filed according to the law.	**開示請求**は、法律に従って行われた。
1251	**recovery** [rɪkʌ́vri]	**（非有体物の）回収**
	The <u>recovery</u> of assets was a result of successful litigation.	資産の**回収**は、訴訟の成功の結果であった。
1252	**amendment act**	**改正法**
	The <u>amendment act</u> was passed by a unanimous legislative vote.	**改正法**は、全会一致で可決された。
1253	**revision** [rɪvíʒən]	**改定**
	A <u>revision</u> to the contract was agreed upon by both parties.	契約書の**改定**は、両者によって合意された。

RANK 3

1254	**replace** [rɪpléɪs] Even if a third party has appointed an administrator for the property, if the replacement of that administrator is required, the family court may appoint an administrator.	改任 第三者が管理者を指定したときであっても、これを**改任**する必要がある場合において、家庭裁判所は、管理者を選任できる。
1255	**sales representative** The sales representative was arrested.	外務員 **外務員**が逮捕された。
1256	**injuring party** The injuring party is liable for compensatory damages.	加害者 **加害者**は、填補的損害賠償責任を負う。
1257	**request for valuation** A request for valuation is subject to the jurisdiction of the rehabilitation court.	価額決定の請求 **価額決定の請求**に係る事件は、再生裁判所が管轄する。
1258	**scientific knowledge** The case hinges on the application of scientific knowledge.	科学的知見 この事件は、**科学的知見**の応用にかかっている。
1259	**determination of the price** The determination of the price was based on an independent appraisal.	価格の決定 **価格の決定**は、独立した鑑定に基づいて行われた。
1260	**reimbursement of value** The court ordered reimbursement of value.	価額の償還 裁判所は、**価額の償還**を命じた。
1261	**party at a distance** The party at a distance participated via teleconference, as permitted by court rules.	隔地者 **隔地者**は、裁判所規則で認められている通り、電話会議を通じて参加した。
1262	**rating** [réɪtɪŋ] The rating of the company's bonds affects its borrowing costs.	格付 社債の**格付**は、借入コストに影響する。
1263	**fixed due date** If a fixed due date is assigned to the performance of an obligation, the obligor is liable for delay from the time that due date arrives.	確定期限 債務の履行について**確定期限**があるときは、債務者は、その期限の到来した時から遅滞の責任を負う。

RANK 3

1264	**processing (processed)** [prάːsesɪŋ]	加工（された）
	If a person adds labor to another person's movables, the ownership of the <u>processed</u> thing belongs to the owner of the material.	他人の動産に工作を加えた者があるときは、その<u>加工</u>物の所有権は、材料の所有者に帰属する。
1265	**defective manifestation of intention**	瑕疵ある意思表示
	A <u>defective manifestation of intention</u> may render a contract voidable.	<u>瑕疵ある意思表示</u>があると、契約が無効になることがある。
1266	**money lender**	貸金業者
	The <u>money lender</u> must comply with laws and regulations.	<u>貸金業者</u>は、法令を遵守しなければならない。
1267	**taxable income**	課税所得
	<u>Taxable income</u> is reported annually to the authority.	<u>課税所得</u>は、毎年当局へ報告される。
1268	**tax base**	課税標準
	The <u>tax base</u> calculation directly impacts tax liabilities.	<u>課税標準</u>の計算は、納税義務に直接影響する。
1269	**falsify** [fɔ́ːlsəfàɪ]	仮装
	<u>Falsifying</u> medical certificates is subject to criminal punishment.	診断書の<u>仮装</u>（虚偽）作成は、刑事罰に処せられる。
1270	**surcharge** [sɚtʃɑ́ːrdʒ]	課徴金（独占禁止法） ※一般的な課徴金の表現にはadministrative monetary penaltyを用いる。
	A <u>surcharge</u> was imposed by the J-FTC.	日本の公正取引委員会によって、<u>課徴金</u>が課された。
1271	**totaling** [tóʊtəlɪŋ]	合算
	<u>Totaling</u> all expenses is necessary for the final accounting.	すべての経費の<u>合算</u>は、最終的な会計に必要である。
1272	**installment sales**	割賦販売
	<u>Installment sales</u> agreements require disclosure of interest rates.	<u>割賦販売</u>契約では、金利の開示が義務付けられている。
1273	**share transfer plan**	株式移転計画
	The <u>share transfer plan</u> was approved by the board of directors.	<u>株式移転計画</u>は、取締役会で承認された。
1274	**demand for a share(, etc.) cash-out**	株式等売渡請求
	The <u>demand for a share (, etc.) cash-out</u> was resolved through arbitration.	<u>株式等売渡請求</u>は、仲裁によって解決された。

RANK 3

1275	**statement of changes in net assets**	**株主資本等変動計算書**
	The statement of changes in net assets is essential for financial transparency.	株主資本等変動計算書は、財務の透明性を高めるために不可欠である。
1276	**simplified rehabilitation**	**簡易再生**
	Simplified rehabilitation proceedings expedite bankruptcy resolution.	簡易再生は、倒産の解決を迅速化する。
1277	**summary delivery (summary transfer)**	**簡易の引渡し**
		※民法の英訳には「summary delivery」が用いられている。
	If a transferee is actually holding the thing under possession, the transfer of possessory rights may be effected by the parties' manifestations of intention alone (summary delivery).	譲受人が現に占有物を所持する場合には、占有権の譲渡は、当事者の意思表示のみによってすることができる（**簡易の引渡し**）。
1278	**simplified distribution**	**簡易配当**
	Permission for a simplified distribution may not be granted if an interim distribution has been made.	簡易配当の許可は、中間配当をした場合は、することができない。
1279	**relevant administrative organ**	**関係行政機関**
	The relevant administrative organ reviewed compliance with regulations.	関係行政機関が、規制の遵守状況を審査した。
1280	**custody (care)** [kʌ́stədi]	**監護**
		※民法の英訳ではcustodyとcareがそれぞれ条文ごとに「監護」に当てられている。
	A person who exercises parental authority holds the right, and bears the duty, to care for and educate the child.	親権を行う者は、子の**監護**及び教育をする権利を有し、義務を負う。
1281	**audit committee**	**監査委員会**
	Each committee, including the nominating committee, audit committee, or compensation committee is composed of three or more committee members.	指名委員会、**監査委員会**又は報酬委員会の各委員会は、委員3人以上で組織する。
1282	**audit certification**	**監査証明**
	Audit certification is required for publicly traded companies.	上場企業には、**監査証明**が必要である。
1283	**audit corporation**	**監査法人**
	An audit corporation conducted the annual financial review.	監査法人が、年次財務レビューを実施した。

1284	**surveillance** [sərvéɪləns]	監視
	<u>Surveillance</u> measures comply with privacy laws.	<u>**監視**</u>の措置は、個人情報保護法に準拠している。
1285	**inspector** [ìnspéktər]	①監事、②検査役
	The court may fix the amount of the remuneration that the stock company after the formation pays to such an <u>inspector</u>.	裁判所は、成立後の株式会社が<u>**検査役**</u>に対して支払う報酬の額を定めることができる。
1286	**custom** [kʌ́stəm]	慣習
	<u>Custom</u> dictates the informal resolution of certain disputes.	<u>**慣習**</u>により、特定の紛争は非公式に解決される。
1287	**customary law**	慣習法
	<u>Customary law</u> influences legal decisions in specific jurisdictions.	<u>**慣習法**</u>は、特定の法域における法的決定に影響を及ぼす。
1288	**expert examination**	鑑定（末尾㉝参照）
	<u>Expert examination</u> was requested to verify the authenticity of the document.	文書の真正性を確認するため、<u>**鑑定**</u>が要請された。
1289	**expert opinion**	鑑定（末尾㉝参照）
	The <u>expert opinion</u> contributed significantly to the case.	<u>**鑑定**</u>（意見）は、本件に大きく貢献した。
1290	**expert testimony**	鑑定（末尾㉝参照）
	<u>Expert testimony</u> is admissible.	<u>**鑑定**</u>（証言）は認められる。
1291	**expert** [ékspərt]	鑑定人
	The <u>expert</u> analyzed forensic evidence.	<u>**鑑定人**</u>は、法医学的証拠を分析した。
1292	**request for an expert examination**	鑑定の嘱託
	A <u>request for an expert examination</u> was filed with the court.	裁判所に対して、<u>**鑑定の嘱託**</u>を行った。
1293	**official gazette**	官報
	The <u>official gazette</u> published the new regulations.	<u>**官報**</u>は新しい規制を公表した。

RANK 3

1294	**assembly (council)** [káʊnsəl]	①地方公共団体の議会、②行政機関としての会議 ※憲法（英語）は「assemblies」を用いている。
	The local public entities shall establish <u>assemblies</u> as their deliberative organs, in accordance with law.	地方公共団体には、法律の定めるところにより、その議事機関として<u>議会</u>を設置する。
1295	**computation of a period of time**	期間の計算
	The <u>computation of a period of time</u> is governed by statute.	<u>期間の計算</u>は、法令によって定められている。
1296	**burden of risk**	危険負担
	The <u>burden of risk</u> shifts upon delivery of goods.	<u>危険負担</u>は、商品の引渡し時に移転する。
1297	**other than on the date**	期日外
	In cases of taking measures to ask for an explanation <u>other than on the date</u> for oral argument, the presiding judge may direct a court clerk to take that measure.	裁判長は、口頭弁論の<u>期日外</u>において、釈明のための処置をする場合には、裁判所書記官に命じて行わせることができる。
1298	**interim conference procedure**	期日間整理手続
	The <u>interim conference procedure</u> facilitated settlement discussions.	<u>期日間整理手続</u>は、和解の話し合いを促進した。
1299	**change of date**	期日の変更
	A <u>change of date</u> for the trial was granted by the judge.	裁判官は、<u>期日の変更</u>を認めた。
1300	**summons for appearance date**	期日の呼出し
	The <u>summons for appearance date</u> must be strictly adhered to.	<u>期日の呼出し</u>は、厳守しなければならない。
1301	**perjury** [pə́ːrdʒəri]	偽証
	<u>Perjury</u> undermines the integrity of judicial proceedings.	<u>偽証</u>は、司法手続の完全性を損なう。
1302	**charging instrument**	起訴状（末尾⑩参照）
	The <u>charging instrument</u> delineates the charges against the defendant.	<u>起訴状</u>には、被告人に対する罪状が明記されている。
1303	**bailment** [béilmənt]	寄託
	A <u>bailment</u> becomes effective if one of the parties asks the other party to keep a certain thing in custody, and the other party gives consent to keeping it in custody.	<u>寄託</u>は、当事者の一方がある物を保管することを相手方に委託し、相手方がこれを承諾することによって、その効力を生ずる。

RANK 3

1304	**bailor** [béɪlər]	寄託者
	The <u>bailor</u> retains ownership rights during the bailment period.	<u>寄託者</u>は、期間中、所有権を保持する。
1305	**res judicata**	既判力
	<u>Res judicata</u> prevents the same case from being tried twice.	<u>既判力</u>は、同じ事件が二度審理されることを防ぐ。
1306	**mandamus action**	義務付けの訴え
	"<u>Mandamus action</u>" means an action seeking an order to the effect that an administrative authority should make an original administrative disposition or an administrative determination.	「<u>義務付けの訴え</u>」とは、行政庁がその処分又は裁決をすべき旨を命ずることを求める訴訟をいう。
1307	**company disappearing in an absorption-type merger**	吸収合併消滅会社
	The <u>company disappearing in an absorption-type merger</u> ceases to exist.	<u>吸収合併消滅会社</u>は、消滅する。
1308	**company surviving an absorption-type merger**	吸収合併存続会社
	The <u>company surviving an absorption-type merger</u> acquires all assets and liabilities.	<u>吸収合併存続会社</u>は、すべての資産及び負債を取得する。
1309	**right to remedy over (reimbursement)**	求償権（末尾⓫参照）
	The provisions of the preceding two paragraphs do not preclude the employer or supervisor from exercising their <u>right to reimbursement</u> against the employee.	前二項の規定は、使用者又は監督者から被用者に対する<u>求償権</u>の行使を妨げない。
1310	**imminent and unlawful infringement**	急迫不正の侵害
	An act a person was compelled to take to protect the rights of oneself or any other person against <u>imminent and unlawful infringement</u> is not punishable.	<u>急迫不正の侵害</u>に対して、自己又は他人の権利を防衛するため、やむを得ずにした行為は、罰しない。
1311	**former act**	旧法
	The <u>former act</u> is superseded by the new legislation.	<u>旧法</u>は、新法に取って代わられる。
1312	**dormant company**	休眠会社
	A <u>dormant company</u> remains legally existent without active operations.	<u>休眠会社</u>とは、積極的な営業活動を行わず、法的に存在し続ける会社のことである。

RANK 3

1313	**contribution** [kɑ̀:ntrəbjúːʃən] Contribution among joint tortfeasors adjusts their financial obligations.	①寄与（例：寄与分）、②寄附金 共同不法行為者間の**寄与**は、その金銭的債務を調整するものである。
1314	**common-benefit claim** The opponent's claim for court costs against the creditor in rehabilitation proceedings is classed as a common-benefit claim.	共益債権 相手方の再生債権者に対する訴訟費用請求権は、**共益債権**とする。
1315	**expenses for common benefit** Expenses for common benefit are distributable among beneficiaries.	共益費用 **共益費用**は、受益者間で分配可能である。
1316	**extortion** [ekstɔ́:rʃən] A person who extorts another person to deliver property is punished by imprisonment for not more than 10 years (extortion).	恐喝 人を恐喝して財物を交付させた者は、10年以下の懲役に処する（**恐喝**）。
1317	**deliberation** [dɪlìbəréɪʃən] A bar association must respond to a consultation or deliberation by the Japan Federation of Bar Associations.	協議 弁護士会は、日本弁護士連合会から諮問又は**協議**を受けた事項につき答申をしなければならない。
1318	**inducement** [ɪndúːsmənt] Inducement to commit a crime implicates liability.	①教唆、②誘引 犯罪の**教唆**は責任を伴う。
1319	**abettor** [əbétər] An abettor is criminally liable for encouraging the offense.	教唆者 **教唆者**は、犯罪を助長した刑事責任を負う。
1320	**mutual legal assistance** Mutual legal assistance facilitates cross-border law enforcement.	共助 **共助**は、国境を越えた法執行を容易にする。
1321	**coprincipal (in crime)** A coprincipal in crime shares equal liability.	共同正犯 犯罪の**共同正犯**は、同等の責任を負う。
1322	**joint suit** A joint suit consolidates claims of multiple plaintiffs.	共同訴訟 **共同訴訟**は、複数の原告の請求を統合するものである。

1323	**joint mortgage**	共同抵当
	A <u>joint mortgage</u> secures a loan for co-borrowers.	<u>共同抵当</u>は、共同借主のための債務を担保するものである。
1324	**joint tort**	共同不法行為
	<u>Joint tort</u> liability holds multiple parties responsible for damage.	<u>共同不法行為</u>責任は、複数の当事者に損害賠償責任を負わせるものである。
1325	**joint guarantor**	共同保証人
	A <u>joint guarantor</u> shares responsibility for loan repayment.	<u>共同保証人</u>は、ローン返済の責任を分担する。
1326	**duress** [dɔ́res]	強迫
	<u>Duress</u> invalidates agreements made under coercion.	<u>強迫</u>は、強制の下でなされた合意を無効にする。
1327	**intimidation** [ìntɪmɪdéɪʃən]	脅迫
	A person who, through assault or <u>intimidation</u> forcibly engages in intercourse with another person of not less than thirteen years of age is guilty of the crime of forcible sexual intercourse, and is punished by imprisonment for a definite term of not less than 5 years.	13歳以上の者に対し、暴行又は<u>脅迫</u>を用いて性交をした者は、強制性交等の罪とし、5年以上の有期懲役に処する。
1328	**complicity** [kəmplísəti]	共犯（共犯関係）
	<u>Complicity</u> in a crime implicates all involved parties.	<u>共犯（共犯関係）</u>は、すべての関係者を巻き込むこととなる。
1329	**enjoyment** [ənʤɔ́ɪmənt]	享有
	<u>Enjoyment</u> of property rights is protected by law.	財産権の<u>享有</u>は、法律によって保護されている。
1330	**property in co-ownership**	共有物
	<u>Property in co-ownership</u> necessitates consensus for significant decisions.	<u>共有物</u>は、重要な決定には同意が必要である。
1331	**partition of property in co-ownership**	共有物の分割
	<u>Partition of property in co-ownership</u> may require legal intervention.	<u>共有物の分割</u>には、法的介入が必要な場合がある。
1332	**co-ownership interest**	共有持分
	<u>Co-ownership interest</u> specifies each owner's share in the property.	<u>共有持分</u>は、不動産に対する各所有者の持分を特定する。

RANK 3

RANK 3

1333 compulsion [kəmpʌ́lʃən]

A person who intimidates another person using threat to harm the life, body, freedom, reputation or property of another person, causing the other person to perform an act which the person had no obligation to perform, is punished by imprisonment for not more than 3 years (<u>compulsion</u>).

強要

生命、身体、自由、名誉若しくは財産に対し害を加える旨を告知して脅迫して、人に義務のないことを行わせた者は、3年以下の懲役に処する（<u>強要</u>）。

1334 notice of grounds for rejection

<u>Notice of grounds for rejection</u> must be clearly articulated.

拒絶理由通知

<u>拒絶理由通知</u>は、明瞭に記載されなければならない。

1335 prohibitory injunction

A <u>prohibitory injunction</u> prevents a party from taking specific actions.

禁止命令

<u>禁止命令</u>は、当事者が特定の行動をとることを阻止するものである。

1336 financial institution

<u>Financial institutions</u> are regulated to protect consumer interests.

金融機関

<u>金融機関</u>は、消費者の利益を守るために規制されている。

1337 financial instruments intermediary service

<u>Financial instruments intermediary service</u> requires regulatory compliance.

金融商品仲介業

<u>金融商品仲介業</u>には、規制遵守が必要である。

1338 intermediation for financial instruments

<u>Intermediation for financial instruments</u> involves facilitating transactions.

金融商品仲介行為

<u>金融商品仲介行為</u>には、取引の円滑化が含まれる。

1339 financial instruments firms association

<u>Financial instruments firms association</u> sets industry standards.

金融商品取引業協会

<u>金融商品取引業協会</u>が、業界基準を設定している。

1340 financial instruments business operator

<u>Financial instruments business operators</u> are subject to stringent oversight.

金融商品取引業者

<u>金融商品取引業者</u>は、厳しい監督下に置かれる。

1341 lottery ticket (drawing of lots)

A person who sells a <u>lottery ticket</u> is punished by imprisonment for not more than 2 years or a fine of not more than 1,500,000 yen.

富くじ

<u>富くじ</u>を発売した者は、2年以下の懲役又は150万円以下の罰金に処する。

1342 partnership property

<u>Partnership property</u> is governed by the partnership agreement.

組合財産

<u>組合財産</u>は、組合契約によって管理される。

1343	**passage** [pǽsədʒ]	経過
	This does not apply after the <u>passage</u> of three years from the filing date of application.	出願の日から3年を<u>経過</u>した後は、この限りでない。
1344	**progress** [prá:grəs]	経過
	When the entire period of suspended execution of the sentence in whole <u>progresses</u> without rescission, the sentence ceases to be effective.	刑の全部の執行猶予の言渡しを取り消されることなくその猶予の期間を<u>経過</u>したときは、刑の言渡しは、効力を失う。
1345	**term (of sentence)** [tə́:rm]	刑期
	<u>Term of sentence</u> is determined by judicial discretion.	<u>刑期</u>は、司法の裁量によって決定される。
1346	**posting** [póʊstɪŋ]	掲示
	<u>Posting</u> of legal notices must meet statutory requirements.	法的通知の<u>掲示</u>は、法定要件を満たさなければならない。
1347	**penal institution**	刑事施設
	A <u>penal institution</u> rehabilitates and punishes offenders.	<u>刑事施設</u>は、犯罪者を更生させ、処罰する。
1348	**disqualification** [dɪskwɑ̀:ləfəkéɪʃən]	欠格
	<u>Disqualification</u> from holding certain positions may follow conviction.	有罪判決を受けると、特定の役職に就く<u>欠格</u>事由となる。
1349	**clearing** [klírɪŋ]	決済(相殺勘定の決済)
	<u>Clearing</u> transactions reduces settlement risk.	取引の決済をすることで、<u>決済</u>リスクを軽減できる。
1350	**censorship** [sénsərʃɪp]	検閲
	No <u>censorship</u> shall be maintained, nor shall the secrecy of any means of communication be violated.	<u>検閲</u>は、これをしてはならない。通信の秘密は、これを侵してはならない。
1351	**depreciation** [dɪpriːʃiéɪʃən]	償却(減価償却)
	<u>Depreciation</u> of assets is considered in calculating taxable income.	資産の<u>減価償却</u>費は、課税所得の計算において考慮される。

RANK 3

1352	**offender caught in the act**	**現行犯人**
	A person who is caught in the act of committing or is caught having just committed an offense is an <u>offender caught in the act</u>.	現に罪を行い、又は現に罪を行い終った者を**現行犯人**とする。
1353	**present danger**	**現在の危難**
	An act a person was compelled to take to avert a <u>present danger</u> is not punishable only when the harm produced by such act does not exceed the harm to be averted.	**現在の危難**を避けるため、やむを得ずにした行為は、これによって生じた害が避けようとした害の程度を超えなかった場合に限り、罰しない。
1354	**raw material**	**原材料**
	<u>Raw material</u> import regulations ensure quality and compliance.	**原材料**の輸入規制は、品質及び法令遵守を確保する。
1355	**original work(s)**	**原作品**
	The author of a work has the right to use the author's true name or pseudonym to indicate the name of the author on the <u>original work</u>.	著作者は、その著作物の**原作品**に、その実名若しくは変名を著作者名として表示する権利を有する。
1356	**inhabited building**	**現住建造物**
	A person who sets fire to and burns a building which is being used as a dwelling or for which a person is actually present is punished by the death penalty or imprisonment for life or for a definite term of not less than 5 years (arson of <u>inhabited buildings</u>).	放火して、現に人が住居に使用し又は現に人がいる建造物を焼損した者は、死刑又は無期若しくは5年以上の懲役に処する（**現住建造物**等放火）。
1357	**actual enrichment**	**現に受けている利益**
	<u>Actual enrichment</u> obtained through unjust means is subject to restitution.	不当な手段で得た**現に受けている利益**は、返還の対象となる。
1358	**to the extent actually enriched**	**現に利益を受けている限度において**
	Compensation is limited <u>to the extent actually enriched</u> by the defendant.	補償は、被告が**現に利益を受けている限度において**行われる。
1359	**probate** [próʊbèɪt]	**（遺言書の）検認**
	<u>Probate</u> proceedings are essential for the distribution of a decedent's estate.	**検認**手続は、被相続人の遺産を分配するために必要である。
1360	**pledge of right**	**権利質**
	A <u>pledge of right</u> is secured against a debtor's assets.	**権利質**は、債務者の資産を担保とする。

1361	**creator** [kriéɪtər]		考案者
	If the Commissioner of the Japan Patent Office finds that the <u>creator</u> is having difficulty paying the registration fees due to poverty, the Commissioner may reduce the registration fees.		特許庁長官は、**考案者**が貧困により登録料を納付する資力がないと認めるときは、登録料を軽減できる。
1362	**public interest**		公益
	<u>Public interest</u> guides legislation and regulatory measures.		**公益**（公共の利益）は、法律や規制措置の指針となる。
1363	**public interest incorporated foundation**		公益財団法人
	A <u>public interest incorporated foundation</u> operates under oversight for societal benefit.		**公益財団法人**は、社会の利益のために管理の下に運営される。
1364	**public interest incorporated association**		公益社団法人
	<u>Public interest incorporated associations</u> fulfill roles deemed necessary for community welfare.		**公益社団法人**は、地域社会の福祉に必要とされる役割を担っている。
1365	**public interest corporation**		公益法人
	<u>Public interest corporations</u> serve functions vital to the public's welfare.		**公益法人**は、公共の福祉に不可欠な機能を果たしている。
1366	**council system**		合議制
	The <u>council system</u> facilitates democratic decision-making within organizations.		**合議制**は、組織内の民主的な意思決定を促進する。
1367	**allegation and evidence**		攻撃防御方法
	<u>Allegation and evidence</u> form the basis of legal arguments in trial.		**攻撃防御方法**は、裁判における法的主張の基礎となる。
1368	**a court in charge of an appeal**		抗告裁判所
	<u>A court in charge of an appeal</u> reviews lower court decisions for errors.		**抗告裁判所**は、下級審の決定に誤りがないかを審査する。
1369	**action for judicial review of administrative disposition**		抗告訴訟
	<u>Action for judicial review of administrative disposition</u> challenges government decisions.		**抗告訴訟**は、政府の決定を争うものである。
1370	**uttering** [ʌ́tərɪŋ]		行使（偽造文書等の行使）
	<u>Uttering</u> false documents is a criminal offense.		虚偽文書の**行使**は、犯罪行為である。

RANK 3

1371	**deduction** [dɪdʌ́kʃən] <u>Deduction</u> from taxable income requires valid documentation.	控除 課税所得からの<u>控除</u>には、有効な書類が必要である。
1372	**authentic instrument (notarized deeds)** A person, who makes a false statement before a public employee and thereby causes the employee to make a false entry in <u>notarized deeds</u> is punished by imprisonment for not more than 5 years or a fine of not more than 500,000 yen.	公正証書（末尾㉞参照） 公務員に対し虚偽の申立てをして、<u>公正証書</u>の原本に不実の記載をさせた者は、5年以下の懲役又は50万円以下の罰金に処する。
1373	**(corporate) reorganization proceedings** <u>Corporate reorganization proceedings</u> aim to rehabilitate financially distressed companies.	更生手続 <u>会社更生手続</u>は、財政難に陥った企業を再生させることを目的としている。
1374	**demotion** [dɪmóʊʃən] <u>Demotion</u> as a disciplinary measure must follow due process.	降任 懲戒処分としての<u>降任</u>は、適正手続きに従わなければならない。
1375	**in a fair and sincere manner** Transactions must be conducted <u>in a fair and sincere manner</u> to ensure trust.	公平かつ誠実に 信頼を確保するためには、取引は<u>公平かつ誠実に</u>行われなければならない。
1376	**detention warrant** A <u>detention warrant</u> is issued based on probable cause.	勾留状 <u>勾留状</u>は、正当な理由に基づいて発行される。
1377	**international application** <u>International applications</u> for patents require navigating multiple jurisdictions.	国際出願 特許の<u>国際出願</u>では、複数の法域での支援を要する。
1378	**information for personal identification** <u>Information for personal identification</u> is protected under privacy laws.	個人識別情報 <u>個人識別情報</u>は、個人情報保護法により保護されている。
1379	**this Act comes into effect as of ...** <u>This Act comes into effect as of</u> the specified date, introducing new regulations.	この法律は…から施行する <u>この法律</u>は指定された日付<u>から施行され</u>、新たな規則を導入する。
1380	**adviser** [ædváɪzər] An <u>adviser</u> provides expertise in specific legal matters.	顧問 <u>顧問</u>は、特定の法律問題に関する専門知識を提供する。

1381	**pledge of claim**	債権質
	A <u>pledge of claim</u> secures a loan against the borrower's receivables.	**債権質**は、借り手の債権を担保に融資を行うものである。
1382	**action by the subrogee**	債権者代位訴訟
	The company decide to file an <u>action by the subrogee</u>.	当該会社は、**債権者代位訴訟**を提起した。
1383	**instrument evidencing claims**	債権証書
	An <u>instrument evidencing claims</u> must be presented during debt recovery.	債権回収の際には、**債権証書**を提示しなければならない。
1384	**period for filing of proofs of claims**	債権届出期間
	A bankruptcy creditor who seeks to participate in bankruptcy proceedings must file notification to the court within a <u>period for filing proofs of claims</u>.	破産手続に参加しようとする破産債権者は、**債権届出期間**内に、裁判所に届け出なければならない。
1385	**investigation and allowance of claims**	債権の調査及び確定
	<u>Investigation and allowance of claims</u> is on schedule.	**債権の調査及び確定**は、予定通り進捗している。
1386	**filing of proofs of claims**	債権の届出
	The court must, upon making an order of commencement of bankruptcy proceedings, specify items such as the period for a <u>filing of proof of claims</u>.	裁判所は、破産手続開始の決定と同時に、**債権の届出**のための期間などの事項を定めなければならない。
1387	**redelivery** [rìːdilívəri]	再交付
	The <u>redelivery</u> of the patent certificate is prescribed by Order of the Ministry of Economy, Trade and Industry.	特許証の**再交付**については、経済産業省令で定める。
1388	**defense of demand**	催告の抗弁
	The guarantor may request the obligee to demand performance of the principal obligor first (<u>defense of demand</u>).	保証人は、まず主たる債務者に催告をすべき旨を請求することができる（**催告の抗弁**）。
1389	**assets disclosure procedure**	財産開示手続
	An enforcement court must order implementation of an <u>asset disclosure procedure</u> against an obligor, upon petition by an obligee of a monetary claim who has an authenticated copy of an enforceable title of obligation.	執行裁判所は、執行力のある債務名義の正本を有する金銭債権の債権者の申立てにより、債務者について、**財産開示手続**を実施する旨の決定をしなければならない。

RANK 3

1390	**request for re-examination**	**再審査請求**
	The duties of an attorney are to conduct actions regarding a litigation case, <u>request for re-examination</u> and conduct other general legal practices.	弁護士は、訴訟事件、**再審査請求**その他一般の法律事務を行うことを職務とする。
1391	**incorporated foundation**	**財団法人**
	An <u>incorporated foundation</u> operates for a specific non-commercial purpose.	**財団法人**は、特定の非営利目的のために運営される。
1392	**award** [əwɔ́ːrd]	**(仲裁の場合) 裁定**
	An arbitration <u>award</u> has the same effect as a labor agreement.	仲裁**裁定**は、労働協約と同一の効力を有する。
1393	**be present in court**	**在廷**
	The court may have the public prosecutor or defense counsel appear for the trial date and order said person to <u>be present in court</u>.	裁判所は、検察官又は弁護人に対し、公判期日に出頭し、かつ、**在廷**を命ずることができる。
1394	**demand by litigation**	**裁判上の請求**
	<u>Demand by litigation</u> initiates formal legal action against a party.	**裁判上の請求**は、当事者に対して正式な法的措置を開始するものである。
1395	**resale price**	**再販売価格**
	<u>Resale price</u> maintenance is scrutinized under competition law.	**再販売価格**の維持は、競争法の下で精査される。
1396	**right to demand rescission of fraudulent act**	**詐害行為取消権**
	An obligee may demand the court to rescind an act which the obligor commits knowing that it will prejudice the obligee (<u>right to demand rescission of fraudulent act</u>).	債権者は、債務者が債権者を害することを知ってした行為の取消しを裁判所に請求することができる（**詐害行為取消請求**）。
1397	**action for rescission of fraudulent act**	**詐害行為取消訴訟**
	<u>Action for rescission of fraudulent act</u> seeks to annul contracts obtained by fraud.	**詐害行為取消訴訟**は、詐害行為によって取得された契約の取消しを求めるものである。
1398	**visa** [víːzə]	**査証**
	<u>Visa</u> regulations dictate the conditions under which foreign nationals may enter the country.	**査証**の規制は、外国人が入国できる条件を規定するものである。

RANK 3

1399	**assessment** [əsésmənt]	査定
	The property's <u>assessment</u> reflects its market value for tax purposes.	不動産の**査定**額は、税務上の市場価値を反映している。
1400	**intervenor** [ìntərvínər]	参加人
	The <u>intervenor</u> filed a motion to participate in the case.	**参加人**は、この訴訟への参加を申し立てた。
1401	**remaining creditors**	残存債権者
	<u>Remaining creditors</u> will receive payment after primary debts are settled.	**残存債権者**は、主要な債務が清算された後に支払いを受ける。
1402	**fund settlement**	資金決済
	The <u>fund settlement</u> occurred smoothly, concluding the financial transaction.	**資金決済**は、スムーズに行われ、金融取引は終了した。
1403	**suspension of prescription**	時効の停止
	Prescription is not to run while execution of the sentence is suspended or stayed in accordance with laws and regulations (<u>suspension of prescription</u>).	時効は、法令により執行を猶予し、又は停止した期間内は、進行しない（**時効の停止**）。
1404	**tolling of statute of limitations**	時効の停止
	<u>Tolling of statute of limitations</u> was supported by the court.	裁判所は、**時効の停止**を支持した。
1405	**with the same care a person would exercise over the person's own property**	自己の財産におけるのと同一の注意義務をもって
	Under the agreement, the contractor must manage <u>with the same care they would exercise over their own property</u>.	契約上、受託者は、**自己の財産におけるのと同一の注意義務をもって**管理しなければならない。
1406	**bearer** [bérər]	持参人
	The <u>bearer</u> of the document is entitled to claim.	書類の**持参人**は、請求する権利を有する。
1407	**self-denounce**	自首する
	He decided to <u>self-denounce</u> to the authorities.	彼は、当局に**自首する**ことを決めた。
1408	**fire caused by negligence**	失火
	A <u>fire caused by negligence</u> led to significant damages.	**失火**により大きな損害が生じた。

RANK 3

#	English	Japanese
1409	**objection to (a disposition of) execution**	執行異議
	The <u>objection to a disposition of execution</u> was filed timely.	<u>執行異議</u>は、適時に行われた。
1410	**court execution officer**	執行官
	The <u>court execution officer</u> proceeded with the asset seizure.	<u>執行官</u>は、資産の差押えを進めた。
1411	**executive agency**	執行機関
	The <u>executive agency</u> revised its policy on public health.	<u>執行機関</u>は、公衆衛生に関する方針を改定した。
1412	**execution court**	執行裁判所
	The party shall use the official depository located in the territorial jurisdiction of the district court of jurisdiction in the locality of the <u>execution court</u>.	当事者は、<u>執行裁判所</u>の所在地を管轄する地方裁判所の管轄区域内の供託所を利用しなければならない。
1413	**notarial instrument authorizing execution**	執行証書
	The <u>notarial instrument authorizing execution</u> was duly prepared.	<u>執行証書</u>が、正式に作成された。
1414	**stay of execution**	執行停止
	The <u>stay of execution</u> provided temporary relief to the debtor.	<u>執行停止</u>は、債務者を一時的に救済した。
1415	**enforcement judgment (execution judgment)**	執行判決（外国裁判所判決）
	The lawyer is checking whether it falls a foreign court judgment for which an <u>enforcement judgment</u> has become final and binding.	弁護士は、確定した<u>執行判決</u>のある外国裁判所の判決を確認している。
1416	**payer** [péɪər]	支払者
	The <u>payer</u> fulfilled the obligation under the tax law promptly.	<u>支払者</u>は、速やかに税法上の義務を果たした。
1417	**report of payment**	支払調書
	The <u>report of payment</u> was duly delivered.	<u>支払調書</u>は、適切に送付された。
1418	**holograph** [hάləgræf]	自筆証書
	His will was found in a <u>holograph</u>, entirely handwritten.	彼の遺書は、すべて手書きの<u>自筆証書</u>だった。

RANK 3

1419	**private document**	私文書
	If a private document has been signed by, or bears the seal of the principal, it is presumed to be of authentic provenance.	私文書は、本人の署名又は押印があるときは、真正に成立したものと推定する。
1420	**reduction of the stated capital**	資本金の額の減少
	Reduction of the stated capital was approved in the meeting.	資本金の額の減少が、会議において承認された。
1421	**benevolent intervention in another's affairs**	事務管理
	Facts of benevolent intervention in another's affairs was recognized by the court.	事務管理の事実が、裁判所によって認定された。
1422	**fingerprint** [fíŋgərprìnt]	指紋
	The fingerprint was crucial evidence in the criminal case.	この指紋は、刑事事件の決定的な証拠となった。
1423	**land leasehold right**	借地権
	The land leasehold right was transferred to the new lessee.	借地権は、新しい賃借人に譲渡された。
1424	**order for clarification**	釈明処分
	The order for clarification demanded further details on the argument.	釈明処分は、主張のさらなる詳細を要求した。
1425	**bond register**	社債原簿
	The bond register was updated with the new issuance.	社債原簿は、新規発行に伴い更新された。
1426	**incorporated association**	社団法人
	The incorporated association announced its annual general meeting.	社団法人が、年次総会を発表した。
1427	**legatee** [lègətíː]	受遺者
	The legatee accepted the inheritance as per the will.	受遺者は、遺言に従って相続を受け入れた。
1428	**income** [ínkʌm]	収益
	His income sources varied across several investments.	彼の収益は、いくつかの投資にまたがっている。
1429	**proceeds** [prəsídz]	犯罪収益
	"Proceeds of crime, etc." means proceeds of crime and property derived from proceeds of crime.	「犯罪収益等」とは、犯罪収益及び犯罪収益に由来する財産を含む。

RANK 3

#	English	Japanese
1430	**accessory** [æksésəri] The <u>accessory</u> to the crime was also arrested.	<u>従犯</u> ※動産の「従物」の意味もある（1945参照）。 <u>従犯</u>も、逮捕された。
1431	**sufficient grounds** There were <u>sufficient grounds</u> for the lawsuit.	<u>十分な理由</u> 訴訟には、<u>十分な理由</u>があった。
1432	**inhabitants tax** <u>Inhabitants tax</u> was calculated based on residency status.	<u>住民税</u> <u>住民税</u>は、在留資格に基づいて計算された。
1433	**resident record** The <u>resident record</u> was updated following the move.	<u>住民票</u> <u>住民票</u>は、引っ越し後に更新された。
1434	**(criminal) acceptance of bribe** <u>Criminal acceptance of bribes</u> led to the official's resignation.	<u>収賄</u> <u>収賄</u>により、この公務員は辞任した。
1435	**sentenced person** A "<u>sentenced person</u>" means a person who has been sentenced to imprisonment, a person who has been sentenced to imprisonment without work, or a person who has been sentenced to penal detention.	<u>受刑者</u> <u>受刑者</u>とは、懲役受刑者、禁錮受刑者又は拘留受刑者をいう。
1436	**donee** [douníː] The <u>donee</u> graciously accepted the charitable donation.	<u>受贈者</u> <u>受贈者</u>は、この慈善寄付を快く受け入れた。
1437	**recipient** [rəsípiənt] If the value of the testamentary gift is exceeds the value of a donee's share in inheritance, the <u>recipient</u> may not receive the share in inheritance.	<u>受遺者</u> 遺贈の価額が、相続分の価額を超えるときは、<u>受遺者</u>は、その相続分を受けることができない。
1438	**publication of (an) application** If a request for the examination of an application is filed prior to the <u>publication of the application</u>, the Commissioner of the Japan Patent Office must publish an indication of this in the patent gazette at the time of <u>publication of the application</u>, the commissioner must publish this in the patent gazette thereafter without delay.	①（an ありの場合）<u>出願公開</u>、②（an なしの場合）<u>出願公表</u> 特許庁長官は、<u>出願公開</u>前に出願審査の請求があったときは<u>出願公開</u>の際、その旨を特許公報に掲載しなければならない。

RANK 3

1439	**extra wages**	**割増賃金**
	Extra wages were paid for overtime work according to regulations.	時間外労働に対して、**割増賃金**が支払われた。
1440	**examination of applications**	**出願審査**
	Examination of applications for the grant began last week.	先週から、**出願審査**の審査が始まった。
1441	**print right**	**出版権**
	The owner of print rights exclusively holds all or part of rights to the work that is subject to those print rights, pursuant to the act of establishment.	出版権者は、設定行為で定めるところにより、その**出版権**の目的である著作物について、権利の全部又は一部を専有する。
1442	**principal registration**	**主登記**
	Principal registration of the property was completed.	不動産の**主登記**が、完了した。
1443	**acquisitive prescription**	**取得時効**
	Acquisitive prescription granted her ownership after continuous use.	彼女は、継続的な使用により、**取得時効**によって所有権を取得した。
1444	**main text (of judgment)**	**主文**
	Res judicata applies only with regard to the contents of a final and binding judgment that are included in the main text.	確定判決は、**主文**に包含するものに限り、既判力を有する。
1445	**competent government agency**	**主務官庁**
	The competent government agency reviewed the regulatory impact.	**主務官庁**は、規制の影響を調査した。
1446	**competent minister**	**主務大臣**
	The competent minister endorsed the new education policy.	**主務大臣**は、新しい教育政策を支持した。
1447	**capacity to accept/receive**	**受領能力**
	His capacity to accept/receive the gift was confirmed.	**受領能力**が確認された。
1448	**compliance obligation**	**遵守義務**
	The Act on Welfare and Management of Animals sets out compliance obligations with standards.	動物の愛護及び管理に関する法律は、基準**遵守義務**を定める。
1449	**observance obligation**	**遵守義務**
	The Water Pollution Prevention Act sets out observance obligations of standards for controlling total emissions.	水質汚濁防止法は、総量規制基準の**遵守義務**を規定する。

RANK 3

1450	**quasi-loan (for consumption)**	準消費貸借
	If any person has an obligation to pay money or deliver other things under any arrangement, and the parties agree to regard such a thing as the subject matter of a loan for consumption, it is deemed that this establishes a loan for consumption (quasi-loan for consumption).	金銭その他の物を給付する義務を負う者がある場合において、当事者がその物を消費貸借の目的とすることを約したときは、消費貸借は、これによって成立したものとみなす（準消費貸借）。
1451	**injury** [índʒəri]	傷害
	The injury was reported to the police.	傷害は、警察に報告された。
1452	**summons** [sʌ́mənz]	召喚（状）
	A summons was issued to the defendant by the court.	裁判所から被告に対して、召喚状が出された。
1453	**refusal to testify**	証言拒絶
	The witness's refusal to testify complicated the trial.	証人の証言拒絶は、裁判を複雑にした。
1454	**final appellate court**	上告裁判所
	The case reached the final appellate court for review.	この事件は、上告裁判所に持ち込まれた。
1455	**(written) statement of reasons (for final appeal)**	上告趣意書
	The written statement of reasons for the final appeal was submitted.	上告趣意書が提出された。
1456	**acceptance of final appeal**	上告受理
	The acceptance of the final appeal moved the case forward.	上告受理により、事件は前進した。
1457	**petition for acceptance of final appeal**	上告受理の申立て
	The petition for acceptance of final appeal has been filed.	上告受理の申立てが行われた。
1458	**petition of (a) final appeal**	上告状
	A final appeal shall be filed through the submission of a petition of a final appeal with the court of prior instance.	上告の提起は、上告状を原裁判所に提出してしなければならない。
1459	**appellant (of final appeal)** [əpélənt]	上告人
	The appellant of the final appeal sought to overturn the judgment.	上告人は、判決の破棄を求めた。

RANK 3

#	English	Japanese
1460	**negotiation** [nɪɡòʊʃíéɪʃən] The method falls using the price decided by <u>negotiation</u> between the customers.	①譲渡（末尾⑲参照）、②**交渉** その方法は、顧客の間の**交渉**に基づく価格を用いる方法に該当する。
1461	**share with restriction on transfer** <u>Shares with restriction on transfer</u> limit ownership changes.	**譲渡制限株式** **譲渡制限株式**は、所有者の変更を制限する。
1462	**recognition** [rèkəɡníʃən] <u>Recognition</u> of the treatment was essential for its enforcement.	①**承認**、②認定 条約の執行には、条約の**承認**が不可欠だった。
1463	**deposit of fungibles** Due to the <u>deposit of fungibles</u>, the bailee must return the thing that is the same kind, quality and quantity as the bailed thing.	**消費寄託** **消費寄託**のため、受寄者は、寄託された物と種類、品質及び数量の同じ物をもって返還しなければならない。
1464	**commodity futures transaction** A <u>commodity futures transaction</u> was executed on the exchange.	**商品先物取引** **商品先物取引**が、取引所で行われた。
1465	**Commodity Derivatives Transaction Act** The <u>Commodity Derivatives Transaction Act</u> regulates market activities.	**商品先物取引法** **商品先物取引法**は、市場活動を規制している。
1466	**commodity investment management** <u>Commodity investment management</u> requires expert knowledge.	**商品投資顧問業** **商品投資顧問業**には、専門知識が必要である。
1467	**commodity exchange** The <u>commodity exchange</u> facilitated trading among investors.	**商品取引所** **商品取引所**は、投資家間の取引を促進した。
1468	**information and communications technology** <u>Information and communications technology</u> transformed the legal profession.	**情報通信技術** **情報通信技術**は、法曹界を一変させた。
1469	**petty bench** The Supreme Court conducts proceedings and reaches judicial decisions through the grand bench or a <u>petty bench</u>.	**小法廷** 最高裁判所は、大法廷又は**小法廷**で審理及び裁判をする。
1470	**action for future performance** An <u>action for future performance</u> was filed to ensure contract fulfillment.	**将来の給付の訴え** 契約の履行を確実にするため、**将来の給付の訴え**が提起された。

RANK 3

1471	**claim that may arise in the future**	将来の請求権
	The <u>claim that may arise in the future</u> was denied.	<u>将来の請求権</u>は、否定された。
1472	**clerk** [klə́ːrk]	書記官
	The <u>clerk</u> organized the case files for the judge.	<u>書記官</u>は、裁判官のために事件ファイルを整理した。
1473	**provisional disposition prohibiting the disposal of property**	処分禁止の仮処分
	<u>Provisional disposition prohibiting the disposal of property</u> was granted.	<u>処分禁止の仮処分</u>が決定された。
1474	**action for revocation of original administrative disposition**	処分の取消しの訴え
	An <u>action for revocation of original administrative disposition</u> was initiated.	<u>処分の取消しの訴え</u>が開始された。
1475	**infringement lawsuit**	侵害訴訟
	The <u>infringement lawsuit</u> sought to protect intellectual property rights.	<u>侵害訴訟</u>は、知的財産権の保護を求めたものである。
1476	**association or foundation without legal personality**	人格のない社団又は財団
	The <u>association or foundation without legal personality</u> operated in the community.	<u>人格のない社団又は財団</u>が地域社会で運営されていた。
1477	**good faith principle (principle of good faith)**	信義則（信義誠実の原則）
	The <u>good faith principle</u> underpins contract law.	<u>信義則（信義誠実の原則）</u>は、契約法を支えている。
1478	**trial decision**	審決
	The <u>trial decision</u> was announced after deliberation.	審議の結果、<u>審決</u>が発表された。
1479	**written decision**	審決書
	The <u>written decision</u> detailed the facts.	<u>審決書</u>には、事実が詳細に記されている。
1480	**request for administrative review**	審査請求
	The <u>request for administrative review</u> aimed at reversing the decision.	<u>審査請求</u>は、決定を覆すことを目的としていた。
1481	**diminished capacity**	心神耗弱
	<u>Diminished capacity</u> affected the defendant's liability.	<u>心神耗弱</u>は、被告人の責任に影響した。

RANK 3

1482	**insanity** [ínsǽnəti]	心神喪失
	Insanity was argued as a defense in the trial.	裁判では、**心神喪失**が、抗弁として主張された。
1483	**consolidation-type merger agreement**	新設合併契約
	The consolidation-type merger agreement was finalized.	**新設合併契約**が最終版となった。
1484	**company disappearing in a consolidation-type merger**	新設合併消滅会社
	The company disappearing in a consolidation-type merger ceased to exist.	**新設合併消滅会社**は、消滅した。
1485	**company incorporated in a consolidation-type merger**	新設合併設立会社
	The company incorporated in a consolidation-type merger took on new roles.	**新設合併設立会社**は、新たな役割を担うことになった。
1486	**company splitting in an incorporation-type split**	新設分割会社
	The company splitting in an incorporation-type split diversified.	**新設分割会社**は、多角化した。
1487	**incorporation-type company split plan**	新設分割計画
	The incorporation-type company split plan outlined the division.	**新設分割計画**では、分割の概要を説明した。
1488	**company incorporated in an incorporation-type split**	新設分割設立会社
	The company incorporated in an incorporation-type split was investigated.	**新設分割設立会社**は、調査を受けた。
1489	**taking unlawful possession**	侵奪
	Taking unlawful possession of real estate resulted in legal action.	不動産**侵奪**は、法的措置につながった。
1490	**degree of kinship**	親等
	The degree of kinship influenced inheritance rights.	**親等**が、相続権に影響した。
1491	**credit rating**	信用格付
	The credit rating affected the company's borrowing costs.	**信用格付**は、同社の借入コストに影響を与えた。

RANK 3

#	英語	日本語
1492	**credit union**	信用金庫
	The <u>credit union</u> offered financial services to its members.	<u>信用金庫</u>は、組合員に金融サービスを提供していた。
1493	**margin transaction**	信用取引
	The <u>margin transaction</u> was carefully monitored for risk.	<u>信用取引</u>について、リスクは慎重に監視された。
1494	**principal place of daily activity**	生活の本拠
	The <u>principal place of daily activity</u> determined domicile.	<u>生活の本拠</u>が、居住地を決定した。
1495	**action to oppose execution**	請求異議の訴え
	An <u>action to oppose execution</u> was filed to prevent asset seizure.	資産の差押えを防ぐため、<u>請求異議の訴え</u>が提起された。
1496	**completion of liquidation**	清算結了
	The <u>completion of liquidation</u> marked the company's end.	<u>清算結了</u>により、この会社は終わりを告げた。
1497	**liquidator** [líkwɪdèɪtər]	清算人
	The <u>liquidator</u> was appointed to dissolve the company.	<u>清算人</u>は、会社清算のために任命された。
1498	**board of liquidators**	清算人会
	The <u>board of liquidators</u> oversaw the dissolution process.	<u>清算人会</u>が、清算手続を監督した。
1499	**adult** [ədʌ́lt]	成人
	In Japan, a person becomes an <u>adult</u> at 18, gaining full legal rights and responsibilities.	日本では18歳で<u>成人</u>となり、完全な法的権利と責任を得る。
1500	**manufacture** [mæ̀njəfǽktʃər]	製造
	The <u>manufacturing</u> process adhered to strict quality standards.	<u>製造</u>の工程は、厳格な品質基準に従った。
1501	**manufacturer** [mæ̀njəfǽktʃərər]	製造者
	The <u>manufacturer</u> issued a recall for the defective units.	<u>製造者</u>は、欠陥のある製品ユニットに関して、リコールを発表した。
1502	**product** [prɑ́:dəkt]	製造物
	The <u>product</u> warranty covered repairs and replacements.	<u>製造物</u>の保証は、修理及び交換を対象としていた。

#	Term	Japanese
1503	**supervisor of guardian of adult** The <u>supervisor of the guardian of an adult</u> was appointed by the court.	**成年後見監督人** **成年後見監督人**は、裁判所によって任命された。
1504	**guardian of adult** The <u>guardian of an adult</u> managed the ward's financial affairs.	**成年後見人** **成年後見人**は、被後見人の金銭管理を行った。
1505	**adult ward** The <u>adult ward</u> received legal protection.	**成年被後見人** **成年被後見人**は、法的な保護を受けた。
1506	**government** [gʌ́vərmənt] The <u>government</u> initiated infrastructure improvement projects.	**政府** **政府**は、インフラ整備プロジェクトを開始した。
1507	**government contract** The <u>government contract</u> was awarded after a competitive bidding process.	**政府契約** **政府契約**は、競争入札の末に結ばれた。
1508	**life insurance** <u>Life insurance</u> policies were revised.	**生命保険** **生命保険**契約が更新された。
1509	**director at incorporation** The <u>director at incorporation</u> played a key role in the company's founding.	**設立時取締役** **設立時取締役**は、会社設立において重要な役割を果たした。
1510	**share issued at incorporation** <u>Shares issued at incorporation</u> formed the company's initial capital.	**設立時発行株式** **設立時発行株式**は、会社の最初の資本金となった。
1511	**pronounce judgment** The court is set to <u>pronounce judgment</u> next week.	**宣告する** 裁判所は、来週判決を**宣告する**予定だ。
1512	**swear** [swér] Witnesses <u>swear</u> to tell the truth before testifying.	**宣誓** 証人は、証言する前に真実を語ることを**宣誓**する。
1513	**alternative obligation** If the subject matter of the claim is to be determined by a choice being made from among more than one performance (<u>alternative obligation</u>), the right to choose belongs to the obligor.	**選択債権** 債権の目的が数個の給付の中から選択によって定まるとき（**選択債権**）の場合、その選択権は、債務者に属する。

RANK 3

#	English	Japanese
1514	**share subject to class-wide call**	全部取得条項付種類株式
	Shares subject to class-wide call were outlined in the bylaws.	全部取得条項付種類株式は、定款に定められている。
1515	**transfer of possession**	占有移転
	Transfer of possession was confirmed by the lawyer.	占有移転が、弁護士によって確認された。
1516	**action for recovery of possession**	占有回収の訴え
	An action for recovery of possession was filed to reclaim property.	財産を取り戻すために占有回収の訴えが提起された。
1517	**possessory action**	占有の訴え
	The possessory action disputed the rightful ownership.	占有の訴えは、正当な所有権を争うものであった。
1518	**action for maintenance of possession**	占有保持の訴え
	If a possessor is obstructed from possession, the possessor may claim for the discontinuation of the obstruction by filing an action for maintenance of possession.	占有者がその占有を妨害されたときは、占有保持の訴えにより、その妨害の停止を請求することができる。
1519	**action for preservation of possession**	占有保全の訴え
	The possessor may demand the prevention of the obstruction by filing an action for preservation of possession.	占有者は、占有保全の訴えにより、その妨害の予防を請求することができる。
1520	**exclusive (patent) license**	専用実施権
	The exclusive patent license was negotiated between two tech companies.	専用実施権は、2つのテック企業間で交渉された。
1521	**exclusive (trademark) license**	専用使用権
	The exclusive trademark license allowed for brand expansion.	専用使用権により、ブランドの拡大が可能になった。
1522	**sending back**	送還
	When the Minister of Justice has ordered the sending back, the Minister of Justice must notify the incoming sentenced person to that effect in writing.	法務大臣は、送還の命令をしたときは、当該受入受刑者に書面でその旨を通知しなければならない。
1523	**administrator of an estate**	相続財産の管理人
	The administrator of an estate managed the deceased's assets.	相続財産の管理人は。被相続人の財産を管理する。

1524	**referral (refer)** [rɪfə́ːrəl]	送致（する）
	When a public prosecutor receives a suspect <u>referred</u>, the public prosecutor must give the suspect an opportunity for explanation.	検察官は、**送致**された被疑者を受け取ったときは、弁解の機会を与えなければならない。
1525	**proceedings to arrange issues and evidence**	争点及び証拠の整理手続
	The <u>proceedings to arrange issues and evidence</u> streamlined the trial.	**争点及び証拠の整理手続**は、裁判を効率化した。
1526	**(criminal) offer of bribe**	贈賄
	The <u>criminal offer of bribe</u> led to immediate arrest.	**贈賄**は、直ちに逮捕につながった。
1527	**immediate appeal from/against a ruling**	即時抗告
	The <u>immediate appeal against the ruling</u> challenged the decision.	この決定を不服として、**即時抗告**が行われた。
1528	**good faith acquisition**	即時取得
	The <u>good faith acquisition</u> was recognized by the court.	**即時取得**は、裁判所に認められた。
1529	**person concerned in a case**	訴訟関係人
	The accused or any other <u>person concerned in a case</u> may request, at said person's own cost, a transcript or an extract of the written decision or the trial record in which the judicial decision is recorded.	被告人その他**訴訟関係人**は、自己の費用で、裁判書又は裁判を記載した調書の謄本又は抄本の交付を請求することができる。
1530	**notice of suit**	訴訟告知
	The <u>notice of suit</u> was officially served.	**訴訟告知**は、正式に送達された。
1531	**third party notice**	訴訟告知
	<u>Third party notice</u> was issued to involve additional stakeholders.	さらなる利害関係者を巻き込むため、**訴訟告知**がなされた。
1532	**intervention** [ìntərvénʃən]	訴訟参加
	<u>Intervention</u> was sought by a non-party with a vested interest.	**訴訟参加**は、既得権益を持つ非当事者によって求められた。
1533	**control of court proceedings**	訴訟指揮
	<u>Control of court proceedings</u> ensures fair and orderly litigation.	**訴訟指揮**は、公正で秩序ある訴訟を担保する。

RANK 3

#	English	Japanese
1534	**original party's withdrawal from suit**	訴訟脱退
	The <u>original party's withdrawal from the suit</u> was officially recorded.	元の当事者の**訴訟脱退**が、正式に記録された。
1535	**suspension of (litigation/court) proceedings**	訴訟手続の中止
	If there are grounds for a <u>suspension of litigation proceedings</u> with regard to one of the co-litigants, the suspension is valid against all of them.	共同訴訟人の1人について**訴訟手続の中止**の原因があるときは、その中止は、全員についてその効力を生ずる。
1536	**stay of court proceedings**	訴訟手続の停止
	If a petition to disqualify is filed, litigation proceedings shall be stayed until the ruling on the petition becomes final and binding (<u>stay of litigation proceedings</u>).	除斥の申立てがあったときは、その申立てについての決定が確定するまで訴訟手続を停止しなければならない（**訴訟手続の停止**）。
1537	**expedited trial proceedings**	即決裁判手続
	<u>Expedited trial proceedings</u> aimed to resolve the case quickly.	**即決裁判手続**は、事件の早期解決を目指したものだった。
1538	**continuation** [kəntìnjuéɪʃən]	続行
	A resolution for the <u>continuation</u> is passed at the creditors meeting.	債権者集会において、**続行**について決議があった。
1539	**loss compensation**	損失補てん
	<u>Loss compensation</u> is prohibited under the law.	**損失補てん**は、法律で禁止されている。
1540	**thing received (in exchange for)**	対価
	The <u>thing received in exchange</u> was deemed equivalent in value.	**対価**は、同等の価値とみなされた。
1541	**outward direct investment**	対外直接投資
	<u>Outward direct investment</u> was made into a foreign subsidiary.	海外子会社への**対外直接投資**が行われた。
1542	**third party beneficiary contract**	第三者のためにする契約
	The <u>third party beneficiary contract</u> benefited a non-contracting party.	**第三者のためにする契約**は、契約当事者でない者を利するものであった。
1543	**retirement allowance**	退職手当
	The <u>retirement allowance</u> was disbursed as per company policy.	**退職手当**は、会社の方針に従って支払われた。
1544	**severance pay**	退職手当
	<u>Severance pay</u> was negotiated during the termination process.	**退職手当**は、解雇の過程において交渉された。

1545	**inward direct investment**	対内直接投資
	Inward direct investment increased the company's capital resources.	対内直接投資により、同社の資本は増加した。
1546	**second instance**	第二審
	The second instance court viewed the appeal.	第二審は、この控訴を審理した。
1547	**grand bench**	大法廷
	The grand bench deliberated on the constitutional matter.	大法廷は、憲法問題について審理した。
1548	**arrester** [əréstər]	逮捕者
	The arrester was commended for their quick response.	逮捕者は、迅速な返答を命じられた。
1549	**arrest warrant**	逮捕状
	The judge issued an arrest warrant based on presented evidence.	裁判官は、提示された証拠に基づいて逮捕状を発した。
1550	**durable years**	耐用年数
	The building's durable years are 22 years.	その建物の耐用年数は、22年である。
1551	**large volume holding**	大量保有
	Large volume holding significantly impacted market prices.	大量保有は、市場価格に大きな影響を与えた。
1552	**presence (attendance)** [əténdəns]	立会い
	The search for assets is not valid unless conducted in the presence of the guardian supervisor, if there is one.	財産の調査は、後見監督人があるときは、その立会いをもってしなければ、その効力を生じない。
1553	**on-site inspection**	立入検査
	The on-site inspection verified compliance with health standards.	立入検査では、衛生基準の遵守が確認された。
1554	**order to provide security**	担保提供命令
	The court issued an order to provide security.	裁判所は、担保提供命令を出した。
1555	**servitude** [sə́:rvətù:d]	地役権
	The property was subject to a right of servitude.	この土地には、地役権が設定されていた。
1556	**servitude holder**	地役権者
	The servitude holder was granted access for maintenance purposes.	地役権者は、保全のために立ち入りを許可された。

RANK 3

#	Term	Japanese
1557	**causing death**	**致死**
	A person who causes the death of another person due to negligence is punished by a fine of not more than 500,000 yen (<u>causing death</u> due to negligence).	過失により人を死亡させた者は、50万円以下の罰金に処する（過失**致死**）。
1558	**decentralization** [dɪsèntrəlɪzéɪʃən]	**地方分権**
	<u>Decentralization</u> aimed to distribute authority more evenly.	**地方分権**は、権限をより均等に分配することを目的としていた。
1559	**interlocutory confirmation suit**	**中間確認の訴え**
	The <u>interlocutory confirmation suit</u> sought to clarify legal standings.	**中間確認の訴え**では、法的主張を明確にすることを求めた。
1560	**interim dividend**	**中間配当**
	Shareholders received an <u>interim dividend</u> this fiscal quarter.	株主は、当四半期に**中間配当**を受け取った。
1561	**interlocutory judgment**	**中間判決**
	The <u>interlocutory judgment</u> allowed the case to proceed.	**中間判決**は、訴訟の続行を認めた。
1562	**arbitration committee member**	**仲裁委員**
	The <u>arbitration committee member</u> reviewed the case details.	**仲裁委員**は、事件の詳細を検討した。
1563	**arbitral award**	**仲裁判断**
	The <u>arbitral award</u> was issued concluding the dispute.	紛争を終結させる**仲裁判断**が下された。
1564	**small and medium-sized enterprise**	**中小企業**
	A <u>small and medium-sized enterprise</u> launched a new product line.	**中小企業**が、新しい製品ラインを立ち上げた。
1565	**written statement**	**調書（陳述書）**
	The <u>written statement</u> detailed the witness's account.	**調書（陳述書）**には、目撃者の証言が詳細に記されていた。
1566	**subsequent distribution**	**追加配当**
	<u>Subsequent distribution</u> of assets was scheduled for next month.	**追加配当**は、来月に予定されていた。
1567	**subsequent completion**	**追完**
	<u>Subsequent completion</u> of the delivery was anticipated by year-end.	履行の**追完**は、年末までと予想されていた。
1568	**non-exclusive (patent) license**	**通常実施権（特許）**
	The <u>non-exclusive patent license</u> allowed multiple companies to use the invention.	**通常実施権（特許）**により、複数の企業が発明を使用できるようになった。

#	Term	Japanese
1569	**non-exclusive (trademark) license** The <u>non-exclusive trademark license</u> was granted to several distributors.	**通常使用権（商標）** **通常使用権（商標）**が、複数の販売業者に付与された。
1570	**conspire** [kənspáɪər] The suspects <u>conspired</u> to commit the crime.	**通謀する** 被疑者たちは、**通謀して**犯行に及んだ。
1571	**service wherever (the person) may be found** <u>Service wherever the person may be found</u> ensured legal notice.	**出会送達** **出会送達**は、法的な通知を確実にする。
1572	**stay** [stéɪ] The <u>stay</u> of proceedings gave the defendant time to prepare.	**停止** 訴訟手続の**停止**は、被告に準備の時間を与えた。
1573	**fixtures** [fíkstʃərz] <u>Fixtures</u> in the leased property were cataloged.	**定着物** 賃貸物件の**定着物**は、一覧化された。
1574	**qualified institutional investor** <u>Qualified institutional investors</u> participated in the funding round.	**適格機関投資家** 資金調達ラウンドには、**適格機関投資家**が参加した。
1575	**derivatives transaction** The <u>derivatives transaction</u> was carefully analyzed for risk.	**デリバティブ取引** **デリバティブ取引**のリスクは、慎重に分析された。
1576	**natural disaster** The community prepared for the <u>natural disaster</u> with evacuation plans.	**天災** そのコミュニティは避難計画を立てて、**天災**に備えた。
1577	**electronic public notice** <u>Electronic public notice</u> increased accessibility to information.	**電子公告** **電子公告**により、情報へのアクセシビリティが向上した。
1578	**electronic signature** The <u>electronic signature</u> validated the document.	**電子署名** **電子署名**が、文書を真正にした。
1579	**electronic or magnetic record** The <u>electronic or magnetic record</u> was securely stored.	**電磁的記録** **電磁的記録**は、安全に保管された。

RANK 3

1580	**investment** [ìnvéstmənt]	投資、運用
	The <u>investment</u> in renewable energy promised long-term returns.	再生可能エネルギーへの**投資**は、長期的なリターンを約束した。
1581	**discretionary investment contract**	投資一任契約
	The <u>discretionary investment contract</u> provided customized portfolio management.	**投資一任契約**は、カスタマイズされたポートフォリオ管理を提供した。
1582	**investment management business**	投資運用業
	The <u>investment management business</u> expanded its client base.	**投資運用業**は、顧客基盤を拡大した。
1583	**investment equities**	投資口
	The price of <u>investment equities</u> were deided for growth potential.	**投資口**の価格は、成長の可能性を考慮して決定された。
1584	**investment advisory contract**	投資顧問契約
	The <u>investment advisory contract</u> outlined the consultant's responsibilities.	**投資顧問契約**には、コンサルタントの責任が概説されていた。
1585	**investment business limited partnership**	投資事業有限責任組合
	The <u>investment business limited partnership</u> explored new markets.	**投資事業有限責任組合**は、新市場を開拓した。
1586	**investor** [ìnvéstər]	投資者
	The <u>investor</u> reviewed the portfolio's quarterly performance.	**投資者**は、ポートフォリオの四半期ごとの運用実績を確認した。
1587	**public law related action**	当事者訴訟
	The <u>public law related action</u> challenged the regulation.	**当事者訴訟**は、この規制に異議を唱えた。
1588	**standing** [stǽndɪŋ]	当事者適格
	<u>Standing</u> (to sue) was granted based on affected interests.	影響を受ける利益に基づき、**当事者適格**が認められた。
1589	**capacity to be a party**	当事者能力
	The <u>capacity to be a party</u> was confirmed for the corporation.	法人について、**当事者能力**が確認された。
1590	**investment advisory business**	投資助言業務
	The <u>investment advisory business</u> offers strategic market insights.	**投資助言業務**は、戦略的な市場洞察を提供する。

RANK 3

1591	**investment trust**	投資信託
	The investment trust diversified into international equities.	投資信託は、国際株式に分散投資した。
1592	**investment corporation**	投資法人
	The investment corporation announced a merger with a competitor.	投資法人が、競合他社との合併を発表した。
1593	**family company**	同族会社
	The family company celebrated fifty years in business.	同族会社は、創業50周年を迎えた。
1594	**attainment** [ətéɪnmənt]	到達
	The attainment of the sales target triggered bonuses.	売上目標に到達すると、ボーナスが支給される。
1595	**misappropriation** [mìsəpròʊpriéɪʃən]	盗用
	Misappropriation of funds led to an internal audit.	資金の盗用が、内部監査につながった。
1596	**whenever** [wenévər]	とき（末尾㉕参照）
	The policy applies whenever the need arises.	この指針は、必要性が生じたときに、いつでも適用される。
1597	**monopolistic situation**	独占的状態
	The monopolistic situation prompted regulatory scrutiny.	独占的状態は、規制当局の監視を促した。
1598	**acquisition or loss (of rights)**	得喪
	The acquisition or loss of rights is governed by the Civil Code.	権利の得喪は、民法によって規定されている。
1599	**silent partnership**	匿名組合
	The silent partnership agreement detailed profit sharing without direct involvement.	匿名組合では、直接的な関与を伴わない利益分配が詳細に定められていた。
1600	**silent partner**	匿名組合員
	The silent partner contributed capital while remaining uninvolved in management.	匿名組合員は、経営に関与しないまま資本を提供した。
1601	**impartiality** [ìmpɑːrʃiǽlɪti]	独立性（第三者性）
	Impartiality is crucial for the fairness of judicial proceedings.	独立性（第三者性）は、司法手続の公正性にとって重要である。

RANK 3

1602	**trial for patent invalidation**	特許無効審判
	The <u>trial for patent invalidation</u> contested the patent's originality.	**特許無効審判**では、特許の独創性が争われた。
1603	**action for revocation of administrative disposition**	取消訴訟
	The <u>action for revocation of administrative disposition</u> challenged the decision.	**取消訴訟**は、決定を争うものであった。
1604	**right of segregation**	取戻権
	The <u>right of segregation</u> allows creditors to separate their assets.	**取戻権**により、債権者は資産を分離することができる。
1605	**broker** [bróʊkər]	仲立人
	The <u>broker</u> facilitated the sale, earning a commission.	**仲立人**は、売却を仲介し、手数料を得た。
1606	**secondary use**	二次使用
	<u>Secondary use</u> of copyrighted material requires authorization.	著作物の**二次使用**には、許可が必要である。
1607	**certify** [sə́ːrtəfàɪ]	認定する
	The university will <u>certify</u> the completion of your studies.	大学が、修了を**認定する**。
1608	**taxpayer** [tǽkspèɪər]	納税義務者
	The <u>taxpayer</u> complied with all filing requirements on time.	**納税義務者**は、すべての提出要件を期限内に遵守した。
1609	**disposal** [dɪspóʊzəl]	廃棄
	The <u>disposal</u> of hazardous waste followed environmental regulations.	有害廃棄物の**廃棄**は、環境規制に従った。
1610	**abolish** [əbɑ́ːlɪʃ]	（制度を）廃止する
	The outdated law was <u>abolished</u> by the new legislation.	この時代遅れの法律は、新しい法律によって**廃止された**。
1611	**close** [klóʊs]	（事業や営業所を）廃止する
	The company decided to <u>close</u> its underperforming retail stores.	同社は、不採算小売店舗の**廃止**を決定した。

RANK 3

#	英語	日本語
1612	**repeal** [rɪpíːl] The controversial law was <u>repealed</u> after widespread protest.	（規定などを）廃止する 物議を醸したこの法律は、広範な抗議の後、**廃止された**。
1613	**opposition to distribution** An obligee who has filed an <u>opposition to distribution</u> must file an action of opposition to distribution.	配当異議 **配当異議**の申出をした債権者は、配当異議の訴えを提起しなければならない。
1614	**reversal** [rɪvə́ːrsəl] The appellate court's <u>reversal</u> changed the outcome of the case.	破棄 控訴裁判所の**破棄**判決によって、この事件の結果は一変した。
1615	**bankruptcy trustee** The <u>bankruptcy trustee</u> managed the liquidation of assets.	破産管財人 **破産管財人**は、資産の清算を管理した。
1616	**bankruptcy creditor** The <u>bankruptcy creditor</u> filed a claim for outstanding debts.	破産債権者 **破産債権者**は、未払い債務の請求を行った。
1617	**bankrupt** [bǽŋkrəpt] The company was declared <u>bankrupt</u> after failing to pay debts.	①破産者、②破産 同社は債務返済に失敗し、**破産**宣告を受けた。
1618	**bankruptcy proceedings** <u>Bankruptcy proceedings</u> began to settle the company's financial obligations.	破産手続 会社の債務を清算するために、**破産手続**が始まった。
1619	**applicable penal statute** Several counts and <u>applicable penal statutes</u> may be entered in a conjunctive or alternative way.	罰条 数個の訴因及び**罰条**は、予備的に又は択一的にこれを記載することができる。
1620	**penal provision** The <u>penal provision</u> imposed a fine for the offense.	罰則 **罰則**は、違反に対して罰金を課すというものであった。
1621	**non-permanent resident** The <u>non-permanent resident</u> applied for an extension of stay.	非永住者 **非永住者**が、在留延長を申請した。
1622	**aggrieved party** The <u>aggrieved party</u> sought compensation for damages.	被害者（末尾❾参照） **被害者**は、損害賠償を求めた。

RANK 3

#	Word	Japanese
1623	**nontaxable** [nɑntǽksəbəl] The donation was confirmed as <u>nontaxable</u> by the tax office.	非課税 この寄付は税務署によって、**非課税**であることが確認された。
1624	**acceptor** [əkséptər] The <u>acceptor</u> of the bill of exchange guaranteed payment.	引受人（末尾㉗参照） 為替手形の**引受人**は、支払いを保証した。
1625	**ward** [wɔ́ːrd] The court appointed a guardian to protect the <u>ward</u>'s interests.	被後見人 裁判所は、**被後見人**の利益を守るために後見人を任命した。
1626	**appellee** [æ̀pəlíː] The <u>appellee</u> defended the trial court's decision on appeal.	被控訴人 **被控訴人**は、控訴審で原審の判決を擁護した。
1627	**ratification** [rætəfəkéɪʃən] <u>Ratification</u> is retroactive to the time of the conclusion of the contract.	①批准、②追認（民法） **追認**は、契約の時にさかのぼってその効力を生ずる。
1628	**decedent** [desídənt] The <u>decedent</u>'s estate was distributed among the heirs.	被相続人 **被相続人**の遺産は、相続人の間で分配された。
1629	**secured claim** The <u>secured claim</u> was prioritized in bankruptcy proceedings.	被担保債権 **被担保債権**は、破産手続において優先された。
1630	**insured** [ɪnʃʊ́rd] The <u>insured</u> filed a claim after the car accident.	被保険者 **被保険者**は、交通事故後に保険金を請求した。
1631	**person under curatorship** The <u>person under curatorship</u> was protected by legal guardians.	被保佐人 **被保佐人**は、保佐人によって保護されていた。
1632	**person under assistance** The <u>person under assistance</u> received support.	被補助人 **被補助人**は、支援を受けていた。
1633	**apparent manager** The <u>apparent manager</u> acted on behalf of the company.	表見支配人 **表見支配人**が、会社を代表して行動した。

1634	**apparent representative executive officer**	表見代表執行役
	The <u>apparent representative executive officer</u> signed the agreement.	<u>表見代表執行役</u>が、契約書に署名した。
1635	**apparent authority**	表見代理
	<u>Apparent authority</u> led third parties to believe in the representative's power.	<u>表見代理</u>によって、第三者は代表の権限を信じるようになった。
1636	**label (labeling)** [léɪbl]	表示
	<u>Labeling</u> requirements ensured product information transparency.	<u>表示</u>要件により、製品情報の透明性が確保された。
1637	**mark** [mάːrk]	表示
	The <u>mark</u> protects the brand.	この<u>表示</u>はブランドを保護する。
1638	**rumor** [rúːmər]	風説
	<u>Rumor</u> about the merger affected the stock price.	合併の<u>風説</u>は、株価に影響した。
1639	**indivisible claim**	不可分債権
	If an <u>indivisible claim</u> becomes a divisible claim, each obligee may request the performance only of the share of the claim to which each obligee is entitled, and if an <u>indivisible obligation</u> becomes a divisible obligation, each obligor is liable only for the share of the obligation for which each obligor is liable.	<u>不可分債権</u>が可分債権となったときは、各債権者は自己が権利を有する部分についてのみ履行を請求することができ、<u>不可分債務</u>が可分債務となったときは、各債務者はその負担部分についてのみ履行の責任を負う。
1640	**indivisible obligation**	不可分債務
	（1639の例文参照）	（1639の例文参照）
1641	**supplemental registration**	付記登記
	A registration of change or registration of correction of a right may be made by the <u>supplemental registrations</u>.	権利の変更の登記又は更正の登記は、<u>付記登記</u>によってすることができる。
1642	**reinstatement** [rìːɪnstéɪtmənt]	復職
	<u>Reinstatement</u> to the previous position was requested after wrongful termination.	不当解雇後、前職への<u>復職</u>を求められた。

RANK 3

1643	**reproduction** [rìprədʌ́kʃən]	**複製**
	Reproduction of the artwork without permission infringed copyright.	作品の無断**複製**は、著作権を侵害する。
1644	**unfair trade practice**	**不公正な取引方法**
	The **unfair trade practice** was investigated by the authorities.	**不公正な取引方法**は、当局によって調査された。
1645	**false statement**	**不実記載**
	The **false statement** misled investors about company profits.	**不実記載**は、会社の利益について投資家に誤解を与えた。
1646	**unfair competition**	**不正競争**
	Unfair competition laws protect businesses and consumers.	**不正競争**に関する法規制は、企業と消費者を保護する。
1647	**unauthorized use**	**不正使用**
	Unauthorized use of the trademark was contested in court.	商標の**不正使用**は、裁判で争われた。
1648	**real right**	**物権**
	No **real right** may be established other than those prescribed by laws including this Code.	**物権**は、この法律その他の法律に定めるもののほか、創設することができない。
1649	**extension of a security interest to the proceeds of the collateral**	**物上代位**
	As an **extension of a security interest to the proceeds of the collateral**, a statutory lien may also be exercised against things including monies that the obligor is to receive as a result of the sale the subject matter of the statutory lien.	**物上代位**として、先取特権は、その目的物の売却によって債務者が受けるべき金銭その他の物に対しても、行使することができる。
1650	**misleading representation**	**不当表示**
	Misleading representation can lead to administrative investigation.	**不当表示**は、行政調査を招きうる。
1651	**unjust enrichment**	**不当利得**
	Unjust enrichment occurred.	**不当利得**が発生した。
1652	**unspecified and large number of persons**	**不特定多数の者**
	The lawsuit involved an **unspecified and large number of persons**.	この訴訟は、**不特定多数の者**を巻き込んだものだった。

1653	**installment (amount)** [instɔ́:lmənt]	賦払金	
	The <u>installment amount</u> was agreed upon at the contract signing.	賦払金は、契約締結時に合意された。	
1654	**book-entry**	振替	
	<u>Book-entry</u> securities simplify the transfer of ownership in that jurisdiction.	振替証券は、その法域において、所有権の移転を簡素化する。	
1655	**divisible claim**	分割債権	
	A <u>divisible claim</u> can be enforced in parts.	分割債権は、分割して行使することができる。	
1656	**bar association**	弁護士会	
	The <u>bar association</u> regulates the practice of law.	弁護士会は、弁護士業務を規制している。	
1657	**compilation** [kɑ̀:mpəléɪʃən]	編集物	
	The <u>compilation</u> of laws was updated annually.	編集物は、毎年更新されている。	RANK 3
1658	**arson** [ɑ́:rsən]	放火	
	<u>Arson</u> is a serious criminal offense involving property damage.	放火は、器物の損害を伴う重大な犯罪である。	
1659	**(criminal) assault** [əsɔ́lt]	暴行	
	<u>(Criminal) assault</u> may involve intentionally harming another person.	暴行は、故意に他人を傷つけることを含むこともある。	
1660	**accessoryship**	幇助	
	<u>Accessoryship</u> entails aiding in the commission of a crime.	幇助とは、犯罪の遂行を手助けすることである。	
1661	**statutory agent**	法定代理人	
	The <u>statutory agent</u> acts on behalf of the child.	法定代理人は、その子どもを代理して行動する。	
1662	**organized crime group**	暴力団	
	<u>Organized crime groups</u> are subject to strict legal scrutiny.	暴力団は、厳格な法的監視の対象となる。	
1663	**member of an organized crime group**	暴力団員	
	A <u>member of an organized crime group</u> faces enhanced penalties.	暴力団員は、罰則の強化に直面した。	

1664	**retain** [rɪtéɪn]	①保管する、②保存する
	When a partition is completed, each of the persons that participated in the partition must <u>retain</u> the instruments regarding things each of them acquired.	分割が完了したときは、各分割者は、その取得した物に関する証書を<u>保存</u>しなければならない。
1665	**insurance business**	保険業
	The <u>insurance business</u> is heavily regulated.	<u>保険業</u>は、厳しく規制されている。
1666	**insurance proceeds**	保険金
	<u>Insurance proceeds</u> are paid out upon a claim's approval.	<u>保険金</u>は、請求が承認された時点で支払われる。
1667	**insurance policy**	保険契約
	The <u>insurance policy</u> outlines coverage terms.	<u>保険契約</u>には、補償条件の概要が記載されている。
1668	**policyholder** [pá:ləsihòʊldər]	保険契約者
	The <u>policyholder</u> is the individual insured under the policy.	<u>保険契約者</u>とは、保険の被保険者個人である。
1669	**insurer** [ìnʃʊ́rər]	保険者
	The <u>insurer</u> provides coverage according to the policy terms.	<u>保険者</u>は、保険約款に従って補償を提供する。
1670	**insurance sales**	保険募集
	<u>Insurance sales</u> must comply with regulatory standards.	<u>保険募集</u>は、規制基準に従わなければならない。
1671	**insurance agent**	保険募集人
	An <u>insurance agent</u> facilitates the purchase of policies.	<u>保険募集人</u>は、保険契約の購入を促進する。
1672	**insurance premium**	保険料
	<u>Insurance premiums</u> are paid to maintain coverage.	<u>保険料</u>は、補償を維持するために支払う。
1673	**assistant in court**	補佐人
	An <u>assistant in court</u> supports legal proceedings.	<u>補佐人</u>は、法的手続をサポートする。
1674	**offering** [ɔ́:fərɪŋ]	募集
	<u>Offering</u> a new financial instrument involves comprehensive market analysis.	新しい金融商品を<u>募集</u>するには、包括的な市場分析が必要である。

RANK 3

1675	**substituted service** <u>Substituted service</u> ensures legal notice when direct service fails.	**補充送達** <u>補充送達</u>は、直接送達ができなかった場合に法的通知を確実にする。
1676	**objection to provisional remedy** <u>Objection to provisional remedy</u> challenges its necessity.	**保全異議** <u>保全異議</u>は、保全の必要性を問うものである。
1677	**appeal pertaining to provisional remedy** <u>Appeal pertaining to provisional remedy</u> seeks judicial review.	**保全抗告** <u>保全抗告</u>は、司法審査を求める。
1678	**execution of provisional remedy** <u>Execution of provisional remedy</u> was enforced.	**保全執行** <u>保全執行</u>が行われた。
1679	**provisional order** A <u>provisional order</u> aims to maintain the status quo during litigation.	**保全処分** <u>保全処分</u>は、訴訟中の現状維持を目的とする。
1680	**revocation of provisional remedy** It is not required for the obligor's consent to be obtained in order to withdraw a petition for an order for a provisional remedy, even after an objection to the provisional remedy or a petition for <u>revocation of provisional remedy</u> is filed.	**保全取消し** 保全命令の申立てを取り下げるには、保全異議又は<u>保全取消し</u>の申立てがあった後においても、債務者の同意を得ることを要しない。
1681	**order for provisional remedy** An <u>order for a provisional remedy</u> is issued by a court upon petition.	**保全命令** <u>保全命令</u>は、申立てにより、裁判所が行う。
1682	**non-penal confiscation** If the court rescinds bail, it may order the <u>non-penal confiscation</u> of the bail bond.	**没取** 保釈を取り消す場合には、裁判所は、保証金の<u>没取</u>を命じることができる。
1683	**maturity** [mət͡ʃúrəti] <u>Maturity</u> signifies the due date for payment.	**満期** <u>満期</u>とは、支払いの期日を意味する。
1684	**pre-sentencing detention** The days spent in <u>pre-sentencing detention</u> may be included in whole or in part into the sentence imposed.	**未決勾留** <u>未決勾留</u>の日数は、その全部又は一部を本刑に算入することができる。
1685	**without (good) reason/cause** Entering <u>without (good) reason/cause</u> may result in liability.	**みだりに** <u>みだりに</u>侵入すると、責任を問われる可能性がある。

RANK 3

1686	**deemed daily wage amount** <u>Deemed daily wage amount</u> is used for compensation calculations.	みなし賃金日額 みなし賃金日額は、報酬計算に使用される。
1687	**life imprisonment without work** <u>Life imprisonment without work</u> is a severe penalty.	無期禁錮 無期禁錮は、厳しい刑罰である。
1688	**debt instrument payable to bearer** A <u>debt instrument payable to bearer</u> may include gift certificates and train tickets.	無記名債権 無記名債権には、ギフトカードや乗車券が含まれうる。
1689	**unauthorized agency** <u>Unauthorized agency</u> involves acting without authority.	無権代理 無権代理とは、権限を持たずに行動することを指す。
1690	**allotment without contribution** <u>Allotment without contribution</u> is a form of company's incentive plan.	無償割当て 無償割当ては、会社のインセンティブプランの一形態である。
1691	**entry of a name change** <u>Entry of a name change</u> was requested.	名義書換 名義書換が、請求された。
1692	**dismissal by a bar to prosecution** <u>Dismissal by a bar to prosecution</u> ends criminal proceedings.	免訴 免訴は、刑事手続を終了させる。
1693	**subject matter** The <u>subject matter</u> was identified in the contract.	目的物 目的物は、契約者において特定された。
1694	**prospectus** [prəspéktəs] The <u>prospectus</u> provides detailed investment information.	目論見書 目論見書には、詳細な投資情報が記載されている。
1695	**document of title** A <u>document of title</u> represents rights.	有価証券 有価証券は、権利を表象する。
1696	**securities registration statement** <u>Securities registration statement</u> is filed with regulatory bodies.	有価証券届出書 有価証券届出書が、規制当局に提出された。
1697	**annual securities report** The <u>annual securities report</u> discloses a company's financial status.	有価証券報告書 有価証券報告書は、企業の財務状況を開示するものである。

1698	**with/for definite term**	有期
	The contract was signed <u>with definite term</u> of five years.	契約期間は、**有期**の5年間である。
1699	**limited liability partner**	有限責任組合員
	The <u>limited liability partner</u> contributed capital without managing the business.	その**有限責任組合員**は、事業を管理することなく資本を拠出した。
1700	**limited liability business partnership**	有限責任事業組合
	The <u>limited liability business partnership</u> protects members from excessive losses.	**有限責任事業組合**は、組合員を過大な損失から守る。
1701	**member with limited liability**	有限責任社員
	A <u>member with limited liability</u> cannot lose more than their investment.	**有限責任社員**は、投資額以上の損失を被ることはない。
1702	**contract for value**	有償契約
	The <u>contract for value</u> stipulates mutual obligations of exchange.	**有償契約**は、相互の義務を定めている。
1703	**act for value**	有償行為
	Every <u>act for value</u> requires consideration to be legally binding.	あらゆる**有償行為**は、法的拘束力を持つために対価を必要とする。
1704	**onerous act**	有償行為
	An <u>onerous act</u> involves obligations or burdens.	**有償行為**には、義務又は負担が伴う。
1705	**adopted child**	養子
	The <u>adopted child</u> was legally recognized as a family member.	**養子**は、法的に家族として認められた。
1706	**digest** [dáɪdʒést]	要旨
	The <u>digest</u> summarized important case laws.	**要旨**には、重要な判例がまとめられていた。
1707	**adoption** [ədɑ́ːpʃən]	養子縁組
	<u>Adoption</u> procedures were finalized in family court.	**養子縁組**の手続は、家庭裁判所で行われた。
1708	**foreseeability** [fɔːsìːəbíləti]	予見可能性
	<u>Foreseeability</u> is critical in assessing negligence.	**予見可能性**は、過失を評価する上で重要である。
1709	**coupon** [kúːpɔ̀ːn]	利札
	<u>Coupons</u> may be attached to bond certificates.	社債券には、**利札**を付けることができる。

RANK 3

#	Term	Japanese
1710	**summary proceedings** Summary proceedings expedite minor legal disputes.	略式手続 略式手続は、軽微な法的紛争を迅速化する。
1711	**summary order** The summary order quickly resolved the case.	略式命令 略式命令により、本件はすぐに解決した。
1712	**right of retention** The right of retention allows creditors to hold property as security.	留置権 留置権により、債権者は財産を担保として保持することができる。
1713	**obtain** [əbtéɪn] A person who accepts free of charge stolen property or any other property obtained through an act equivalent to an offense against property is punished by imprisonment for not more than 3 years.	領得する 盗品その他財産に対する罪に当たる行為によって領得された物を無償で譲り受けた者は、3年以下の懲役に処する。
1714	**cumulative voting** Cumulative voting rights strengthen minority shareholder influence.	累積投票 累積投票は、少数株主の影響力を強化する。
1715	**spread** [spréd] It is prohibited for any person to spread rumors for the purpose of causing a fluctuation in the market price.	流布 何人も、相場の変動を図る目的をもって、風説を流布してはならない。
1716	**consolidated financial statements** Consolidated financial statements show the entire corporate group's financial health.	連結計算書類 連結計算書類は、企業グループ全体の財務の健全性を示している。
1717	**consolidated subsidiary company** The consolidated subsidiary company was fully integrated into financial reporting.	連結子会社 連結子会社は、財務報告において、完全に統合された。
1718	**joint and several obligation** Joint and several obligation makes co-debtors liable for the full debt.	連帯債務 連帯債務とは、連帯債務者が債務全額について責任を負うことである。
1719	**joint and several obligor** A joint and several obligor may be pursued for the entire debt.	連帯債務者 連帯債務者は、債務全額を追及される可能性がある。
1720	**joint and several suretyship** Joint and several suretyship involves co-signers guaranteeing the debt.	連帯保証 連帯保証は、連帯保証人が債務を保証するものである。

RANK 3

1721	**collective agreement**	労働協約
	The <u>collective agreement</u> outlined negotiated working conditions.	**労働協約**では、労働条件について取り決められた。
1722	**working conditions**	労働条件
	<u>Working conditions</u> were improved following union negotiations.	労働組合との交渉により、**労働条件**が改善された。
1723	**labor tribunal decision**	労働審判
	The <u>labor tribunal decision</u> ended the workplace dispute.	**労働審判**の決定は、職場紛争に終止符を打った。
1724	**labor dispute**	労働争議
	The <u>labor dispute</u> was mediated to prevent strikes.	**労働争議**は、ストライキを防ぐために調停された。
1725	**obscenity** [əbsénɪti]	わいせつ
	Material deemed as <u>obscenity</u> was removed from publication.	**わいせつ**と判断されたものは、出版から削除された。

RANK 3

法律英単語® I 2100
RANK4

#	Entry	Japanese
1726	**family employees of a blue return taxpayer** Family employees of a blue return taxpayer enjoy certain tax benefits.	**青色事業専従者** **青色事業専従者**は、一定の税制上の優遇措置を受けることができる。
1727	**blue return** Blue return filers adhere to stringent accounting standards.	**青色申告** **青色申告**者は、厳格な会計基準を遵守している。
1728	**arrangement (arrange)** [əréɪndʒmənt] A person who arranges disposal for compensation a stolen property is punished by imprisonment for not more than 10 years and a fine of not more than 500,000 yen.	**あっせん（盗品のあっせん）** 盗品の有償の処分の**あっせん**をした者は、10年以下の懲役及び50万円以下の罰金に処する。
1729	**influence** [ínfluəns] A public employee who accepts a bribe as consideration for the influence which the employee exerted, in response to a request, upon another public employee so as to cause the other to act illegally is punished by imprisonment for not more than 5 years.	**あっせん（収賄）** 公務員が請託を受け、他の公務員に職務上不正な行為をさせるように**あっせん**をすることの報酬として、賄賂を収受したときは、5年以下の懲役に処する。
1730	**mediator** [mídièɪtər] The Labour Relations Commission must each appoint candidates for mediators and prepare a list thereof.	**斡旋員** 労働委員会は、**斡旋員**候補者を委嘱し、その名簿を作製して置かなければならない。
1731	**allocate** [ǽləkèɪt] A time payment is allocated to cover the late charges sequentially in chronological order.	**（資金・日数を）充当する** 遅延損害金については、発生が早いものから順次に**充当する**。
1732	**national security** National security concerns influenced the policy change.	**安全保障** **安全保障**上の懸念が、政策変更に影響を与えた。
1733	**abandonment (abandon)** [əbǽndənmənt] A person who abandons another person with illness in need of support is punished by imprisonment for not more than 1 year.	**遺棄（する）** 疾病のために扶助を必要とする者を**遺棄**した者は、1年以下の懲役に処する。
1734	**disputing party** If making an assessment decision, the court must interrogate the disputing parties.	**異議者** 裁判所は、査定の裁判をする場合には、**異議者**を審尋しなければならない。

RANK 4

#	Term	Japanese
1735	**creditor who has an objection**	**異議のある債権者**
	The <u>creditor who had an objection</u> did not state an objection within the period.	**異議のある債権者**は、期間内に異議を述べなかった。
1736	**person filing an objection**	**（書面による）異議申立人**
	Any grounds not pleaded by a <u>person filing an opposition</u> may be examined in proceedings on an opposition to a granted patent.	特許異議の申立てについての審理においては、特許**異議申立人**が申し立てない理由についても、審理することができる。
1737	**person raising an objection**	**（口頭による）異議申立人**
	The <u>person raising an objection</u> expressed dissatisfaction with the decision.	**異議申立人**は、決定に不満を示した。
1738	**childcare leave**	**育児休業**
	<u>Childcare leave</u> policies supported working parents.	**育児休業**の政策は、働く親を支援した。
1739	**lost property**	**遺失物**
	<u>Lost property</u> was returned to its rightful owner.	**遺失物**は、本来の持ち主に戻された。
1740	**mental capacity**	**意思能力**
	<u>Mental capacity</u> is essential for entering into contracts.	契約締結には、**意思能力**が不可欠である。
1741	**solatium** [souléiʃiəm]	**慰謝料**
	The <u>solatium</u> was awarded for emotional distress.	精神的苦痛に対する**慰謝料**が支払われた。
1742	**design** [dɪzáin]	**意匠**
	The new <u>design</u> revolutionized product appeal.	この新しい**意匠**は、製品の魅力を一変させた。
1743	**design right**	**意匠権**
	The inventor registered a <u>design right</u> for the new product's unique appearance.	発明者は、新製品のユニークな外観について**意匠権**を登録した。
1744	**holder of a design right**	**意匠権者**
	The <u>holder of a design right</u> intended to protect their innovation.	**意匠権者**は、彼らのイノベーションを保護しようと企図した。
1745	**creator of a design**	**意匠の創作をした者**
	A <u>creator of a design</u> that is industrially applicable may have a design registration made for the design.	工業上利用することができる**意匠の創作をした者**は、その意匠について意匠登録を受けることができる。

RANK 4

1746	**bequest** [bɪkwést]	遺贈
	The <u>bequest</u> included a significant charitable donation.	<u>遺贈</u>には、多額の慈善寄付が含まれていた。
1747	**legacy** [légəsi]	遺贈
	The <u>legacy</u> left to the museum enriched its collection.	美術館への<u>遺贈</u>は、美術館のコレクションを豊かにした。
1748	**decision of transfer**	移送の裁判
	The <u>decision of transfer</u> was approved by the judge.	<u>移送の裁判</u>は、裁判官によって認められた。
1749	**surviving family (member)**	遺族
	<u>Surviving family members</u> are entitled to the estate.	<u>遺族</u>は、遺産を受け取る権利がある。
1750	**occasional income**	一時所得
	<u>Occasional income</u> must be reported during tax season.	<u>一時所得</u>は、確定申告の時期に申告しなければならない。
1751	**extreme** [ekstrím]	著しい
	No co-owner may make changes (excluding those that do not involve <u>extreme</u> changes to the shape) to the property in co-ownership.	各共有者は共有物に変更（形状の<u>著しい</u>変更を伴わないものを除く）を加えることができない。
1752	**partial amendment**	一部改正
	The law underwent a <u>partial amendment</u> this year.	この法律は、今年<u>一部改正</u>された。
1753	**disposal by a sale en bloc**	一括売却 （例：破産法第78条第2項第4号）
	The <u>disposal by a sale en bloc</u> was completed efficiently.	<u>一括売却</u>による処分は、効率的に完了した。
1754	**general incorporated foundation**	一般財団法人
	The <u>general incorporated foundation</u> supports various charitable activities.	<u>一般財団法人</u>は、さまざまな慈善活動を支援している。
1755	**general priority claim**	一般の優先権がある債権 （例：民事再生法第122条第1項）
	A claim for which a general statutory lien or any other <u>general priority claim</u> is a claim with general priority.	一般の先取特権その他<u>一般の優先権がある債権</u>は、一般優先債権とする。

1756	**general period for payment**	**一般弁済期間** （例：民事再生法第199条）
	If a rehabilitation plan is unlikely to be confirmed, it may be provided for that during a certain period within the <u>general period for payment</u>, payment is required only for part of principal of a home loan claim during the grace period to pay the principal.	再生計画の認可の見込みがない場合には、**一般弁済期間**の範囲内で定める期間中は、住宅資金貸付債権の元本の一部のみを支払うものとすることができる。
1757	**pharmaceutical** [fɑ̀ːrməsúːtɪkəl]	**医薬品**
	<u>Pharmaceutical</u> advancements have improved quality of life.	**医薬品**の進歩は、生活の質を向上させた。
1758	**quasi-pharmaceutical products**	**医薬部外品**
	<u>Quasi-pharmaceutical products</u> are regulated for consumer safety.	**医薬部外品**は、消費者の安全のために規制されている。
1759	**right of common**	**入会権**
	The <u>right of common</u> allows access to shared resources.	**入会権**は、共有する資源へのアクセスを可能にする。
1760	**article left behind**	**遺留した物**
	The <u>article left behind</u> was stored in the lost and found.	**遺留した物**は、遺失物係に保管された。
1761	**affinity** [əfínəti]	**姻族**
	Relationships of <u>affinity</u> are terminated by divorce.	**姻族**関係は、離婚によって終了する。
1762	**relatives by marriage**	**姻族**
	<u>Relatives by marriage</u> are considered part of the extended family.	**姻族**は、拡大した家族の一員とみなされる。
1763	**spoliation** [spòuliéiʃən]	**隠滅**
	<u>Spoliation</u> of evidence can result in legal penalties.	証拠**隠滅**は、法的処罰の対象となる。
1764	**incoming sentenced person**	**受入受刑者**
	The <u>incoming sentenced person</u> was processed at the facility.	**受入受刑者**は、施設で対応をうけた。
1765	**receipt** [rɪsíːt]	**受取証書**
	The <u>receipt</u> must be presented for returns and exchanges.	返品及び交換には、**受取証書**の提示が必要である。

RANK 4

1766	**endorsement** [endɔ́:rsmənt]	裏書
	The <u>endorsement</u> on the back of the check authorizes transfer.	小切手裏面への**裏書**は、譲渡を許可するものである。
1767	**endorser** [ɪndɔ́:rsər]	裏書人
	The <u>endorser</u> guarantees payment to the check's holder.	**裏書人**は、小切手の所持人に対する支払いを保証する。
1768	**uninterrupted series of endorsements**	裏書の連続
	The <u>uninterrupted series of endorsements</u> traced the check's history.	**裏書の連続**は、手形の履歴をたどっている。
1769	**forwarding agency**	運送取扱営業
	The <u>forwarding agency</u> arranged transport for the export goods.	**運送取扱営業者**が、輸出貨物の輸送を手配した。
1770	**freight** [fréɪt]	運送品
	<u>Freight</u> charges were calculated based on weight and distance.	**運送品**の料金は、重量及び距離に基づいて計算された。
1771	**cargo insurance**	運送保険
	<u>Cargo insurance</u> provides coverage against loss or damage.	**運送保険**は、紛失又は損害に対する補償を提供するものである。
1772	**maker of cinematographic works**	映画製作者
	The <u>maker of cinematographic works</u> holds copyright.	**映画製作者**が、著作権を有する。
1773	**cinematographic work(s)**	映画の著作物
	<u>Cinematographic works</u> are protected under intellectual property law.	**映画の著作物**は、知的財産法で保護されている。
1774	**health committee**	衛生委員会
	An employer must establish a <u>health committee</u>.	事業者は、**衛生委員会**を設けなければならない。
1775	**general safety and health supervisor**	統括安全衛生責任者
	The position of <u>general safety and health supervisor</u> must be filled by the person in charge of overall management for implementing the undertaking at the relevant site.	**統括安全衛生責任者**は、当該場所においてその事業の実施を統括管理する者をもって充てなければならない。

RANK 4

1776	epidemiological survey	疫学的調査
	The <u>epidemiological survey</u> helped trace the outbreak's source.	<u>疫学的調査</u>によって、発生源を突き止めることができた。
1777	adoption [ədáːpʃən]	縁組
	<u>Adoption</u> processes prioritize the child's best interests.	養子<u>縁組</u>の手続は、子どもの最善の利益を優先する。
1778	fire spread	延焼
	<u>Fire spread</u> rapidly due to dry conditions.	火災は、乾燥状態のため急速に<u>延焼</u>した。
1779	tax on delinquency	延滞税
	<u>Tax on delinquency</u> is imposed for late payments.	支払いが遅れると、<u>延滞税</u>が課される。
1780	contamination [kəntæmənéɪʃən]	（放射能、毒物等による）汚染
	<u>Contamination</u> of the water supply prompted a boil order.	水道の<u>汚染</u>により、煮沸消毒命令が出された。
1781	pollution [pəlúːʃən]	汚染
	<u>Pollution</u> reduction targets were set by the new policy.	新政策によって、<u>汚染</u>削減目標が設定された。
1782	musical work(s)	音楽の著作物
	<u>Musical works</u> does not require copyright registration for protection.	<u>音楽の著作物</u>の保護には著作権登録が必要ではない。
1783	pardon [páːrdən]	恩赦
	A <u>pardon</u> was granted to the reformed inmate.	改心した受刑者には、<u>恩赦</u>が与えられた。
1784	a foreign currency denominated bond	外貨建債券
	<u>A foreign currency denominated bond</u> attracts international investors.	<u>外貨建債券</u>は、海外の投資家を惹きつける。
1785	instigation of foreign aggression	外患誘致
	The <u>instigation of foreign aggression</u> was condemned.	<u>外患誘致</u>は、非難された。
1786	nursing care	介護
	<u>Nursing care</u> facilities are regulated to ensure quality service.	<u>介護</u>施設は、サービスの質を保証するために規制されている。

RANK 4

1787	**foreign tax credit**	外国税額控除
	The <u>foreign tax credit</u> prevents double taxation.	<u>外国税額控除</u>は、二重課税を防止する。
1788	**foreign lawyer**	外国弁護士
	<u>Foreign lawyers</u> can practice in certain jurisdictions.	<u>外国弁護士</u>は、特定の法域で業務を行うことができる。
1789	**foreign law joint enterprise**	外国法共同事業
	A <u>foreign law joint enterprise</u> facilitates cross-border legal services.	<u>外国法共同事業</u>は、国境を越えた法律サービスを促進する。
1790	**registered foreign lawyer**	外国法事務弁護士
	<u>Registered foreign lawyers</u> provide expertise in international law.	<u>外国法事務弁護士</u>は、国際法に関する専門知識を提供する。
1791	**office of registered foreign lawyer**	外国法事務弁護士事務所
	The <u>office of registered foreign lawyer</u> serves international clients.	<u>外国法事務弁護士事務所</u>は、国際的なクライアントにサービスを提供している。
1792	**certified care worker**	介護福祉士
	<u>Certified care workers</u> are trained in providing elderly care.	<u>介護福祉士</u>は、高齢者介護を提供するための訓練を受けている。
1793	**nursing care insurance**	介護保険
	<u>Nursing care insurance</u> supports the costs of long-term care.	<u>介護保険</u>は、介護費用をサポートする。
1794	**post-commencement claim**	開始後債権
	A claim on assets arising from a cause that has occurred after the commencement of rehabilitation proceedings is classed as <u>post-commencement claim</u>.	再生手続開始後の原因に基づいて生じた財産上の請求権は、<u>開始後債権</u>とする。
1795	**petition to commence**	開始の申立て
	The <u>petition to commence</u> bankruptcy was filed by the creditor.	破産<u>開始の申立て</u>は、債権者が行った。
1796	**marine accident**	海難
	The mission of the Japan <u>Marine Accident</u> Tribunal is conduct an inquiry to take disciplinary action against a marine technician.	<u>海難</u>審判所は、海技士に対する懲戒を行うための海難の審判を行うことを任務とする。
1797	**developing area**	開発途上地域
	<u>Developing areas</u> benefit from targeted investment and aid.	<u>発展途上地域</u>は、的を絞った投資や援助から利益を得ている。

RANK 4

1798	**recuse oneself** Judges must <u>recuse themselves</u> from cases involving conflicts of interest.	**（裁判官を）回避する** 裁判官は、利益相反に関わる事件を**回避する**義務を負う。
1799	**petition for the court to determine the price (petition for determination of the price)** The <u>petition for determination of the price</u> was filed by the shareholder.	**価格の決定の申立て** **価格の決定の申立て**は、株主が行った。
1800	**chemical substance** The regulation of <u>chemical substances</u> ensures public safety.	**化学物質** **化学物質**の規制は、公共の安全を確保するものである。
1801	**cabinet meeting** The <u>cabinet meeting</u> discussed national security strategies.	**閣議** **閣議**では、国家安全保障戦略が話し合われた。
1802	**cabinet decision** A <u>cabinet decision</u> was made to increase educational funding.	**閣議決定** 教育資金の増額が、**閣議決定**された。
1803	**relevant expertise** <u>Relevant expertise</u> is required for the project's success.	**学識経験** プロジェクトの成功には、**学識経験**が必要である。
1804	**ascertainment** [æsərtéinmənt] <u>Ascertainment</u> of facts is crucial for fair judgment.	**確知** 公正な判断のためには、事実の**確知**が重要である。
1805	**procedures to fix** The provision sets out handling of the <u>procedures to fix</u> a bankruptcy claim.	**確定手続** その条項は、破産手続終了の場合における破産債権の**確定手続**の取扱いを定めたものである。
1806	**fire insurance** <u>Fire insurance</u> claims surged after the wildfire.	**火災保険** 山火事の後、**火災保険**の請求が急増した。
1807	**additional tax** <u>Additional tax</u> is levied on undisclosed income.	**加算税** 非開示所得には、**加算税**が課される。
1808	**additional tax for under report** <u>Additional tax for under report</u> was assessed on the corporation.	**過少申告加算税** **過少申告加算税**が課された。

1809	**register of lost share certificates**	株券喪失登録簿
	The <u>register of lost share certificates</u> was updated.	**株券喪失登録簿**を更新した。
1810	**widow deduction**	寡婦控除
	The <u>widow deduction</u> provides tax relief for surviving spouses.	**寡婦控除**は、残された配偶者の税負担を軽減するものである。
1811	**widower deduction**	寡夫控除
	The <u>widower deduction</u> was claimed on the annual tax return.	**寡夫控除**は、毎年、確定申告された。
1812	**inland bill of lading**	貨物引換証
	Works to prepare documents concerning foreign trade (such as <u>inland bills of lading</u>, bills of lading) are regulated.	外国貿易に関する文書（**貨物引換証**、船荷証券など）の作成の業務は、法律により規制されている。
1813	**provisional detention**	仮拘禁
	He is subject to a <u>provisional detention</u> permit that has been issued pursuant to the provisions of the Act of Extradition.	彼は、逃亡犯罪人引渡法の規定により発せられた**仮拘禁**許可状に従う。
1814	**provisional designation**	仮指定
	<u>Provisional designation</u> of the area as protected was approved.	保護地域としての**仮指定**が、承認された。
1815	**parole** [pəróʊl]	仮釈放
	<u>Parole</u> may be revoked.	**仮釈放**の処分は、取り消すことができる。
1816	**provisional release**	仮放免・仮出場
	A person under penal detention may be provisionally released by a disposition of a government agency at any time when circumstances so warrant (<u>provisional release</u>).	拘留に処せられた者は、情状により、いつでも、行政官庁の処分によって仮に出場を許すことができる（**仮出場**）。
1817	**summary criminal trial**	簡易公判手続
	The <u>summary criminal trial</u> expedited minor offenses.	**簡易公判手続**は、軽微な犯罪の処理を迅速化するものであった。
1818	**unlawful confinement**	監禁
	<u>Unlawful confinement</u> charges were filed against the kidnapper.	誘拐犯には、**監禁**罪が適用された。
1819	**surveillance action (disposition)**	観察処分
	Commission must revoke a <u>surveillance disposition</u> when it finds that is no longer necessary to continuously reveal the status of the organization's activities.	公安審査委員会は、**観察処分**について、当該団体の活動状況を継続して明らかにする必要がなくなったと認められるときは、これを取り消さなければならない。

1820	**written expert opinion**	鑑定書
	The <u>written expert opinion</u> supported the legal argument.	**鑑定書**は、法的な主張を裏付けるものだった。
1821	**expert witness**	鑑定証人
	The <u>expert witness</u> testified on technical matters.	**鑑定証人**は、技術的な事柄について証言した。
1822	**detention for (expert) examination**	鑑定留置
	When a <u>detention</u> warrant <u>for expert examination</u> is executed against an accused under detention, the execution of detention is deemed to be suspended while said accused is under detention for expert examination.	勾留中の被告人に対し**鑑定留置**状が執行されたときは、被告人が留置されている間、勾留は、その執行を停止されたものとする。
1823	**writ of detention for expert examination**	鑑定留置状
	A <u>writ of detention for expert examination</u> was issued.	**鑑定留置状**が発された。
1824	**interest on tax refund**	還付加算金 （例：国税通則法第58条）
	<u>Interest on tax refund</u> compensates for the delay.	**還付加算金**は、その遅滞を補うものである。
1825	**naturalization** [nǽtʃərələzéɪʃən]	帰化
	To undergo <u>naturalization</u>, permission of the Minister of Justice must be obtained.	**帰化**をするには、法務大臣の許可を得なければならない。
1826	**dangerous driving**	危険運転
	<u>Dangerous driving</u> resulted in a severe accident.	**危険運転**が重大事故につながった。
1827	**port of call**	寄港地
	The immigration inspector may affix a seal of verification for landing at the <u>port of call</u> in the passport possessed by a foreign national.	入国審査官は、外国人の所持する旅券に**寄港地**上陸の許可の証印ができる。
1828	**standard claim**	基準債権 （例：民事再生法第231条）
	During rehabilitation for individuals with small-scale debts, the court may issue an order of disconfirmation of the rehabilitation plan considering the amount of <u>standard claims</u>.	小規模個人再生においては、裁判所は、**基準債権**等の基準を考慮して、再生計画不認可を決定できる。
1829	**basic personal exemption**	基礎控除
	<u>Basic personal exemption</u> reduces taxable income.	個人**基礎控除**は、課税所得を減らす。

RANK 4

1830	**challenge** [tʃǽləndʒ]	忌避する
	If there are circumstances involving a judge which could prejudice the impartiality of a judicial decision, a party may <u>challenge</u> that judge.	裁判官について裁判の公正を妨げるべき事情があるときは、当事者は、その裁判官を**忌避する**ことができる。
1831	**evade** [ɪvéɪd]	忌避する
	A person refuses, interferes with, or <u>evades</u> an inspection will be subject to criminal sanction.	検査を拒み、妨げ、若しくは**忌避する**者は、刑事罰に処せられる可能性がある。
1832	**act of endowment**	寄附行為（財団法人を設立する行為）
	A person that intends to establish an incorporated educational Institution must apply for authorization from the competent authority with regard to the <u>articles of endowment</u>.	学校法人を設立しようとする者は、**寄附行為**について所轄庁の認可を申請しなければならない。
1833	**articles of endowment**	寄附行為（財団法人の根本規則）
	The <u>articles of endowment</u> were legally documented.	**寄附行為**は、法的に文書化されていた。
1834	**compensation for absence from work**	休業補償
	<u>Compensation for absence from work</u> was provided.	**休業補償**が、支給された。
1835	**in case of urgency**	急速を要する場合
	In executing a search warrant when searching the body of a female, the executing officer must have a female adult attend the execution of said warrant; provided however, that this does not apply <u>in case of urgency</u>.	女子の身体について捜索状の執行をする場合には、成年の女子をこれに立ち会わせなければならない。但し、**急速を要する場合**は、この限りでない。
1836	**boundary** [báʊndəri]	境界
	The <u>boundary</u> dispute was resolved through mediation.	**境界**紛争は、調停によって解決された。
1837	**weapon** [wépən]	凶器
	The <u>weapon</u> was confiscated by the police.	**凶器**は、警察に押収された。
1838	**mutual aid pension**	共済年金
	The <u>mutual aid pension</u> supports community members.	**共済年金**は、地域住民を支えている。

RANK 4

1839	**joint revolving mortgage** The <u>joint revolving mortgage</u> facilitated home purchases.	**共同根抵当** **共同根抵当**は、住宅購入を容易にした。
1840	**coercion** [kəʊ́ːrʃən] <u>Coercion</u> in the contract negotiations was investigated.	**強要** 契約交渉における**強要**が、調査された。
1841	**appeal with permission** <u>Appeal with permission</u> was granted by the appellate court.	**許可抗告** 控訴審で、**許可抗告**が認められた。
1842	**maximum amount** A revolving mortgagee may exercise the relevant revolving mortgage up to the <u>maximum amount</u>.	**極度額** 根抵当権者は、**極度額**を限度として、その根抵当権を行使することができる。
1843	**amount of contribution** The <u>amount of contribution</u> to an estate may not exceed the amount remaining after the value of legacies is deducted from the value of the property held by the decedent at the time the succession opens.	**寄与分** **寄与分**は、被相続人が相続開始の時において有した財産の価額から遺贈の価額を控除した残額を超えることができない。
1844	**seizure with an order to produce a copy of records** <u>Seizure with an order to produce a copy of records</u> was executed.	**記録命令付差押え** **記録命令付差押え**が、実行された。
1845	**close relative** <u>Close relatives</u> were notified of the legal proceedings.	**近親者** **近親者**には、法的手続を通知した。
1846	**mayor of special ward** The <u>mayor of the special ward</u> implemented new policies.	**区長（特別区の場合）** **区長**は、新しい政策を実施した。
1847	**light vehicle** <u>Light vehicle</u> taxes were adjusted to encourage efficiency.	**軽車両** **軽車両**に課される税は、効率化を促進するために調整された。
1848	**disaster of extreme severity** The <u>disaster of extreme severity</u> prompted a state of emergency.	**激甚災害** **激甚災害**が、非常事態宣言を促した。
1849	**quarantine** [kwɔ́ːrəntin] <u>Quarantine</u> measures were implemented to control the outbreak.	**検疫** 感染症の蔓延（まんえん）を抑えるために**検疫**措置が実施された。

RANK 4

1850	**amortization** [ǽmərtɪzéɪʃən]	減価償却（無形固定資産の場合）
	Amortization of the loan will be completed in 20 years.	減価償却は、20年で完了する。
1851	**depreciable assets**	減価償却資産
	Depreciable assets are recorded at cost less accumulated depreciation.	減価償却資産は、取得原価から減価償却累計額を差し引いた額で計上される。
1852	**healthy and cultured living**	健康で文化的な生活
	The initiative promotes healthy and cultured living for all citizens.	この取組みは、すべての市民の健康で文化的な生活を促進するものである。
1853	**court of prior instance**	原裁判所
	The court of prior instance had jurisdiction before the appeal.	控訴前の管轄権は、原裁判所にあった。
1854	**inspection organization**	検査機関
	The inspection organization certified the safety standards were met.	検査機関は、安全基準を満たしていることを証明した。
1855	**defense of debtor's solvency**	検索の抗弁
	The defense of debtor's solvency was crucial for the case.	債務者の検索の抗弁は、この訴訟にとって極めて重要であった。
1856	**public prosecutor's assistant officer**	検察事務官
	The public prosecutor's assistant officer gathered evidence for the trial.	検察事務官は、裁判のために証拠を集めた。
1857	**coroner's inspection**	検視
	The coroner's inspection determined the cause of death.	検視により死因が特定された。
1858	**Chief Prosecutor**	検事正
	The Chief Prosecutor led the high-profile criminal investigation.	検事正が、注目の犯罪捜査を指揮した。
1859	**Prosecutor General**	検事総長
	Prosecutor General's monthly salary is set out as 1,486,000 yen.	検事総長の俸給月額は、148万6,000円と定められている。
1860	**nuclear damage**	原子力損害
	Compensation for nuclear damage is governed by specific legislation.	原子力損害の補償は、特定の法律によって規定されている。
1861	**qualified acceptance**	限定承認
	A person seeking to rescind a qualified acceptance must file a statement with the family court to that effect.	限定承認をしようとする者は、その旨を家庭裁判所に申述しなければならない。

RANK 4

1862	**motorized bicycle**	原動機付自転車
	The <u>motorized bicycle</u> must comply with traffic regulations.	<u>原動機付自転車</u>は、交通規則を遵守しなければならない。
1863	**building coverage ratio**	建ぺい率
	The <u>building coverage ratio</u> is regulated by zoning laws.	<u>建ぺい率</u>は、ゾーニングに関する法令によって規制されている。
1864	**public safety commission**	公安委員会
	The <u>public safety commission</u> is responsible for maintaining public order.	<u>公安委員会</u>は、治安維持に責任を負う。
1865	**rape** [réɪp]	強姦（不同意性交）
	<u>Rape</u> is a grave criminal offense punishable by law.	<u>強姦（不同意性交）</u>は、法律で罰せられる重大な犯罪である。
1866	**discipline committee**	綱紀委員会（弁護士法第58条）
	The <u>discipline committee</u> reviewed the breach of conduct.	<u>綱紀委員会</u>は、違反を審査した。
1867	**reduction of pay**	降給
	<u>Reduction of pay</u> was a disciplinary measure.	<u>降給</u>は、懲戒処分だった。
1868	**aircraft and railway accidents investigation commission**	航空・鉄道事故調査委員会
	The <u>aircraft and railway accidents investigation commission</u> reports on transport safety.	<u>航空・鉄道事故調査委員会</u>は、輸送の安全について報告する。
1869	**guardianship** [gáːrdiənʃɪp]	後見
	The mandatary was subject to a decision for the commencement of <u>guardianship</u>.	受任者は、<u>後見</u>開始の審判を受けた。
1870	**ruling for commencement of guardianship**	後見開始の審判
	The <u>ruling for commencement of guardianship</u> was issued by the court.	裁判所から、<u>後見開始の審判</u>が下された。
1871	**supervisor of guardian**	後見監督人
	The spouse, lineal blood relative, or sibling of the guardian may not become the <u>supervisor of that guardian</u>.	後見人の配偶者、直系血族及び兄弟姉妹は、<u>後見監督人</u>となることができない。

RANK 4

1872	**guardian** [gáːrdiən]	後見人
	If there is a legitimate reason, the <u>guardian</u> of an adult may resign from the role of guardian, with the permission of the family court.	<u>後見人</u>は、正当な事由があるときは、家庭裁判所の許可を得て、その任務を辞することができる。
1873	**navigation** [nævəgéɪʃən]	航行
	The Minister of Land, Infrastructure, Transport and Tourism designates pathways through airspace, as airways, appropriate for the <u>navigation</u> of aircraft.	国土交通大臣は、航空機の<u>航行</u>に適する空中の通路を航空路として指定する。
1874	**open account**	交互計算 (例：商法第529条)
	Either of the parties to an <u>open account</u> may terminate the account at any time.	各当事者は、いつでも<u>交互計算</u>の解除をすることができる。
1875	**public bond**	公債
	<u>Public bond</u> offerings finance government projects.	<u>公債</u>は、政府のプロジェクトに資金を提供する。
1876	**structure** [strʌ́ktʃər]	工作物
	The <u>structure</u>'s integrity was confirmed by engineers.	<u>工作物</u>の完全性は、エンジニアによって確認された。
1877	**public and corporate bond**	公社債
	<u>Public and corporate bonds</u> are investment options.	<u>公社債</u>は、投資オプションである。
1878	**public health**	公衆衛生
	<u>Public health</u> initiatives aim to prevent disease.	<u>公衆衛生</u>の取り組みは、病気を予防することを目的としている。
1879	**spouse qualified for tax deduction**	控除対象配偶者
	A <u>spouse qualified for tax deduction</u> reduces taxable income.	<u>控除対象配偶者</u>は、課税所得を減らすことができる。
1880	**rehabilitation** [rìːəbìlətéɪʃən]	更生（犯罪者）
	<u>Rehabilitation</u> programs support recovery and reintegration.	<u>更生</u>プログラムは、回復と社会復帰を支援する。
1881	**public hearing**	公聴会
	The <u>public hearing</u> allowed for community input on the proposal.	<u>公聴会</u>では、この提案に対する地域住民の意見が求められた。

RANK 4

1882	**obstruction of performance of public duty**	**公務執行妨害**
	<u>Obstruction of performance of public duty</u> is a punishable offense.	<u>公務執行妨害</u>は、罰せられるべき犯罪である。
1883	**torture** [tɔ́:rtʃər]	**拷問**
	<u>Torture</u> is prohibited by international human rights laws.	<u>拷問</u>は、国際人権法によって禁止されている。
1884	**retail** [rítèɪl]	**小売業**
	<u>Retail</u> businesses were affected by the economic downturn.	<u>小売業</u>は、景気後退の影響を受けた。
1885	**check** [tʃék]	**小切手**
	The <u>check</u> was processed by the bank without issues.	<u>小切手</u>は、問題なく銀行で処理された。
1886	**action on checks**	**小切手訴訟**
	<u>Action on checks</u> can involve legal proceedings for non-payment.	<u>小切手訴訟</u>は、不払いに対する法的手続を伴うことがある。
1887	**Japanese Government Bonds**	**国債**
	<u>Japanese Government Bonds</u> are a safe investment option.	<u>日本国債</u>は、安全な投資オプションである。
1888	**National Tax Tribunal**	**国税不服審判所**
	The <u>National Tax Tribunal</u> adjudicates tax disputes.	<u>国税不服審判所</u>は、税務紛争を裁く。
1889	**domestic source income**	**国内源泉所得**
	<u>Domestic source income</u> is subject to national taxation.	<u>国内源泉所得</u>は、国内課税の対象となる。
1890	**national referendum**	**国民審査**
	The national government must take other necessary measures so that persons with disabilities are able to smoothly vote at an election, <u>national referendum</u>, or poll.	国は、選挙、<u>国民審査</u>又は投票において、障害者が円滑に投票できるようにするため、必要な施策を講じなければならない。
1891	**national pension**	**国民年金**
	Documents proving the payment status of <u>national pension</u> insurance premiums are required.	<u>国民年金</u>の保険料の納付状況を証する文書が義務付けられている。
1892	**national government asset**	**国有財産**
	<u>National government asset</u> management is critical for fiscal health.	<u>国有財産</u>の管理は財政の健全化にとって極めて重要である。

RANK 4

1893	**national university corporation**	**国立大学法人**
	The <u>national university corporation</u> advances higher education.	<u>国立大学法人</u>は、高等教育を発展させる。
1894	**individual rehabilitation commissioner**	**個人再生委員**
	An <u>individual rehabilitation commissioner</u> may receive remuneration determined by the court.	<u>個人再生委員</u>は、裁判所が定める報酬を受けることができる。
1895	**family register**	**戸籍**
	An original and a duplicate is made for each <u>family register</u>.	<u>戸籍</u>は、正本及び副本を設ける。
1896	**treasury** [tréʒəri]	**国庫**
	Ownerless immovables belong to the national <u>treasury</u>.	所有者のない不動産は、<u>国庫</u>に帰属する。
1897	**fixed asset tax**	**固定資産税**
	<u>Fixed asset tax</u> is levied on property owners.	<u>固定資産税</u>は、不動産所有者に課税される。
1898	**confusion / merger** [kənfjúːʒən]	**混同**
	If there is a <u>merger</u> between one of the joint and several obligees and the obligor, the obligor is deemed to have performed the obligation.	連帯債権者の1人と債務者との間に<u>混同</u>があったときは、債務者は、弁済をしたものとみなす。
1899	**mixture** [míkstʃər]	**混和**
	The provisions of the preceding two Articles apply mutatis mutandis if the things of different owners are <u>mixed</u> together and can no longer be distinguished.	前二条の規定は、所有者を異にする物が<u>混和</u>して識別することができなくなった場合について準用する。
1900	**disaster recovery project**	**災害復旧事業**
	The <u>disaster recovery project</u> aimed to rebuild the affected community.	<u>災害復旧事業</u>は、被災したコミュニティの再建を目的としていた。
1901	**re-appeal from an appeal from a ruling**	**再抗告**
	A <u>re-appeal from an appeal from a ruling</u> is rare in the legal system.	<u>再抗告</u>は、法制度上まれなことである。
1902	**retrial** [ritráiəl]	**再審**
	The <u>retrial</u> was granted based on new evidence.	<u>再審</u>は、新たな証拠に基づいて認められた。

RANK 4

1903	**order of commencement of retrial**	再審開始の決定
	The order of commencement of retrial was broadcasted nation-widely.	再審開始の決定は、国中に広く報道された。
1904	**action for retrial**	再審の訴え
	The action for retrial challenged the original verdict.	再審の訴えは、（確定した）判決を争うものであった。
1905	**minimum wage**	最低賃金
	The government revised the minimum wage upwards.	政府は、最低賃金を上方修正した。
1906	**repeat conviction**	再犯
	Repeat conviction may result in harsher sentences.	再犯には、より厳しい判決が下される可能性がある。
1907	**judicial divorce**	裁判上の離婚
	Judicial divorce proceedings concluded with the court's decision.	裁判上の離婚手続は、裁判所の決定で終了した。
1908	**judicial research official**	裁判所調査官
	The judicial research official assisted in case law analysis.	裁判所調査官は、判例分析を手伝った。
1909	**omission in a judicial decision**	裁判の脱漏
	If there has been an omission in a judicial decision with regard to the burden of court costs, the court reaches a judicial decision on the burden of court costs in the form of a ruling.	訴訟費用の負担の裁判を脱漏したときは、裁判所は、その訴訟費用の負担について、決定で、裁判をする。
1910	**residence** [rézɪdəns]	在留
	The purpose of the Immigration Control and Refugee Recognition Act includes to provide for fair management over the residence of foreign nationals in Japan.	出入国管理及び難民認定法の目的は、本邦に在留する外国人の在留の公正な管理を図ることを含む。
1911	**period of stay**	在留期間
	The period during which a foreign national may reside ("period of stay") is determined for each status of residence by the Ministry of Justice Order.	外国人が在留することのできる期間（在留期間）は、各在留資格について、法務省令で定める。
1912	**status of residence**	在留資格
	The status of residence determines eligibility for various services.	在留資格によって、さまざまなサービスを受ける資格が決まる。

RANK 4

1913	**certificate of status of residence**	在留資格証明書
	The <u>certificate of status of residence</u> was required for the application.	申請には、<u>在留資格証明書</u>が必要だった。
1914	**miscellaneous income**	雑所得
	<u>Miscellaneous income</u> must be reported on annual tax returns.	<u>雑所得</u>は、毎年の確定申告において、申告しなければならない。
1915	**gift on donor's death**	死因贈与
	The <u>gift on the donor's death</u> is exempt from certain taxes.	<u>死因贈与</u>は、一定の税金が免除される。
1916	**urbanization control area**	市街化調整区域
	<u>Urbanization control area</u> regulations limit development to preserve nature.	<u>市街化調整区域</u>の規制は、自然を保護するために開発を制限する。
1917	**trade association**	事業者団体
	The <u>trade association</u> represented the collective interests of local businesses.	この<u>事業者団体</u>は、地元企業の利益を代表していた。
1918	**business income**	事業所得
	<u>Business income</u> was significantly higher this quarter.	<u>事業所得</u>は、今期大幅に増加した。
1919	**benefit of prescription**	時効の利益
	The <u>benefit of prescription</u> may not be waived in advance.	<u>時効の利益</u>は、あらかじめ放棄することができない。
1920	**self-contract**	自己契約
	A <u>self-contract</u> involves the same person in dual roles, raising conflict of interest concerns.	<u>自己契約</u>は、同一人物が二重の役割を担うことになり、利益相反の懸念が生じる。
1921	**constructive robbery**	事後強盗
	When a person who has committed the crime of theft uses assault in order to retain the stolen property, the person is dealt with a <u>constructive robbery</u>.	窃盗が、財物を得てこれを取り返されることを防ぐために、暴行をしたときは、<u>事後強盗</u>に該当する。
1922	**capital adequacy ratio**	自己資本規制比率
	The <u>capital adequacy ratio</u> ensures financial institutions have sufficient capital.	<u>自己資本規制比率</u>は、金融機関が十分な資本を有していることを保証するものである。
1923	**deceased (dead person)** [dɪsíst]	死者
	A person who defames a <u>dead person</u> is not punished unless such defamation is based on false facts.	<u>死者</u>の名誉を毀損した者は、虚偽の事実を摘示することによってした場合でなければ、罰しない。

1924	**moral right of performer**	実演家人格権
	The <u>moral right of the performer</u> protects against unauthorized use of performances.	**実演家人格権**は、実演の無断使用から保護するものである。
1925	**illness** [ílnəs]	疾患
	<u>Illness</u> forced the CEO to take a temporary leave.	CEOは、**疾患**のため、一時休養を余儀なくされた。
1926	**appeal against (a disposition of) execution**	執行抗告
	<u>Appeal against a disposition of execution</u> was filed by the debtor.	債務者が、**執行抗告**を行った。
1927	**adjudication of somebody's disappearance**	失踪の宣告
	<u>Adjudication of somebody's disappearance</u> allows for legal proceedings in their absence.	**失踪の宣告**は、不在のまま法的手続を行うことを可能にする。
1928	**utility model right**	実用新案権
	The <u>utility model right</u> encourages innovation in practical devices.	**実用新案権**は、実用的な装置における技術革新を奨励するものである。
1929	**compensation for private sound and visual recording**	私的録音録画補償金
	<u>Compensation for private sound and visual recording</u> supports creators' rights.	**私的録音録画補償金**は、クリエイターの権利を支えるものである。
1930	**automatic public transmission**	自動公衆送信
	<u>Automatic public transmission</u> means a transmission to a member of the public that is made automatically in response to a request from the member of the public.	**自動公衆送信**とは、公衆送信のうち、公衆からの求めに応じ自動的に行うものをいう。
1931	**automatic public transmission server**	自動公衆送信装置
	The <u>automatic public transmission server</u> may contain a risk to trigger "available for transmission".	**自動公衆送信装置**は、送信可能化に該当するリスクを含みうる。
1932	**subject matter jurisdiction**	事物管轄
	When a court deems it appropriate, the court may rule to transfer a case under its jurisdiction to another competent court which has the same <u>subject-matter jurisdiction</u>.	裁判所は、適当と認めるときは、決定を以て、その管轄に属する事件について、**事物管轄**を同じくする他の管轄裁判所に移送することができる。

RANK 4

1933	**bank note (money bill)**	**紙幣**
	A person who counterfeits <u>bank note</u> for the purpose of uttering is punished by imprisonment for life or for a definite term of not less than 3 years.	行使の目的で、**紙幣**を偽造した者は、無期又は3年以上の懲役に処する。
1934	**judicial commissioner**	**司法委員**
	If the court may have a <u>judicial commissioner</u> assist in the attempt to arrange a settlement so that it may hear the commissioner's opinion on the case.	裁判所は、和解を試みるについて**司法委員**に補助をさせて事件につきその意見を聴くことができる。
1935	**judicial police personnel**	**司法警察員**
	<u>Judicial police personnel</u> are involved in criminal investigations.	**司法警察員**は、犯罪捜査に携わる。
1936	**legal apprentice**	**司法修習生**
	<u>Legal apprentices</u> are in the process of becoming licensed lawyers.	**司法修習生**は、弁護士資格を取得する過程にある。
1937	**reduction of punishment in light of extenuating circumstances**	**酌量減軽**
	<u>Reduction of punishment in light of extenuating circumstances</u> considers the defendant's situation.	**酌量減軽**は、被告人の状況を考慮したものである。
1938	**heavy additional tax**	**重加算税**
	<u>Heavy additional tax</u> penalizes deliberate tax evasion.	**重加算税**は、意図的な脱税を罰する。
1939	**workplace** [wɔ́ːrkplèɪs]	**就業場所**
	The <u>workplace</u> introduced new safety protocols.	**就業場所**に、新しい安全のプロトコルが導入された。
1940	**religious corporation**	**宗教法人**
	The <u>religious corporation</u> was registered under the new law.	**宗教法人**は、新法に基づいて登録された。
1941	**bigamy** [bígəmi]	**重婚**
	<u>Bigamy</u> is illegal and punishable by law.	**重婚**は違法であり、法律で罰せられる。
1942	**amended return**	**修正申告**
	The <u>amended return</u> corrected errors in the initial tax filing.	**修正申告**は、最初の税務申告の誤りを訂正したものである。
1943	**revenue stamp**	**収入印紙**
	A <u>revenue stamp</u> is required for official documents.	公的書類には、**収入印紙**が必要である。

RANK 4

1944	**appurtenance** [əpə́ːrtənəns]		**不動産の従物**
	Appurtenance includes items associated with the property.		**不動産の従物**には、不動産に付随する物品が含まれる。
1945	**accessory** [æksésəri]		**動産の従物** ※刑法の「従犯」の意味もある（1430参照）。
	If the distinction of principal and accessory cannot be made between the movables united by accession, the owner of each movable property co-owns the composite thing in proportion to the respective price current at the time of the accession.		付合した動産について主従（**従物**）の区別をすることができないときは、各動産の所有者は、その付合の時における価格の割合に応じてその合成物を共有する。
1946	**detention** [dɪténʃən]		**収容**
	Penal institutions are establishments for committing the detention of any of the persons set out in the laws.		刑事施設は、法律に定める者を**収容**する施設である。
1947	**beneficiary certificates**		**受益証券**
	Beneficiary certificates of loan trusts will fall under the "securities".		貸付信託の**受益証券**は、「有価証券」に該当する。
1948	**quasi-mandate**		**準委任**
	These provisions may apply mutatis mutandis to entrustments of business that do not constitute juridical acts (quasi-mandate).		これらの規定は、法律行為でない事務の委託（**準委任**）について準用される。
1949	**quasi-co-ownership**		**準共有**
	The provisions of co-ownership may apply mutatis mutandis if two or more persons share property rights other than ownership (quasi-co-ownership).		共有の規定は、数人で所有権以外の財産権を有する場合（**準共有**）について準用される。
1950	**quasi-possession**		**準占有**
	The provisions of possession may apply mutatis mutandis if a person exercises their property rights with the intention to do so on their own behalf (quasi-possession).		占有の規定は、自己のためにする意思をもって財産権の行使をする場合（**準占有**）について準用する。
1951	**screen presentation**		**上映**
	"Screen presentation" means projecting a work on a movie screen or other physical object, and includes playing the sounds accompanying the projection that are fixed to a cinematographic work.		**上映**とは、著作物を映写幕その他の物に映写することをいい、これに伴って映画の著作物において固定されている音を再生することを含むものとする。

RANK 4

1952	**servient land**	承役地
	Servient land is subject to the easement rights of another property.	承役地は、他の土地の地役権の対象となる。
1953	**stage performance**	上演
	The author of a work has the exclusive right to give a stage performance or musical performance of the work.	著作者は、その著作物を、**上演**し又は演奏する権利を専有する。
1954	**disability pension**	障害年金
	Disability pension supports those unable to work due to disabilities.	**障害年金**は、障害のために働くことができない人々を支援する。
1955	**accident insurance**	傷害保険
	Accident insurance provides coverage for unexpected injuries.	**傷害保険**は、予期せぬ怪我に対する補償を提供するものである。
1956	**small claim action**	少額訴訟
	Small claim action simplifies resolution of minor disputes.	**少額訴訟**は、軽微な紛争の解決を簡素化する。
1957	**juvenile** [ʤúːvənəl]	少年
	Juvenile delinquency is addressed through rehabilitation rather than punishment.	**少年**非行は、刑罰ではなく更生を通じて対処される。
1958	**juvenile training school**	少年院
	Juvenile training school aims to correct behavioral issues.	**少年院**は、問題行動の矯正を目的としている。
1959	**injury and disease allowance**	傷病手当
	Injury and disease allowance assists workers affected on the job.	**傷病手当**は、業務上影響を受けた労働者を援助する。
1960	**ex officio**	職権で（末尾㉟参照）
	Ex officio actions are taken by authority, not by request.	**職権**による行動は、請求によってではなく、権限によって行われる。
1961	**sua sponte**	職権で（末尾㉟参照）
	A court may conduct an examination of the evidence sua sponte with regard to matters that concern the jurisdiction of the Japanese courts.	裁判所は、日本の裁判所の管轄権に関する事項について、**職権で**、証拠調べをすることができる。
1962	**without any party's request**	職権で（末尾㉟参照）
	Without any party's request, the court can initiate proceedings.	裁判所は、**職権で**、手続きを開始することができる。

RANK 4

1963	**income tax**	**所得税**
	<u>Income tax</u> is levied on annual earnings.	<u>所得税</u>は、年間所得に対して課税される。
1964	**submission of written statements in lieu of examination**	**書面尋問（民事訴訟手続）**
	If neither party has any objection and the court finds it to be appropriate, the court may have a witness submit a paper document in lieu of witness examination (<u>submission of written statements in lieu of examination</u>).	裁判所は、当事者に異議がない場合であって、相当と認めるときは、証人の尋問に代え、書面の提出をさせること（**書面尋問**）ができる。
1965	**parental authority**	**親権**
	<u>Parental authority</u> involves rights and duties towards one's child.	<u>親権</u>には、子供に対する権利及び義務が含まれる。
1966	**request for examination**	**審査請求**
	No <u>request for examination</u> may be filed against a disposition under Article 7.	第7条の規定による処分については、**審査請求**をすることができない。
1967	**body search**	**身体検査**
	<u>Body search</u> must comply with legal standards for privacy.	<u>身体検査</u>は、プライバシーに関する法的基準を遵守しなければならない。
1968	**physically disabled**	**身体障害者**
	Facilities are mandated to be accessible to <u>physically disabled</u> individuals.	施設は、**身体障害者**が利用しやすいようにすることが義務付けられている。
1969	**mental reservation**	**心裡留保**
	The validity of a manifestation of intention is not impaired even if the person making it does so while knowing that it does not reflect that person's true intention (<u>mental reservation</u>).	意思表示は、表意者がその真意ではないことを知ってしたときであっても、そのためにその効力を妨げられない（**心裡留保**）。
1970	**condition at will**	**随意条件**
	A juridical act subject to a condition precedent is void if the condition is dependent only upon the intention of the obligor (<u>condition at will</u>).	停止条件付法律行為は、その条件が単に債務者の意思のみに係るとき（**随意条件**）は、無効とする。
1971	**presumptive heir**	**推定相続人**
	<u>Presumptive heir</u> is expected to inherit unless a will states otherwise.	**推定相続人**は、遺言に別段の記載がない限り、相続が予定されている。
1972	**liquidating stock company**	**清算株式会社**
	The <u>liquidating stock company</u> is in the process of dissolving.	**清算株式会社**は、解散の手続中である。

RANK 4

1973	**clearing organization**	清算機関
	<u>Clearing organizations</u> facilitate the settlement of transactions.	<u>清算機関</u>は、取引の決済を促進する。
1974	**certified public tax accountant**	税理士
	<u>Certified public tax accountants</u> are essential for complex tax issues.	複雑な税務問題には、<u>税理士</u>が欠かせない。
1975	**action to enforce liability**	責任追及等の訴え
	When the stock company does not file an <u>action to enforce liability</u> within sixty days, the shareholder who has made relevant demand may file an action to enforce liability on behalf of the stock company.	株式会社が60日以内に<u>責任追及等の訴え</u>を提起しないときは、当該請求をした株主は、株式会社のために、責任追及等の訴えを提起することができる。
1976	**householder** [háʊshòʊldər]	世帯主
	<u>Householder</u> refers to the head of a household.	<u>世帯主</u>とは、世帯の主を指す。
1977	**steal** [stíːl]	窃取する
	To <u>steal</u> is to take another's property without permission.	<u>窃取する</u>とは、他人の所有物を許可なく奪うことである。
1978	**master** [mǽstər]	船長
	A person aboard a ship may make a will in the presence of the <u>master</u> or crew member, and at least two witnesses.	船舶中に在る者は、<u>船長</u>又は事務員1人及び証人2人以上の立会いをもって遺言書を作ることができる。
1979	**expert advisor**	専門委員
	<u>Expert advisor</u> provides specialized knowledge in cases.	<u>専門委員</u>は、事件において専門的な知識を提供する。
1980	**deportation** [dìpɔrtéɪʃən]	送還
	A person subject to <u>deportation</u> is to be sent to a country of which they are a national.	退去強制を受ける者は、その者の国籍の属する国に<u>送還</u>されるものとする。
1981	**act of dispute**	争議行為
	An employer may not claim compensation against a labor union for damages received through <u>acts of dispute</u> which are justifiable acts.	使用者は、<u>争議行為</u>であって正当なものによって損害を受けたことの故をもって、労働組合に対し賠償を請求することができない。
1982	**tax on aggregate income**	総合課税
	<u>Tax on aggregate income</u> sums up total taxable earnings.	<u>総合課税</u>は、課税所得を合計したものである。

RANK 4

1983	**mutual company**	相互会社（保険業法）
	The term "mutual company" means an association established pursuant to this Act for the purpose of conducting insurance business, whose policyholders are the members.	「相互会社」とは、保険業を行うことを目的として、この法律に基づき設立された保険契約者をその社員とする社団をいう。
1984	**representation of both parties**	双方代理
	Representation of both parties in a deal requires careful ethical consideration.	双方代理には、慎重な倫理的配慮が必要である。
1985	**bilateral contract**	双務契約
	Bilateral contract involves mutual obligations between parties.	双務契約には、当事者間の相互の義務が含まれる。
1986	**gift tax**	贈与税
	Gift tax applies to transfers of property as gifts.	贈与税は、贈与による財産の移転に適用される。
1987	**neighboring relationship**	相隣関係
	Neighboring relationships are regulated under the Civil Code.	相隣関係は、民法において規制されている。
1988	**organized crime**	組織的な犯罪
	Organized crime is combated through legal measures.	組織的な犯罪は、法的措置によって撲滅されている。
1989	**entity conversion**	組織変更
	Entity conversion changes a company's legal structure.	組織変更は、会社の法的構造を変更する。
1990	**fixing amount of court costs**	訴訟費用の確定
	Fixing the amount of court costs ensures fairness in litigation expenses.	訴訟費用の確定により、訴訟費用の公平性を確保する。
1991	**person without capacity to sue or be sued**	訴訟無能力者
	Person without capacity to sue or be sued lacks legal standing.	訴訟無能力者は、法的地位を欠く。
1992	**quitting** [kwítɪŋ]	退職
	Quitting a job is a personal decision to leave employment.	退職は、個人的な決断である。
1993	**separation from employment**	退職
	Separation from employment can be voluntary or involuntary.	退職には、自発的なものと非自発的なものがある。

RANK 4

1994	**leave the court** The accused may not <u>leave the court</u> without the permission of the presiding judge.	**退廷する** 被告人は、裁判長の許可がなければ、**退廷する**ことができない。
1995	**disposition of delinquency** The principal secured by a revolving mortgage is crystallized if the revolving mortgagee has affected an attachment for <u>disposition of delinquency</u> against the mortgaged immovable.	**滞納処分** 根抵当権者が抵当不動産に対して**滞納処分**による差押えをしたとき、根抵当権の担保すべき元本は確定する。
1996	**real estate brokerage** <u>Real estate brokerage</u> facilitates property transactions.	**宅地建物取引業** **宅地建物取引業**は、不動産取引を促進する。
1997	**walk-in inspection** In the cases of conducting <u>walk-in inspection</u>, the immigration inspector must carry an identification card showing their official status.	**立入検査** **立入検査**を行う場合においては、入国審査官は、その身分を示す証票を携帯しなければならない。
1998	**impeachment** [ìmpíːtʃmənt] The judge faced <u>impeachment</u> for misconduct.	**弾劾** その裁判官は、不祥事による**弾劾**に直面していた。
1999	**short-term lease** The <u>short-term lease</u> of movables must not exceed six months.	**短期賃貸借** 動産の**短期賃貸借**は、6ヶ月の期間を超えられない。
2000	**part-time worker** A <u>part-time worker</u> has flexible working hours.	**短時間労働者** **短時間労働者**は、フレキシブルな労働時間を有する。
2001	**unqualified acceptance** An heir inherits the rights and obligations of the decedent without limitation upon <u>unqualified acceptance</u> of the succession.	**単純承認** 相続人は、**単純承認**をしたときは、無限に被相続人の権利義務を承継する。
2002	**collective bargaining** <u>Collective bargaining</u> negotiated better wages.	**団体交渉** **団体交渉**は、賃金を改善した。
2003	**unilateral juridical act** The gift was a <u>unilateral juridical act</u>.	**単独行為** その贈与は、**単独行為**であった。

RANK 4

2004	**fatal** [féɪtəl]	致死、致命	
	The accident was <u>fatal</u>, leading to immediate death.	その事故は、**致命**的なもので、即死に至った。	
2005	**lethal** [líːθəl]	致死	
	The substance proved to be <u>lethal</u> in small doses.	この物質は、少量でも**致死**量であることが証明された。	
2006	**superficies (right)** [sùːpəfíʃiːz]	地上権	
	The site of residence means land used for the residence or a <u>superficies right</u> established on the land.	住宅の敷地とは、住宅の用に供されている土地又は当該土地に設定されている**地上権**をいう。	
2007	**child born in wedlock**	嫡出である子（民法第790条）	
	A <u>child born in wedlock</u> takes the surname of the parents.	**嫡出である子**は、父母の氏を称する。	
2008	**child born out of wedlock**	嫡出でない子（民法第790条）	
	A <u>child born out of wedlock</u> takes the surname of the mother.	**嫡出でない子**は、母の氏を称する。	
2009	**Central Labour Relations Commission**	中央労働委員会	
	The <u>Central Labour Relations Commission</u> resolved the dispute.	**中央労働委員会**が、争議を解決した。	
2010	**stay order**	中止命令	
	The court may change a <u>stay order</u> issued.	裁判所は、**中止命令**を変更することができる。	
2011	**principle of direct trial**	直接主義	
	The <u>principle of direct trial</u> ensures transparency.	**直接主義**は、透明性を確保する。	
2012	**imperial order**	勅令	
	The emperor issued the <u>imperial order</u> in the 1930s.	1930年代、天皇陛下はその**勅令**を下した。	
2013	**neighboring right**	著作隣接権	
	The duration of <u>neighboring rights</u> begins to differ.	**著作隣接権**の存続期間は、それぞれ異なる。	
2014	**collection of delinquent payment**	追徴金（租税等の追徴）	
	Claims for a fine, petty fine, court costs for a criminal case, <u>collection of delinquent payment</u> or civil fine are to be included in the scope of bankruptcy claims.	罰金、科料、刑事訴訟費用、**追徴金**又は過料の請求権は、破産債権に含まれるものとする。	

RANK 4

2015	**periodic payments**		**定期金**
	Periodic payments are due quarterly.		定期金は、四半期ごとに行われる。
2016	**claim for extinguishment of mortgage**		**抵当権消滅請求**
	A third party acquirer of a mortgaged immovables may make a claim for extinguishment of mortgage.		抵当不動産の第三取得者は、**抵当権消滅請求**をすることができる。
2017	**mandatory retirement age**		**定年**
	Mandatory retirement age is set at 65.		**定年**は、65歳である。
2018	**mandatory retirement**		**定年退職**
	He approached his mandatory retirement this year.		彼は、今年、**定年退職**を迎えた。
2019	**negotiable instrument**		**手形**
	The negotiable instrument was endorsed to the new bearer.		**手形**は、新しい持参人に裏書された。
2020	**actions on bills and notes**		**手形訴訟**
	Actions on bills and notes require specialized legal expertise.		**手形訴訟**には、専門的な法律知識が必要である。
2021	**telecommunication** [tèləkəmjùːnɪkéɪʃən]		**電気通信**
	Telecommunication has connected the world.		**電気通信**は、世界をつないできた。
2022	**telecommunications carrier**		**電気通信事業者**
	The telecommunications carrier expanded its network.		**電気通信事業者**は、ネットワークを拡大した。
2023	**natural fruits**		**天然果実**
	The ownership of natural fruits is acquired by the person entitled to obtain them when they are separated from the original thing.		**天然果実**は、その元物から分離する時に、これを収取する権利を有する者に帰属する。
2024	**assignment order**		**転付命令**
	An enforcement court may issue an assignment order.		執行裁判所は、**転付命令**を発することができる。
2025	**commission merchant**		**問屋**
	The commission merchant sold goods on behalf of the producer.		**問屋**は、生産者に代わって、商品を販売した。
2026	**mutual fund**		**投資信託（商品としての投資信託）**
	The mutual fund diversified investor portfolios.		**投資信託**は、投資家のポートフォリオを分散させた。

RANK 4

2027	**simultaneous trial and decision**		同時審判
	The request for a <u>simultaneous trial and decision</u> shall be made by the time of conclusion of oral arguments in the second instance.		<u>同時審判</u>の申出は、控訴審の口頭弁論の終結の時までにしなければならない。
2028	**stolen property**		盗品
	The police recovered <u>stolen property</u> from the scene.		警察は、現場から<u>盗品</u>を回収した。
2029	**objection to demand**		督促異議
	The <u>objection to demand</u> challenged the claim's validity.		<u>督促異議</u>は、請求の正当性を問うものであった。
2030	**demand procedure**		督促手続
	The <u>demand procedure</u> was followed for the outstanding debt.		未払い債務について、<u>督促手続</u>を行った。
2031	**circumstances that afford special credibility**		特に信用すべき情況
	<u>Circumstances that afford special credibility</u> were carefully examined by the court.		<u>特に信用すべき情況</u>について、裁判所は慎重な検討を行った。
2032	**find particularly necessary**		特に必要があると認める
	The regulator struggles to <u>find</u> a reason of <u>particularly necessary</u> to exercise an on-site inspection.		規制当局は、立入検査を<u>特に必要があると認める</u>理由を見つけることに苦労している。
2033	**special controlling company**		特別支配会社
	The "<u>special controlling company</u>" means the relevant other company if nine tenths or more of the voting rights of all shareholders of a stock company are held by other company.		<u>特別支配会社</u>とは、ある株式会社の総株主の議決権の10分の9以上を他の会社が有している場合における当該他の会社をいう。
2034	**intervention as independent party**		独立当事者参加
	<u>Intervention as an independent party</u> was granted by the court.		<u>独立当事者参加</u>が、裁判所によって、認められた。
2035	**gambling** [gǽmbəlɪŋ]		賭博
	A person who <u>gambles</u> is punished by a fine of not more than 500,000 yen.		<u>賭博</u>をした者は、50万円以下の罰金に処する。
2036	**Japan Federation of Bar Associations**		日本弁護士連合会
	The <u>Japan Federation of Bar Associations</u> promotes legal ethics.		<u>日本弁護士連合会</u>は、法曹倫理の普及に努めている。

RANK 4

2037	**bid** [bíd]	入札
	The <u>bid</u> was submitted before the deadline.	<u>入札</u>は、締切前に行われた。
2038	**bidding process**	入札
	The <u>bidding process</u> was transparent and competitive.	<u>入札</u>プロセスは、透明かつ競争的だった。
2039	**sealed bidding**	入札
	The court clerk caused a sale to be implemented through <u>sealed bidding</u> but no lawful purchase offer was made.	裁判所書記官は、<u>入札</u>の方法により売却を実施させたが、適法な買受けの申出がなかった。
2040	**tender** [téndər]	入札
	The <u>tender</u> was accepted for the construction project.	建設プロジェクトの<u>入札</u>が、受諾された。
2041	**bid rigging**	入札談合
	<u>Bid rigging</u> undermines fair market competition.	<u>入札談合</u>は、公正な市場競争を損なう。
2042	**sale by private contract**	任意売却
	The <u>sale by private contract</u> was completed discreetly.	<u>任意売却</u>は、慎重に完了した。
2043	**acknowledgment of parentage**	認知
	The <u>acknowledgment of parentage</u> was filed with the court.	<u>認知</u>が、裁判所に申し立てられた。
2044	**filiation** [filiéiʃən]	認知
	<u>Filiation</u> affects inheritance rights.	<u>認知</u>は、相続権に影響する。
2045	**agricultural cooperative**	農業協同組合
	The <u>agricultural cooperative</u> supported local farmers.	<u>農業協同組合</u>は、地元の農家を支援した。
2046	**dividend income**	配当所得
	<u>Dividend income</u> was reported on the tax return.	<u>配当所得</u>は、確定申告により申告された。
2047	**assistant judge**	判事補
	An <u>assistant judge</u> may independently reach a judicial decision other than a judgment.	判決以外の裁判は、<u>判事補</u>が単独ですることができる。

RANK 4

2048	**nonprofit corporation**		**非営利活動法人**
	The <u>nonprofit corporation</u> serves the community without profit motives.		その**非営利活動法人**は、営利を目的とせず、地域社会に奉仕する。
2049	**extradition** [èkstrədíʃən]		**引渡し**
	<u>Extradition</u> treaties facilitate the transfer of criminals between countries.		犯罪人**引渡し**に関する条約は、国家間の犯罪者の移送を容易にする。
2050	**appellee (of final appeal)** [æpəlí]		**被上告人**
	The <u>appellee of the final appeal</u> defended the lower court's decision.		**被上告人**は、下級審の判決を擁護した。
2051	**right of rebuttal (to rebut)**		**否認権（嫡出否認）**
	If a husband acknowledges a child to be his child in wedlock after the child is born, he loses the <u>right to rebut</u> the presumption of the child in wedlock.		夫は、子の出生後において、その嫡出であることを承認したときは、その**否認権**を失う。
2052	**uncertain due date**		**不確定期限**
	If an <u>uncertain due date</u> is assigned to the performance of an obligation, the obligor is liable for delay from the time when the obligor receives the request for performance after the due date arrives.		債務の履行について**不確定期限**があるときは、債務者は、その期限の到来した後に履行の請求を受けた時から、遅滞の責任を負う。
2053	**right of reproduction**		**複製権**
	The <u>right of reproduction</u> is protected under copyright laws.		**複製権**は、著作権法で保護されている。
2054	**copy** [ká:pi]		**複製物**
	The author of a cinematographic work has the exclusive right to distribute <u>copies</u> of that cinematographic work.		著作者は、その映画の著作物をその**複製物**により頒布する権利を専有する。
2055	**accession** [əkséʃən]		**①付合、②到達（相続や遺贈の承認の場合）**
	If the distinction of principal and accessory cannot be made between the movables united by accession, the owner of each movable property co-owns the composite thing in proportion to the respective price current at the time of the <u>accession</u>.		付合した動産について主従の区別をすることができないときは、各動産の所有者は、その**付合**の時における価格の割合に応じてその合成物を共有する。

RANK 4

2056	**supplementary provisions**	附則
	Beyond what is prescribed between Article 2 to the preceding Article of these **supplementary provisions**, necessary transitional measures connected with the coming into effect of this Act are provided for by cabinet order.	**附則**第2条から前条までに定めるもののほか、この法律の施行に関して必要な経過措置は、政令で定める。
2057	**legacy with burden**	負担付遺贈
	A **legacy with burden** comes with obligations for the beneficiary.	**負担付遺贈**には、受益者の義務が伴う。
2058	**gift with burden**	負担付贈与
	A **gift with burden** requires the recipient to fulfill certain conditions.	**負担付贈与**は、受け取る側が一定の条件を充足する必要がある。
2059	**third person collateral provider**	物上保証人（末尾㊱参照）
	The court may not make a judicial decision relying on prescription unless a party (in the case of extinctive prescription, including a **third person collateral provider**) invokes it.	時効は、当事者（消滅時効にあっては、**物上保証人**を含む。）が援用しなければ、裁判所がこれによって裁判をすることができない。
2060	**third person mortgagor**	物上保証人（末尾㊱参照）
	The **third person mortgagor** provides a mortgage to secure another's loan.	**物上保証人**は、他人のローンを担保するために抵当権を提供する。
2061	**third person pledgor**	物上保証人（末尾㊱参照）
	A **third person pledgor** pledges assets on behalf of another's debt.	**物上保証人**は、他人の債務に代わって財物を質入れする。
2062	**real estate appraiser**	不動産鑑定士
	A **real estate appraiser** evaluates the value of property.	**不動産鑑定士**は、不動産の価値を評価する。
2063	**pledge of real property**	不動産質
	The **pledge of real property** secures a loan with land or buildings.	**不動産質**は、土地又は建物を担保に融資を行うものである。
2064	**real property income**	不動産所得
	Real property income includes rent from owned property.	**不動産所得**には、所有不動産からの賃料が含まれる。
2065	**duty to support**	扶養義務
	The **duty to support** family members is legally recognized.	家族の**扶養義務**が、法的に認められている。
2066	**average wage**	平均賃金
	The **average wage** is a significant economic indicator.	**平均賃金**は、重要な経済指標である。

2067	**legal professional corporation**	**弁護士法人**
	A legal professional corporation offers specialized legal services.	弁護士法人は、専門的な法律サービスを提供する。
2068	**patent attorney**	**弁理士**
	A patent attorney specializes in intellectual property law.	弁理士は、知的財産法を専門とする。
2069	**universal legacy**	**包括遺贈**
	Universal legacy involves inheriting the entire estate.	包括遺贈は、全財産を相続させることである。
2070	**right of broadcasting**	**放送権**
	The right of broadcasting is protected under copyright laws.	放送権は、著作権法で保護されている。
2071	**observation** [ɑ̀ːbzərvéɪʃən]	**傍聴**
	Observation of court proceedings is open to the public.	裁判の傍聴は、一般に公開されている。
2072	**audience** [ɑ́ːdiəns]	**傍聴人**
	The audience listened intently to the legal arguments presented.	傍聴人は、提示された法的論拠に熱心に耳を傾けた。
2073	**civil fruits**	**法定果実**
	Civil fruits are benefits derived from property ownership, like rent.	法定果実とは、家賃のように所有権から得られる利益のことである。
2074	**statutory superficies**	**法定地上権**
	If the land and a building on that land belong to the same owner, a mortgage is created with respect to that land, and the enforcement of that mortgage causes them to belong to different owners, statutory superficies has been created.	土地及びその上に存する建物が同一の所有者に属する場合において、その土地につき抵当権が設定され、その実行により所有者を異にするに至ったときは、法定地上権が設定される。
2075	**insurance contract**	**保険契約**
	An insurance contract outlines coverage and compensation terms.	保険契約は、補償範囲と補償条件を概説するものである。
2076	**insurance contract holder**	**保険契約者**
	The insurance contract holder is entitled to the benefits of the policy.	保険契約者は、保険金を受け取る権利がある。
2077	**insurance broker**	**保険仲立人**
	An insurance broker acts as an intermediary between insurers and clients.	保険仲立人は、保険会社と顧客の仲介役を務める。

RANK 4

#	英語	日本語
2078	**probation** [prəbéɪʃən] Probation offers an alternative to incarceration for certain offenders.	保護観察 保護観察は、特定の犯罪者に投獄に代わる方法を提供する。
2079	**curator** [kjʊréɪtər] A person subject to a decision for commencement of curatorship becomes a person under curatorship, and a curator is appointed for that person.	保佐人 保佐開始の審判を受けた者は、被保佐人とし、これに保佐人を付する。
2080	**adaptation** [æ̀dəptéɪʃən] Adaptation involves adjusting copyrighted material for new uses.	翻案 翻案とは、著作権で保護された素材を新たな用途のために修正することである。
2081	**prepaid payment instrument** The term "issuer of prepaid payment instruments" means: (i) an issuer of prepaid payment instruments for its own business; and (ii) an issuer of prepaid payment instruments for third-party business.	前払式支払手段 「前払式支払手段発行者」とは、(i) 自家型発行者及び (ii) 第三者型発行者をいう。
2082	**discharge** [dɪstʃɑ́ːrdʒ] Discharge of a debt releases the debtor from further obligation.	免責 債務の免責により、債務者は、債務から解放される。
2083	**divulge** [dɪvʌ́ldʒ] To divulge confidential information breaches laws.	漏らす 機密情報を漏らすことは、法律に違反する。
2084	**kidnapping (by enticement)** Kidnapping by enticement involves luring someone away with deceptive promises.	誘拐 誘拐は、人を欺く約束で誘い出す。
2085	**paid leave** An employer must grant paid leave of 10 working days to a worker.	有給休暇 使用者は、労働者に対して、10労働日の有給休暇を与えなければならない。
2086	**gist** [dʒíst] The gist of the argument was clear and concise.	要旨 議論の要旨は、明確で簡潔だった。
2087	**uncharged offense** An uncharged offense has not led to formal charges.	余罪 余罪は、正式な告発には至っていない。

RANK 4

2088	**prepayment** [pripéɪmənt]	予納
	The petitioner must <u>prepay</u> the amount that the court clerk establishes as the expenses needed for civil enforcement proceedings.	申立人は、民事執行の手続に必要な費用として裁判所書記官の定める金額を<u>予納</u>しなければならない。
2089	**preliminary** [prɪlímənèri]	予備的
	<u>Preliminary</u> discussions set the stage for formal negotiations.	<u>予備的</u>な話し合いが、正式な交渉の段階へつながる。
2090	**successful bidder**	落札者
	The <u>successful bidder</u> was awarded the contract.	<u>落札者</u>が、契約を獲得した。
2091	**securitization** [sɪkjɜ̀rətəzéɪʃən]	流動化、証券化
	<u>Securitization</u> involves converting assets into marketable securities.	<u>証券化</u>には、資産を市場性のある証券に転換することが含まれる。
2092	**repeated convictions**	累犯
	<u>Repeated convictions</u> can result in harsher sentences.	<u>累犯</u>には、より厳しい判決が下される可能性がある。
2093	**divulgation** [dìvəlgéɪʃən]	漏えい ※動詞はdivulge（2083参照）である。
	<u>Divulgation</u> of secrets without consent is illegal.	同意なしに秘密を<u>漏えい</u>することは違法である。
2094	**detention in workhouse in lieu of payment of fine**	労役場留置
	<u>Detention in workhouse in lieu of payment of fine</u> offers an alternative to fines.	<u>労役場留置</u>は、罰金に代わるものである。
2095	**labor relations commission**	労働委員会
	The <u>labor relations commission</u> mediates disputes between employers and employees.	<u>労働委員会</u>は、雇用者と被雇用者の間の紛争を調停する。
2096	**labor standard**	労働基準
	<u>Labor standard</u> laws regulate work conditions.	<u>労働基準</u>法は、労働条件を規制する。
2097	**labor standards office**	労働基準監督署
	The <u>labor standards office</u> enforces employment laws.	<u>労働基準監督署</u>は、労働法を執行する。
2098	**industrial accident**	労働災害
	The <u>industrial accident</u> resulted in significant injuries to workers.	この<u>労働災害</u>により、労働者は大きな負傷を負った。

RANK 4

2099	**working hour**	労働時間
	Working hours are generally limited to 8 hours per day by law.	労働時間は、原則として法律で1日8時間に制限されている。
2100	**industrial accident compensation insurance**	労働者災害補償保険
	Industrial accident compensation insurance covers injuries sustained on the job.	労働災害補償保険は、仕事中の怪我を補償する。
2101	**labor insurance**	労働保険
	Labor insurance provides benefits for work-related accidents and illnesses.	労働保険は、業務上の事故や病気に対する給付を行うものである。
2102	**order in lieu of settlement**	和解に代わる決定
	The order in lieu of settlement expedited the resolution of the dispute.	和解に代わる決定は、紛争の解決を早めた。

RANK 4

法務省の資料(※)に基づく36の類義語知識

(※) 法令用語日英標準対訳辞書

- ❶法務省によれば、the other party/other parties（一般的用法）、opposite party（一般的用法）、counterparty（契約などの相手方）、opponent（対審手続の場合）、adverse party（対立当事者の場合）となる。
- ❷法務省によれば、knowingly（単なる認識を含む場合）、maliciously（害意に近い意味の場合）、迷った場合はin bad faithとなる。
- ❸法務省によれば、delegating party（委託者）、settlor（信託の委託者）、entrustor（その他の事務の委託）、consignor（販売・運送等の委託）となる。
- ❹法務省によれば、unlawfulとillegalは原則同義であるが、illegalは法令違反、unlawfulは公序良俗に反するなどの理由により効果不発生となる。
- ❺法務省によれば、「事務所」「事業所」「事業場」などの物理的な営業が行われる場所はbusiness office、商人の営業の本拠はplace of businessとなる。
- ❻法務省によれば、原則としてcreditor、不動産・物品の場合lessor、金銭の場合lenderとなる。
- ❼法務省によれば、原則としてdebtor、金銭の場合borrower、不動産・物品の場合lesseeとなる。
- ❽法務省によれば、原則company auditor。例外的にauditorも可。しかし、日本監査役協会は、監査役制度の正しい理解を促進するために「Audit & Supervisory Board Member」を推奨している。筆者の経験上、主要国（米国含む。）においては法務省訳が通じない場面が多く、言い換えに賛同する。
- ❾法務省によれば、通常はvictim、民事の場合「aggrieved party」、対として使う場合はinjuring partyとinjured partyとなる。
- ❿法務省によれば、prosecutionは公訴の提起から公判維持活動を含む訴追活動の全過程を意味し、indictmentはアメリカで大陪審起訴を指すため、日本法の「起訴」には用いるべきではない。
- ⓫法務省によれば、原則としてright to reimbursement、保証人の求償権はright to indemnification、賠償責任に係る求償権はright to remedy overとなる。ただし、不法行為に関する条文では「right to reimbursement」が使われていることもある。
- ⓬法務省によれば、事実問題・法律問題を考慮して得られた結論に用いる（司法判断や行政判断にも使われる。）。
- ⓭法務省は、残念ながら、当該単語の使い分けについての詳細な説明を提供していない。また、accountabilityは会社法では「説明責任」として用いられている。
- ⓮法務省によれば、原則としてcease to be effective、期限満了についてはexpireとなる。

- ☐ ⑮ 法務省によれば、債権一般、特に金銭債権の場合はobligee、倒産法の場合はcreditorとなる。
- ☐ ⑯ 法務省によれば、司法の作用を強調する場合はjudicial proceedings、裁判所という機関の手続きに焦点を当てる場合はcourt proceedingsとなる。
- ☐ ⑰ 法務省によれば、一般的な場合はprescription、刑事の公訴時効や刑の時効の場合はstatute of limitationsとなる。
- ☐ ⑱ 法務省によれば、権利の主張はclaim、事実の主張はassertion、刑事訴訟における主張はallegation、一般にはargumentが使われる。
- ☐ ⑲ 法務省によれば、原則としてtransfer、財産権の譲渡はassignment、証券の譲渡はnegotiationとなる。
- ☐ ⑳ 法務省によれば、原則としてtransferor、財産権の譲渡はassignorとなる。
- ☐ ㉑ 法務省によれば、存在や権利の消滅一般はextinction、期間満了による消滅はexpiration、債務の弁済や契約解除・取消による消滅はextinguishment、権利や知的財産権の消滅はlapseとなる。
- ☐ ㉒ 法務省によれば、有罪判決はconviction、訴訟上認定される事実に関する裁判官の心証はdeterminationとなる。しかし、民事訴訟法第247条の「自由な心証により」の英訳には、based on its freedom of personal convictionが使われている。
- ☐ ㉓ 法務省によれば、原本と同義の場合はoriginal、謄本として権限者が作成したものはauthenticated copyとなる。
- ☐ ㉔ 法務省によれば、原則として訴訟・訴えにはlitigationを用いる。
- ☐ ㉕ 法務省によれば、仮定の条件を示す場合はif、確実な条件を示す場合はwhen、繰り返しが予想される場合はwheneverを使う。なお、「とき」は条件を意味し、2つの条件が続く場合は大きな条件に「場合」、小さな条件に「とき」を使う。
- ☐ ㉖ 法務省によれば、判決一般はjudgment、有罪判決はsentence、有罪判決かつ刑の免除を含む場合はjudgment of convictionとなる。
- ☐ ㉗ 法務省によれば、債務の保証人はguarantor、株式の発行者はsubscriber、証券の引受者はunderwriter、手形等はacceptorとなる。
- ☐ ㉘ 法務省によれば、原則としてwrongful、違法・非合法の場合はunlawful、不公正の場合はunfair、無権限の場合はunauthorizedとなる。
- ☐ ㉙ 法務省によれば、原則としてprovisional seizure、債権の場合はprovisional garnishment、有体物の場合はprovisional attachmentとなる。
- ☐ ㉚ 法務省によれば、日本の公証人は大陸法系であるためnotaryとし、英米法系のnotary publicと区別する。
- ☐ ㉛ 法務省によれば、民法上の委任契約はmandatary、権限の委任はdelegateeとなる。
- ☐ ㉜ 法務省によれば、提出期限はperiod for submission、証拠等の期限はperiod for production、攻撃防御方法の期限はperiod for advancementとなる。

- □㉝法務省によれば、動作はexpert examination、証拠方法の類型としてはexpert testimony、鑑定結果に重きを置く場合はexpert opinionとなる。
- □㉞法務省によれば、公務員が適法に作成した証書はauthentic instrument、公証人が作成したものはnotarial instrumentとなるが、刑法上では「notarized deeds」として翻訳されている場合がある。
- □㉟法務省によれば、ex officioは「職務上当然に、職権で」を意味し、sua sponteは「自発的に裁量で」を意味する。
- □㊱法務省によれば、抵当権はthird person mortgagor、質権はthird person pledgor、抵当権・質権以外はthird person collateral providerとなる。しかし、実際の条文では、third-party collateral providerが用いられていることもある（例：民法第145条）。

英 語 索 引

A

a class of shares	99
a court in charge of an appeal	143
a foreign currency denominated bond	185
a third party in good faith	43
abandonment (abandon)	180
abetment	79
abettor	138
ability to pay	94
abolish	166
absorption-type company split	79
absorption-type merger	79
abuse of right	20
acceptance	36
(criminal) acceptance of bribe	150
acceptance of final appeal	152
acceptor	168
access to information	101
accession	211
accessory	150, 201
accessoryship	171
accident	28
accident insurance	202
accomplice	80
accord and satisfaction	109
account	12
accountability	41
accounting	6
accounting advisor	72
accounting books	7
accounting period	83
accounting title	77
accusation	90
accused	58
acknowledgment	113
acknowledgment of claim	40
acknowledgment of parentage	210
acquisition of a business	93
acquisition or loss (of rights)	165
acquisitive prescription	151
acquittal	120
act	20
Act	61
act for value	175
act of dispute	204
act of endowment	190
act that would harm creditors	90
action	5
action by the subrogee	145
action for declaratory judgment	74
action for future performance	153
action for judicial review of administrative disposition	143
action for maintenance of possession	158
action for preservation of possession	158
action for recovery of possession	158
action for rescission of fraudulent act	146
action for retrial	197
action for revocation of administrative disposition	166
action for revocation of original administrative disposition	154
action on checks	195
action to enforce liability	204
action to oppose execution	156
actions on bills and notes	208
actual delivery	84
actual enrichment	84, 142
adaptation	214
addition of claim	106
additional tax	187
additional tax for under report	187
address	32
adjudication of somebody's disappearance	199
administration	15
administrative appeal	80
administrative authority	79
administrative case litigation	79
administrative determination	90
administrative disposition	15
administrative guidance	15
administrative monetary penalty	74
administrative organ	15
administrative procedure	80
administrator of an estate	158
admission	31
admonition	131
adopted child	175
adoption	175, 185
adult	156

adult ward	157
adverse disposition	117
adverse party	68
adviser	144
affiliated company	13
affinity	183
affixing the name and seal	14
after the passage of a period (of time)	78
age of majority	41
agency	46
agent	47
aggrieved party	167
agreement	20
agreement limiting liability	106
agricultural cooperative	210
aircraft and railway accidents investigation commission	193
alien registration	131
all oral arguments and the result of the examination of evidence	22
allegation	33
allegation and evidence	143
alleged facts of crime	115
allocate	180
allotment of share option without contribution	104
allotment of share without contribution	75
allotment without contribution	174
alteration	73
alternative obligation	157
amended return	200
amendment act	131
amendment of claim	128
amortization	192
amount of contribution	191
amount of stated capital	95
amount to be paid in	57
and	6
annex	116
annual general meeting	50
annual securities report	174
annual shareholders meeting	50
(written) answer	52
apparent authority	169
apparent manager	168
apparent representative director	116
apparent representative executive officer	169
appeal	117
(final) appeal	35
appeal (to the court of second instance)	21
appeal against (a disposition of) execution	199
appeal from/against a ruling	86
appeal pertaining to provisional remedy	173
appeal with permission	191
appearance	98
appellant	88
appellant (of final appeal)	152
appellee	168
appellee (of final appeal)	211
applicable penal statute	167
applicant	33
application	33
apply mutatis mutandis	34
appointment	43
appraisal rights	73
appropriation	32
appropriation of profit	122
appropriation of surplus	103
approval	36
approval or disapproval	113
appurtenance	201
arbitral award	162
arbitral tribunal	111
arbitration	110
arbitration agreement	110
arbitration committee member	162
arbitration procedure	111
arbitrator	111
argument	33
arrangement (arrange)	180
arrest	46
arrest warrant	161
arrester	161
arrival	52
arson	171
Article	34
article left behind	183
articles of endowment	190
articles of incorporation	49
as a result of	13
ascertainment	187
(criminal) assault	171
assembly	78
assembly (council)	136
assertion	33
assessment	147
assets	25
assets disclosure procedure	145

assignee	64
assignment	36
assignment order	208
assignor	36
assistance, support	130
assistant	119
assistant in court	172
assistant judge	210
association or foundation without legal personality	154
assumption	100
assumption (of office)	32
assumption of obligation	26
attaching creditor	92
attachment	27
attainment	165
attempt	120
attorney (at law)	60
auction	17
auction applicant	83
audience	213
audit	84
audit certification	134
audit committee	134
audit committee member	76
audit corporation	134
audit report	77
authentic	105
authentic instrument (notarized deeds)	144
authenticated copy	41
author	49
authority	18
authority to ask for clarification	95
authorization to exploit	123
automatic public transmission	199
automatic public transmission server	199
average wage	212
avoid	73
award	146

B

bail	119
bailee	97
bailment	136
bailor	137
balance sheet	109
bank note (money bill)	200
bankrupt	167
bankruptcy	56
bankruptcy creditor	167
bankruptcy proceedings	167
bankruptcy trustee	167
bar association	171
based on	55
basic personal exemption	189
be appointed from among	68
be in office	91
be not required to	39
be present in court	146
be prohibited	30
be subject to a fine	56
bear	60
bearer	147
become effective	23
become final and binding	8
beneficial interest	96
beneficiary	97
beneficiary certificates	201
benefit of prescription	198
benevolent intervention in another's affairs	149
bequest	182
bid	210
bid rigging	210
bidding process	210
bigamy	200
bilateral contract	205
bill	13
binding	88
binding effect	21
blue return	180
board of company auditors	12
board of directors	54
board of liquidators	156
body search	203
(corporate) bond	32
bond (certificate)	24
bond administrator	95
bond register	149
bond with share option	104
bondholder	96
bondholders meeting	96
book-entry	171
books and documents	111
borrower	11
borrowings	75
boundary	190
branch office	30
breach	3

breach of duty of loyalty	114
bribe	123
brief	34
bring to (physical escort)	127
broker	166
brokerage	110
budget	64
building coverage ratio	193
burden of risk	136
business	5
business accounting standards generally accepted as fair and appropriate	69
business for profit	71
business income	198
business office	5
business report	129
business transfer	93
business year	5
by filing an action	70

C

cabinet decision	187
cabinet meeting	187
Cabinet Office Order	54
Cabinet Order	65
calling	72
can be asserted against	108
cancellation	72
(legal) capacity (to act)	85
(legal) capacity (to hold rights)	84
capacity to accept/receive	151
capacity to be a party	164
capacity to sue or be sued	107
capital	31
capital adequacy ratio	198
capital gain	101
capital investor	97
capital reserve	95
cargo	129
cargo insurance	184
carrier	129
carry forward	82
category of evidence	100
cause attributable to (someone)	42
caused by	13
causing death	162
cease and desist order	114
cease to be effective	23
censorship	141

Central Labour Relations Commission	207
certificate	35
certificate of execution	94
certificate of registered information	51
certificate of status of residence	198
certification	55
certified care worker	186
certified date	9
certified public accountant	88
certified public tax accountant	204
certify	166
chairperson	14
challenge	190
change of date	136
Chapter	34
charged fact	21
charged offense	27
charging instrument	136
check	195
chemical substance	187
Chief Prosecutor	192
child born in wedlock	207
child born out of wedlock	207
childcare leave	181
cinematographic work(s)	184
circumstances	101
circumstances that afford special credibility	209
citation (cite)	130
civil fine	76
civil fruits	213
civil suit	63
claim	24, 33, 40
claim for extinguishment of mortgage	208
claim that may arise in the future	154
claims	112
class share	34
class shareholder	34
clearing	141
clearing organization	204
clerk	154
close	166
close relative	191
Code	61
coercion	191
cognizance (acknowledgment of a claim)	113
collateral	109
collection of delinquent payment	207
collection of evidence	100

collective agreement	177	competent minister	151
collective bargaining	206	competitive position	80
collude	49	compilation	171
commercial act(s)	100	complaint	45
commercial custom	34	complaint processing	82
commercial register	34	completion of liquidation	156
commercial registration	34	compliance obligation	151
commission	103	complicity	139
commission merchant	208	compulsion	140
commit	6	compulsory auction	15
Commodity Derivatives Transaction Act	153	compulsory execution	15
commodity exchange	153	compulsory performance	15
commodity futures transaction	153	computation of a period of time	136
commodity investment management	153	concealment (conceal)	127
common interests of the creditors	90	conclusion of oral argument	22
common-benefit claim	138	condition	35
company	7	condition at will	203
company auditor	12	condition precedent	111
company disappearing in a consolidation-type merger	155	condition subsequent	72
		conduct	20
company disappearing in an absorption-type merger	137	confession	31
		confirmation	9
company incorporated in a consolidation-type merger	155	conflict	50
		conflict of interests	64
company incorporated in an incorporation-type split	155	confusion / merger	196
		consent	36
company split	8	consider	104
company splitting in an incorporation-type split	155	consideration	46
		consign	69
company surviving an absorption-type merger	137	consignee	97
		consignor	3
company with accounting advisor(s)	131	consolidated financial statements	176
company with audit and supervisory committee	76	consolidated subsidiary company	176
		consolidation	118
company with board of company auditors	77	consolidation of shares	75
company with board of directors	113	consolidation-type merger	105
company with class shares	99	consolidation-type merger agreement	155
company with committees	126	conspire	163
company with company auditor(s)	77	Constitution	19
company with financial auditor(s)	130	constructive robbery	198
company with nominating committee, etc.	95	constructive transfer with retention of possession	107
comparative negligence	9	consultation	79
compelling reason	121	consumer	101
compensation	61	consumer contract	101
compensation committee	118	contamination	185
compensation for absence from work	190	continuation	160
compensation for loss or damage	46	contract	18
compensation for private sound and visual recording	199	contract for value	175
		contract for work	4
competent government agency	151		

contractor	5
contravention	127
contribute	30
contribution	138
contribution in kind	84
control	31
control of court proceedings	159
convention	102
conviction	105
convocation notice	100
co-owners	81
co-ownership	81
co-ownership interest	139
coprincipal (in crime)	138
copy	211
(certified) copy	52
copyright	48
copyright holder	48
coroner's inspection	192
corporation	61
correction	21
corresponding day	130
corruption	6
cost	59
council system	143
counsel	45
count	107
counterclaim	115
counterfeit	78
counterparty	68
coupon	175
court	62
court clerk	91
court costs	45
court execution officer	148
court of first instance	46
court of prior instance	192
court of second instance	88
court proceedings	25
court with jurisdiction	12
creator	143
creator of a design	181
credit rating	155
credit union	156
creditor	9, 24
creditor who has an objection	181
creditor's (obligee's) right of subrogation	90
crime	57
criminal	114
criminal complaint	24

criminal prosecution	83
cumulative voting	176
curator	214
currency	49
custodian	77
custody (care)	134
custom	135
customary law	135
customs	77

D

damage	45
dangerous driving	189
date for oral argument	22
date for scheduling conference	105
date of payment	31
day corresponding to...	71
de facto	29
death penalty	28
debt	26
debt instrument payable to bearer	174
debtor	11, 26
deceased (dead person)	198
decedent	168
decentralization	162
deception or other wrongful act	127
deception or other wrongful means	127
decision	18
decision of transfer	182
declaration	43
deduction	144
deemed	78
deemed daily wage amount	174
defamation	120
default	26
defect	9
defective manifestation of intention	133
defendant	58
(affirmative) defense	23
defense counsel	60
defense of debtor's solvency	192
defense of demand	145
defense of simultaneous performance	52
definition	49
definitive registration	120
degree of kinship	155
delay	110
delay damages	110
delay in payment	94

delay in performance	122
delayed interest	110
delegate	3
delegatee	98
delegating party	126
delegation	3, 126
delegation of powers	97
deletion	27
deliberation	138
delivery	89
demand	24
demand by litigation	146
demand for a share(, etc.) cash-out	133
demand procedure	209
demotion	144
denial	13, 16
deportation	204
deposit	122
(security) deposit	119
deposit of fungibles	153
deposit with an official depository	80
depreciable assets	192
depreciation	141
derivatives transaction	163
description of evidence	100
design	181
design right	181
destruction	128
detailed regulations	91
detention	86, 201
detention for (expert) examination	189
detention in workhouse in lieu of payment of fine	215
detention warrant	144
determination	38
determination of the price	132
developing area	186
diagnosis	105
digest	175
diminished capacity	154
direct control (over things)	103
direct examination	97
direction	28
director	54
director at incorporation	157
disability pension	202
disadvantageous fact	117
disappearing company	102
disaster of extreme severity	191
disaster recovery project	196

discharge	214
disciplinary action	48
discipline committee	193
disclosure	7
discontinuance	79
discovery	7
discretionary investment contract	164
discretionary provision	113
discriminatory treatment	92
dismissal	7, 13
dismissal by a bar to prosecution	174
dismissal of prosecution	21
dispersion (disperse)	131
disposal	166
disposal by a sale en bloc	182
disposition	37
disposition of delinquency	206
dispute	60
dispute resolution organization	60
disputing party	180
disqualification	141
dissenting shareholder	115
dissolution	7
distribution	117
distribution of profits and losses	45
district court	48
dividend	55
dividend income	210
dividend of surplus	103
divisible claim	171
divisible obligation	117
division of estate	69
divorce	123
divorce by agreement	79
divulgation	215
divulge	214
document of title	174
documentary evidence	103
does not preclude	39
domestic	24
domestic corporation	113
domestic source income	195
domicile	32
donation	44
donee	150
donor	45
dormant company	137
dual criminal liability provision	123
due care of a prudent manager	44
due date	61

duly assert against	108
durable years	161
duress	139
duty	14
duty of care	48
duty of confidentiality	59
duty to support	212

E

effect	23
effective date	41
election	43
electronic or magnetic record	163
electronic public notice	163
electronic signature	163
embezzlement	6
employee	32, 123
employee invention	103
employees pension insurance	87
employer	35
enable the escape (to escape)	128
enactment	106
endorsement	184
endorser	184
enforcement	30
enforcement judgment (execution judgment)	148
Enforcement Order	42
Enforcement Regulation	41
enjoyment	139
enterprise for profit	70
entity conversion	205
entrust	3
entrustee	97
entrustment	3
entrustment of operation	16
entrustor	69
entry of a name change	174
epidemiological survey	185
equitable distribution	90
equity	121
equity capital	93
equity interest	121
equity investor	97
establishment	106
estate	69
etc.	2
evacuation	47
evade	190
eviction	68
evidence	35
ex officio	202
examination	19
examination of a witness	36
examination of applications	151
examination of evidence	35
examination of evidence by court's own authority	103
exceeding	66
except	66
exchange	11
exclusive (patent) license	158
exclusive (trademark) license	158
exclusive jurisdiction	107
execution	30
execution court	148
execution of business	80
execution of provisional remedy	173
executive	80
executive agency	148
executive director	81
executive officer	94
executor	126
exemption	51, 120
exemptions	63
exercise	21
exercise of appraisal rights	74
expedited trial proceedings	160
expenditure	93
expense	59
expenses for common benefit	138
expert	135
expert advisor	204
expert examination	135
expert opinion	135
expert testimony	135
expert witness	189
expiration	37
expiration of a period (of time)	78
expire	23
extension of a security interest to the proceeds of the collateral	170
extinction	102
extinctive prescription	102
extinguishment	102
extortion	138
extra wages	151
extract	102
extradition	211

extreme ... 182

F

fact finding ... 29
facts ... 29
facts to be proved ... 102
fair ... 21
fair competition ... 87
fair practice ... 87
fair trade ... 87
fall under any of ... 55
false manifestation of intention ... 81
false statement ... 170
falsify ... 133
family company ... 165
family court ... 74
family employees of a blue return taxpayer ... 180
family register ... 196
fatal ... 207
filiation ... 210
filing of an objection ... 126
filing of proofs of claims ... 145
final and binding judgment ... 8
final appellate court ... 152
final judgment ... 96
final order ... 96
financial audit report ... 72
financial auditor ... 6
financial institution ... 140
financial instruments ... 82
financial instruments business ... 82
financial instruments business operator ... 140
financial instruments exchange ... 82
financial instruments firms association ... 140
financial instruments intermediary service ... 140
financial statements ... 17, 26
find particularly necessary ... 209
fine ... 56
fingerprint ... 149
fire caused by negligence ... 147
fire insurance ... 187
fire spread ... 185
first day ... 104
first sentence ... 43
fiscal year ... 7
fiscal year end ... 18
fixed asset tax ... 196
fixed due date ... 132
fixed-term labor contract ... 78
fixing amount of court costs ... 205
fixtures ... 163
focused examination of witnesses and parties ... 96
for (the purpose of) profit ... 6
force ... 81, 127
force majeure ... 59
foreign company ... 72
foreign corporation ... 7
foreign country ... 7
foreign law joint enterprise ... 186
foreign lawyer ... 186
foreign national ... 7
foreign tax credit ... 186
foresee ... 64
foreseeability ... 175
forgery ... 79
form ... 58
former act ... 137
forwarding agency ... 184
foundation ... 78
fraud ... 27
freight ... 184
freight (charge) ... 129
freight forwarder ... 129
fruits ... 74
fund ... 28
fund settlement ... 147
fundamental human rights ... 14

G

gambling ... 209
general conditions ... 64
general consumers ... 3
general incorporated association ... 127
general incorporated foundation ... 182
general meeting (of members) ... 95
general meeting of class shareholders ... 99
general partnership company ... 89
general period for payment ... 183
general priority claim ... 182
general provisions ... 44
general safety and health supervisor ... 184
general statutory lien ... 127
general successor ... 69
general venue ... 117
gift ... 45

gift on donor's death	198
gift tax	205
gift with burden	212
gist	214
give	81
good faith acquisition	42, 159
good faith principle (principle of good faith)	154
goods	37
governing law	34
government	157
government contract	157
grace of payment	31
grand bench	161
grant	16
gratuitously	120
gross income	71
gross negligence	32
grounds	92
guarantee	62
guarantee contract	62
guarantee obligation	62
guarantor	58
guardian	194
guardian of adult	157
guardianship	193
guideline	29
guilty	64

H

harm	73
have an exclusive right	85
head office	62
health	130
health committee	184
healthy and cultured living	192
hearing	38
heavy additional tax	200
heir	107
hereinafter referred to as "…"	2
hereinafter the same applies in this …	126
high court	22
hold	119
holder	103
holder of a design right	181
holder of share less than one (share) unit	109
holding company	121
holograph	148
homicide	28

householder	204
human rights	38

I

identity verification	120
if	53
illegal	4
illegal conduct	4
illness	199
immediate appeal from/against a ruling	159
immediately	47
immediately following Article	29
immediately following paragraph	29
immediately preceding Article	43
immediately preceding paragraph	43
imminent and unlawful infringement	137
impartial	87
impartiality	165
impeachment	206
imperial order	207
implementation	30
impose	10
impossibility of performance	122
imprisonment	48
imprisonment without work	16
improvement measure	73
in a fair and sincere manner	144
in bad faith	68
in case of urgency	190
in good faith	40
in good faith and without gross negligence	43
in lieu of	54
in public	88
in the course of trade	80
in writing	37
inability to pay debts (as they become due)	31
inaction	116
incidental	117
income	149
income tax	203
incoming sentenced person	183
incorporated association	149
incorporated foundation	146
incorporation	42
incorporation-type company split	105
incorporation-type company split plan	155
incorporator	62

Term	Page
incur	60
independence	53
indication	116
indirect compulsory execution	77
individual	24
individual rehabilitation commissioner	196
indivisible claim	169
indivisible obligation	169
inducement	138
industrial accident	215
industrial accident compensation insurance	216
industrial property right	86
influence	180
information and communications technology	153
information for personal identification	144
infringement	38
infringement lawsuit	154
inhabitant	33
inhabitants tax	150
inhabited building	142
inheritance	44
injured party	13, 115
injuring party	132
injury	152
injury and disease allowance	202
inland bill of lading	188
inquiry	99
inquiry to opponent	112
insanity	155
insolvency	26
inspection	19
inspection organization	192
inspector	135
installment (amount)	171
installment payments	117
installment sales	133
instigation of foreign aggression	185
institution of prosecution	14
instrument	35
instrument evidencing claims	145
insurance	119
insurance agent	172
insurance broker	213
insurance business	172
insurance contract	213
insurance contract holder	213
insurance policy	172
insurance premium	172
insurance proceeds	172
insurance sales	172
insured	168
insurer	172
intent	2
intention	20
interest	65
interest on tax refund	189
interested party	122
interested person	122
interim conference procedure	136
interim dividend	162
interlocutory confirmation suit	162
interlocutory judgment	162
intermediation	110
intermediation for financial instruments	140
international application	144
interpretation	8
interpreter	49
interrogation	38
intervenor	147
intervention	159
intervention as independent party	209
interview	42
intimidation	139
invention	114
inventor	114
inventory of assets	90
investigation	107
investigation and allowance of claims	145
investigation into violation	4
investment	164
investment advisory business	164
investment advisory contract	164
investment business limited partnership	164
investment corporation	165
investment equities	164
investment management business	164
investment report	70
investment trust	165
investor	164
invocation	71
inward direct investment	161
irreparable damage	73
is in violation of the applicable laws and regulations or the articles of incorporation	118
is presumed	39
issuance	89
issue	56

issue of new shares	38
issue price	56
issued shares	56
issuer	56
item	20

J

Japan Federation of Bar Associations	209
Japanese Government Bonds	195
joint and several obligation	176
joint and several obligor	176
joint and several suretyship	176
joint guarantor	139
joint mortgage	139
joint revolving mortgage	191
joint suit	138
joint tort	139
joint venture	89
jointly and severally	65
judge	25
judgment	57
judgment of conviction	57
judgment on the merits	62
judicial commissioner	200
judicial divorce	197
judicial police personnel	200
judicial precedent	57
judicial proceedings	25
judicial research official	197
juridical person	62
jurisdiction	11
jurisdiction by appearance	71
justifiable	40
juvenile	202
juvenile training school	202

K

kidnapping (by enticement)	214
knowingly	2
known creditor	104

L

label (labeling)	169
labor contract	65
labor dispute	177
labor insurance	216
labor relations commission	215
labor standard	215
labor standards office	215
labor tribunal decision	177
labor union	123
lack of jurisdiction	76
land leasehold right	149
landowner	53
lapse	37
large company	108
large volume holding	161
law	61
lawful	50
laws and regulations	62
lawsuit	45
lease	10
leave the court	206
legacy	182
legacy with burden	212
legal	50
legal apprentice	200
legal professional corporation	213
legally reserved portion (statutory reserved share)	127
legatee	149
legitimate	40
legitimate grounds	41
lend	10
lender	9
less than	63
lessee	11
lessor	9
lethal	207
letter of credit	105
liability	41
license	63
life imprisonment without work	174
life insurance	157
light vehicle	191
likelihood	71
limited liability business partnership	175
limited liability company	88
limited liability partner	175
limited partnership company	86
limited to	54
liquidated damages	46
liquidating distribution	114
liquidating stock company	203
liquidation	106
liquidator	156
list of holders of dischargeable claims	90

listed company	36
litigation	45
litigation representative	45
loan	9
loan (for consumption)	101
loan claim	9
loan for use	101
loan trust	74
local government	110
local public employee	110
loss compensation	160
loss ordinarily incurred from (by)	49
lost property	181
lottery ticket (drawing of lots)	140
lower instance court	8
lump sum payment	69

M

magnetic disk	28
magnetic form	93
main clause	62
main text (of judgment)	151
major shareholder	98
majority	10
maker of cinematographic works	184
maliciously	68
management	5
management (utilization)	129
management committee	128
manager	94
managing member	15
mandamus action	137
mandatary	98
mandate	70
mandatory provision	15
mandatory retirement	208
mandatory retirement age	208
manifestation	59
manifestation of intention	3
manufacture	156
manufacturer	156
margin transaction	156
marine accident	186
mark	169
master	204
matters to be examined upon court's own authority (by the court sua sponte)	104
maturity	173
maximum amount	191

may	39
may not	39
mayor of special ward	191
measure	42
mediation	68
mediator	180
medical certificate	105
meeting of creditors	90
member of an organized crime group	171
member state	75
member with limited liability	175
membership company	121
mental capacity	181
mental reservation	203
merged company	74
merger	10
merger agreement	10
merits	62
minimum wage	197
Ministerial Order	37
minor	120
minutes	14
misappropriation	165
miscellaneous income	198
miscellaneous provision	28
misinterpretation	8
misleading representation	170
misrepresentation	16
mistake	27
mixture	196
model	116
monetary claim	81
monetary debt	82
money and goods	82
money deposit with an official depositary	80
money lender	133
monitoring	77
monopolistic situation	165
moral right	104
moral right of author	111
moral right of performer	199
mortgage	50
mortgaged real property	50
mortgagor	50
most recent business year	91
motion	63
motorized bicycle	193
movables	52
movant	121
municipality	94

musical work(s)	185
must	30
must endeavor to	39
must not	30
mutual aid pension	190
mutual company	205
mutual fund	208
mutual legal assistance	138

N

national government	82
national government asset	195
national government organ	17
national pension	195
national referendum	195
national security	180
National Tax Tribunal	195
national university corporation	196
nationality	24
natural disaster	163
natural fruits	208
naturalization	189
navigation	194
necessity	81
negligence	9
negotiable (debt) instrument payable to order	92
negotiable instrument	208
negotiation	153
neighboring relationship	205
neighboring right	207
new share	38
nominating committee	95
nominative claim	95
non-exclusive (patent) license	162
non-exclusive (trademark) license	163
non-penal confiscation	173
non-performance	26
non-permanent resident	167
nonprofit corporation	211
non-resident	58
nontaxable	168
not exceeding	65
not guilty	120
notarial instrument	87
notarial instrument authorizing execution	148
notary	87
notice of calling	35

notice of grounds for rejection	140
notice of suit	159
notice of termination	8
notification	53
novation	85
novelty	104
nuclear damage	192
nursing care	185
nursing care insurance	186

O

(take an) oath	43
object	64
object of (the) claim	40
objection	2
objection to (a disposition of) execution	148
objection to demand	209
objection to provisional remedy	173
objective	121
obligation	14, 26
obligee	24
obligee's delay in acceptance	98
obligor	26
obscenity	177
observance obligation	151
observation	213
obstruction of performance of public duty	195
obtain	176
occasional income	182
offender	115
offender caught in the act	142
offense	4
offer	63
(criminal) offer of bribe	159
offer of evidence	100
offering	172
offeror	63
office of registered foreign lawyer	186
officer	64
official depository	80
official document	23
official gazette	135
official seal	20
omission in a judicial decision	197
on a regular basis	80
on one's own account	29
onerous act	175
on-site inspection	161

Term	Page
open account	194
open court	22
operating fund	129
operation	5
operation committee	129
opinion	2
opponent	68
opposite party	2
opposition	126
opposition to distribution	167
or less	2
or more	3
oral argument	22, 61
order	83, 99
order commencing ... (proceedings)	112
order for clarification	149
order for improvement	73
order for provisional remedy	173
order in lieu of settlement	216
order of commencement of retrial	197
order to provide security	161
order to submit a document	117
organized crime	205
organized crime group	171
original	41
original party's withdrawal from suit	160
original work(s)	142
other than on the date	136
outline	122
outside company auditor	32
outside director	32
outward direct investment	160
overtime work	28
owner	38
ownership	38

P

Term	Page
paid leave	214
paid money	56
paid-in amount	114
paragraph	20
pardon	185
parent company	6
parental authority	203
parole	188
Part	60
partial amendment	182
participation	92
partition of property in co-ownership	139
partner	82
partnership	17
partnership property	140
part-time worker	206
party	52
party at a distance	132
passage	141
patent	53
patent application	112
patent attorney	213
patent right	53
patented invention	112
patentee	53
payer	148
payment	18
payment date	31
penal institution	141
penal provision	167
penalty	4
pending	17
pension	114
perform the/one's duty (duties)	37
performance	65
performing	85
period (of time)	13
period for advancement	111
period for filing of proofs of claims	145
period for production	111
period for submission	111
period of stay	197
period of time	14
periodic payments	208
perjury	136
permanent establishment	86
permanent residence	129
permanent resident	70
permission	16
person	58
person concerned in a case	159
person entitled to	20
person filing an objection	181
person raising an objection	181
person under assistance	168
person under curatorship	168
person who executes (the) business	81
person who has parental authority	105
person without capacity to sue or be sued	205
personal information	24
personal service	89

petition	101
petition for acceptance of final appeal	152
petition for appeal	88
petition for the court to determine the price (petition for determination of the price)	187
petition of (a) final appeal	152
petition to commence	186
petitioner	121
petty bench	153
petty fine	76
pharmaceutical	183
physically disabled	203
place for payment	94
place of arbitration	111
place of business	5
place of performance	65
place of residence	16
place of the act	85
plaintiff	19
plead	52
pledge	93
pledge of claim	145
pledge of real property	212
pledge of right	142
pledge on movable property	112
pledgee	93
pledgor	94
police officer	17
policy	42
policyholder	172
poll	52
pollution	185
port of call	189
possession	44
possession through agent	109
possessor	103
possessory action	158
possessory right	44
post-commencement claim	186
posting	141
postponement	6
power	18
power of attorney	3
power of judicial decision	25
precedent	57
prefectural governor	113
prefecture	112
preferred equity investment	122
preferred share	122
prejudice	73
preliminary	215
preliminary oral arguments	99
premiums	83
prepaid payment instrument	214
preparatory proceedings	118
prepayment	215
prescription	29
presence (attendance)	161
present danger	142
pre-sentencing detention	173
preservation of evidence	100
presiding judge	25
presumption	39
presumptive heir	203
pretrial conference procedure	89
price	8
prima facie showing	107
principal	12
principal debtor	97
principal obligor	97
principal office	33
principal place of daily activity	156
principal registration	151
principle of direct trial	207
print right	151
private document	149
private monopolization	94
private placement	95
private right	93
privately appointed agent	70
probate	142
probation	214
probative value (of evidence)	102
procedure	51
procedures to fix	187
proceedings	112
proceedings to arrange issues and evidence	159
proceeds	149
processing (processed)	133
product	156
product liability	106
profit and loss statement	107
progress	141
prohibition	17
prohibition of payments	118
prohibitory injunction	140
promptly	39
pronounce judgment	157

pronouncement	69
proof	37
proper	40
property	25
property in co-ownership	139
property right	25
proposal	78
Prosecutor General	192
prospectus	174
prove	65
;provided, however, that ...	47
provisional attachment	75
provisional designation	188
provisional detention	188
provisional disposition	75
provisional disposition prohibiting the disposal of property	154
provisional execution	75
provisional garnishment	75
provisional order	173
provisional payment	76
provisional payment figured by estimate	76
provisional registration	76
provisional release	188
provisional seizure	75
proviso	47
proxy	47
public and corporate bond	194
public bond	194
public charges	85
public company	86
public duty	23
public employee	23
public facility	86
public health	194
public hearing	194
public inspection	96
public interest	21, 143
public interest corporation	143
public interest incorporated association	143
public interest incorporated foundation	143
public law related action	164
public notice	86
public notification	86
public policy	71
public prosecutor	19
public prosecutor's assistant officer	192
public prosecutors office	19
public safety	86
public safety commission	193
public service	23
public welfare	21
publication	83
publication of (an) application	150
punishment	17
purchase and sale	55
purpose	63

Q

qualified acceptance	192
qualified institutional investor	163
quarantine	191
quarterly securities report	94
quasi-co-ownership	201
quasi-loan (for consumption)	152
quasi-mandate	201
quasi-pharmaceutical products	183
quasi-possession	201
quitting	205

R

rape	193
ratification	168
rating	132
raw material	142
real estate appraiser	212
real estate brokerage	206
real property	60
real property income	212
real right	170
re-appeal from an appeal from a ruling	196
reappointment	25
reasonable period of time	44
reassessment	87
receipt	183
recipient	150
recognition	153
recommendation	76
record of oral argument	22
record of preparatory proceedings	118
recording medium	81
recovery	131
rectification	42
recuse oneself	187
redelivery	145
redemption	99
reduction	19
reduction of pay	193

reduction of punishment in light of extenuating circumstances 200
reduction of the stated capital 149
reduction or release of debts 91
re-examination 91
reference 71
reference documents for shareholders meeting 75
referral (refer) 159
refund 57
refusal 16
refusal to testify 152
register 84
register of lost share certificates 188
registered domicile 119
registered foreign lawyer 186
registered mail 73
registered seal certificate 4
registration 51
registration of dissolution 7
registry office 51
regulation 14
Regulation 14
rehabilitation 194
rehabilitation debtor 91
(proposed) rehabilitation plan 91
rehabilitation proceedings 91
reimbursement 34
reimbursement of value 132
reinstatement 169
rejection 16
related company 76
relatives by marriage 183
release 95
relevant 51
relevant administrative organ 134
relevant expertise 187
relevant person 12
religious corporation 200
relocation 70
remain in force 113
remaining creditors 147
remand 92
remote place 130
removal 70
removal (from position/duty) 8
remuneration 118
rendering 69
renewal 21
reorganization 87

(corporate) reorganization proceedings 144
repeal 167
repeat conviction 197
repeated convictions 215
replace 132
re-pledge 112
report of payment 148
representation 59
representation of both parties 205
representative 47
representative director 46
representative executive officer 109
representative liquidator 109
reproduction 170
request 40
request for administrative review 154
request for an expert examination 135
request for disclosure 131
request for examination 203
request for re-examination 146
request for valuation 132
requirement for perfection 108
requirement to duly assert against third parties 108
requirements for perfection of change in rights 84
res judicata 137
resale price 146
rescission 54
rescission right 113
reserve 99
reserve fund 111
residence 197
resident 16
resident record 150
resigning (resignation) 46
resolution 18
responsibility 41
restoration 84
retail 195
retain 172
retention 123
retirement 46
retirement allowance 160
retrial 196
retroactively 27
return of contribution 98
revenue stamp 200
reversal 167
revision 131

revocation	51
revocation of provisional remedy	173
revolving guarantee	114
revolving mortgage	113
reward	61
right	19
right in rem	60
right of avoidance	116
right of broadcasting	213
right of common	183
right of lease	49
right of rebuttal (to rebut)	211
right of reproduction	211
right of retention	176
right of segregation	166
right to defense	61
right to demand rescission of fraudulent act	146
right to grant of patent	112
right to indemnification	79
right to reimbursement	15
right to remedy over (reimbursement)	137
right to represent	47
right to rescind	54
risk	72
robber	88
robbery	88
rules of employment	32
ruling	18, 91
ruling for commencement of guardianship	193
rumor	169

S

salary income	79
sale	5
sale by private contract	210
sales representative	132
sales volume	70
sanitation	130
scientific knowledge	132
screen presentation	201
seal	4
seal impression	4
seal to confirm page continuation	17
sealed bidding	210
search	44
second instance	161
second sentence	22
secondary	96
secondary distribution	70
secondary use	166
secondment	33
secrecy	58
secret	59
Section	42
secured claim	168
secured real property auction	110
securities	64
securities registration statement	174
securitization	215
security	48
security deposit	28
security right	110
seized article	71
seizure	27
seizure warrant	27
seizure with an order to produce a copy of records	191
seizure-prohibition	92
self-contract	198
self-defense	106
self-denounce	147
selling	128
semiannual securities report	114
sending back	158
sentence	57
sentenced person	150
sentencing (sentence)	126
separation from employment	205
serve as	68
service	44
service by publication	87
service contract	6
service wherever (the person) may be found	163
servient land	202
servitude	161
servitude holder	161
set-off	44
settlement	18, 65
settlor	126
severance pay	160
shall	31
share	10
share certificate	10
share certificate-issuing company	74
share exchange	74
share for subscription	119

share issued at incorporation	157
share less than one unit	109
share of an estate	44
share option	38
share option for subscription	119
share option holder	104
share option subject to call	98
share split	74
share subject to call	98
share subject to class-wide call	158
share transfer	74
share transfer plan	133
share unit number	109
share with put option	98
share with restricted voting right	78
share with restriction on transfer	153
shareholder	11
shareholder register	11
shareholder register administrator	75
shareholder subject to a cash-out	128
shareholder, etc. subject to a cash-out	128
shareholders meeting	11
shares of different classes	90
shares subject to a cash-out	128
short-term lease	206
signature	37
silent partner	165
silent partnership	165
simplified distribution	134
simplified rehabilitation	134
simultaneous trial and decision	209
site	92
small and medium-sized enterprise	162
small claim action	202
solatium	181
sole proprietor	90
solicitation	12
special controlling company	209
special provision	112
split company	117
spoliation	183
spouse	55
spouse qualified for tax deduction	194
spread	176
staffing	56
stage performance	202
standard claim	189
standing	164
standing to sue	84
stated capital	32
statement	15
statement of (the) claim(s)	40
statement of accounts	83
statement of changes in net assets	134
(written) statement of reasons (for final appeal)	152
statement of reasons for appeal	88
status of residence	197
statute of limitations	29
statute of limitations for filing an action	98
statutory agent	171
statutory interest	118
statutory interest rate	118
statutory lien	91
statutory superficies	213
stay	163
stay of court proceedings	160
stay of execution	148
stay order	207
steal	204
stock	10
stock company	10
stolen property	209
store	119
structure	194
sua sponte	202
subagent	116
subcontractor	30
subject matter	174
subject matter jurisdiction	199
sublease	51
sublessee	51
sublessor	51
submission of written statements in lieu of examination	203
subpledge	112
subrogation	108
subscriber	58
subscription	58
subscription price	115
Subsection	11
subsequent completion	162
subsequent distribution	162
subsidiary company	23
substitute performance	109
substituted service	173
successful bidder	215
succession	35
sufficient grounds	150
suit	107

summary court	11
summary criminal trial	188
summary delivery (summary transfer)	134
summary order	176
summary proceedings	176
summons	152
summons for appearance date	136
superficies (right)	207
supervising body	12
supervision	12
supervisor	77
supervisor of guardian	193
supervisor of guardian of adult	157
supplemental registration	169
supplementary provisions	212
Supreme Court	24
surcharge	133
surname	128
surplus	103
surveillance	135
surveillance action (disposition)	188
surviving company	108
surviving family (member)	182
suspect	115
suspend	48
suspended execution of the sentence	94
suspension	14, 50
suspension of (litigation/court) proceedings	160
suspension of payments	31
suspension of prescription	147
suspension order	111
suspicion	83
swear	157

T

taking unlawful possession	155
tax	39
tax base	133
tax credit	106
tax on aggregate income	204
tax on delinquency	185
tax return	73
taxable income	133
taxpayer	166
telecommunication	208
telecommunications carrier	208
template	116
tender	210
tender offer (bid)	86
term	13
term (of sentence)	141
term of office	55
termination	8
terms and conditions (of transaction)	54
testator	126
testify	100
the Act on [○○]	54
the date of promulgation	22
the life or (and) person	106
the other party (other parties)	2
the same applies hereinafter	2
the State	82
theft	106
thing received (in exchange for)	160
third party beneficiary contract	160
third party debtor	108
third party notice	159
third party obligor	109
third person collateral provider	212
third person mortgagor	212
third person pledgor	212
this Act comes into effect as of ...	144
threat	72
time limit	78
time of commencement	28
time of performance	61
title	84
title of obligation	91
to the extent actually enriched	142
tolling of statute of limitations	147
tort	60
tortfeasor	60
torture	195
total number of authorized shares	56
total number of authorized shares in a class	114
totaling	133
trade association	198
trade name	35
trade secret	5
trademark	37
trademark registration	101
trademark right	37
transcript	53
transfer	36, 115
transfer of business	93
transfer of possession	158
transfer of possession by instruction	27

transferee ··· 64
transferee company ··· 122
transferor ··· 36
transferor company ··· 36
transitional measure ··· 82
transportation ··· 129
treasury ··· 196
treasury share ··· 93
treaty ··· 102
trial date ··· 22
trial decision ··· 154
trial for patent invalidation ··· 166
trial preparation ··· 89
trial procedure ··· 22
trial record ··· 22
trust ··· 105
trust agreement ··· 105
trustee ··· 97
trustee in bankruptcy ··· 76

U

unauthorized ··· 116
unauthorized agency ··· 174
unauthorized use ··· 170
unavoidable grounds ··· 122
unavoidably ··· 121
uncertain due date ··· 211
uncharged offense ··· 214
under ··· 55
underwriter ··· 115
underwriting ··· 115
unfair ··· 59
unfair competition ··· 170
unfair trade practice ··· 170
unilateral juridical act ··· 206
uninterrupted series of endorsements ··· 184
universal legacy ··· 213
unjust enrichment ··· 170
unknowingly ··· 42
unlawful ··· 4, 59
unlawful confinement ··· 188
unqualified acceptance ··· 206
unspecified and large number of persons ··· 170
upper instance court ··· 99
urbanization control area ··· 198
utility model right ··· 199
uttering ··· 143

V

vacation ··· 68
valid ··· 50
validity ··· 89
value ··· 8, 46
victim ··· 57
violation ··· 4
visa ··· 146
void ··· 63
voluntarily ··· 55
vote ··· 52
voting form ··· 78
voting right ··· 13

W

wage ··· 49
waiver ··· 118
waiver of claim ··· 40
walk-in inspection ··· 206
ward ··· 168
warning ··· 17
warrant ··· 65
warranty ··· 48
warranty against defects ··· 74
weapon ··· 190
when ··· 53
whenever ··· 165
whistleblower ··· 85
whistleblowing ··· 85
wholly owned subsidiary company ··· 12
wholly owning parent company ··· 12
widow deduction ··· 188
widower deduction ··· 188
will ··· 2
(person) with a special interest in a resolution ··· 83
with the same care a person would exercise over the person's own property ··· 147
with/for definite term ··· 175
withdrawal ··· 54
withholding (at source) ··· 19
withholding tax ··· 19
without (good) reason/cause ··· 173
without any party's request ··· 202
without delay ··· 48
without knowledge ··· 43
without negligence ··· 63
work(s) ··· 49

working conditions ··············· 177
working hour ··············· 216
workplace ··············· 200
writ of detention for expert examination ···· 189
writ of physical escort ··············· 85
written decision ··············· 18, 154

written expert opinion ··············· 189
written opinion ··············· 69
written ruling ··············· 83
written statement ··············· 162
wrongful ··············· 59

日本語索引

あ

相手方	2, 68
青色事業専従者	180
青色申告	180
悪意で	2, 68
明渡し	47
明渡し（強制的な）	68
明渡し（自主的）	68
あっせん	68
あっせん（収賄）	180
あっせん（盗品のあっせん）	180
斡旋員	180
あってはならない	30
安全保障	180

い

言渡し	69
言渡し（刑事の場合）	126
言渡し（民事の場合）	69
委員会設置会社	126
…以下	2
以下「…」という	2
以下同じ	2
以下この…において同じ	126
異議	2, 126
遺棄（する）	180
異議者	180
異議のある債権者	181
異議の申立て	126
（書面による）異議申立人	181
（口頭による）異議申立人	181
育児休業	181
意見	2
意見書	69
遺言	2
遺言執行者	126
遺言者	126
遺産	69
遺産の分割	69
意思	2
遺失物	181
意思能力	181
意思表示	3
慰謝料	181
意匠	181
…以上	3
意匠権	181
意匠権者	181
意匠の創作をした者	181
（管轄違いなどによる）移送	36
遺贈	182
移送の裁判	182
遺族	182
委託	3
委託者	69, 126
（販売・運送等の）委託者	3
（権限を代わって行使することを）委託する	3
（信認関係の下で事務を）委託する	3
（商品の販売を）委託する	69
委託料金（コミッション）	103
一時金	69
一時所得	182
著しい	182
一部改正	182
一括売却	182
一般財団法人	182
一般社団法人	127
一般承継人	69
一般消費者	3
一般に公正妥当と認められる企業会計の基準	69
一般の先取特権	127
一般の優先権がある債権	182
一般弁済期間	183
偽りその他不正の行為	127
偽りその他不正の手段	127
移転	36
（主たる事務所の）移転	70
（人・物の場所的な）移転	70
委任	3
委任（民法上の委任契約）	70
委任（権限の委任）	3
委任状	3
委任する	3
委任による代理人	70
違反	3, 4, 127
違反行為	4
違反調査	4
違法な	4

違約金	4
医薬品	183
医薬部外品	183
入会権	183
遺留した物	183
遺留分	127
威力	127
印影	4
印鑑（印章の趣旨）	4
印鑑証明書	4
姻族	183
引致	127
隠匿（する）	127
隠避させる	128
隠滅	128, 183
引用（…する）	130

う

受入受刑者	183
請負	4
請負人	5
受取証書	183
氏	128
訴え	5, 45, 107
訴えによって	70
訴えの変更	128
裏書	184
裏書人	184
裏書の連続	184
売上高	70
売出し	70
売付け	128
売渡し	5
売渡株式	128
売渡株主	128
売渡株主等	128
運営	5
運営委員会	128, 129
運送	129
運送賃	129
運送取扱営業	184
運送取扱人	129
運送人	129
運送品	37, 129, 184
運送保険	184
運用	129, 164
運用資金	129
運用報告書	70

え

映画製作者	184
映画の著作物	184
営業	5
営業所	5
営業年度	5
営業秘密	5
永住	129
永住者	70
衛生	130
衛生委員会	184
営利企業	70
営利事業	71
営利の目的	6
疫学的調査	185
益金	71
役務	44
役務提供委託	6
閲覧	19
遠隔の地	130
延期	6
縁組	185
援護	130
延焼	185
延滞税	185
援用	71, 130

お

押収	27
押収物	71
応訴管轄	71
応当する日	130
横領	6
公の秩序又は善良の風俗	71
犯す	6
汚職	6
（放射能、毒物等による）汚染	185
汚染	185
おそれ	71, 72
親会社	6
及び	6
音楽の著作物	185
恩赦	185

か

| 外貨建債券 | 185 |
| 外患誘致 | 185 |

日本語索引	
（行政機関としての）会議	136
会計	6
会計監査人	6
会計監査人設置会社	130
会計監査報告書	72
会計検査	84
会計参与	72
会計参与設置会社	131
会計帳簿	7
会計年度	7
解雇	7
介護	185
戒告	131
外国	7
外国会社	72
外国人	7
外国人登録	131
外国税額控除	186
外国弁護士	186
外国法共同事業	186
外国法事務弁護士	186
外国法事務弁護士事務所	186
外国法人	7
介護福祉士	186
介護保険	186
解散（する）	131
解散（例：法人または議会）	7
解散の登記	7
開示	7
開始後債権	186
開示請求	131
開始の申立て	186
会社	7
（文言の）解釈	8
解釈の誤り	8
会社分割	8
（債権の）回収	72
（非有体物の）回収	131
解除	72
解職	8
解除条件	72
害する	73
改正法	131
改善措置	73
改善命令	73
改定	131
買取請求権	73
海難	186
解任	7
改任	132
開発途上地域	186
回避する	73
（裁判官を）回避する	187
回復することができない損害	73
改変	73
外務員	132
買戻し	99
解約（将来に向かって契約を失効）	8
解約の申入れ	8
加害	72
加害者	132
価格（金銭的価値）	8
価格（品物の価格・値段）	8
価額決定の請求	132
科学的知見	132
価格の決定	132
価格の決定の申立て	187
価額の償還	132
化学物質	187
書留郵便	73
下級審	8
閣議	187
閣議決定	187
学識経験	187
確知	187
隔地者	132
格付	132
確定期限	132
確定申告	73
確定する（裁判・判決等）	8
確定手続	187
確定判決	8
確定日付	9
確認	9
確認の訴え	74
可決	36
加工（された）	133
火災保険	187
加算税	187
瑕疵	9
瑕疵ある意思表示	133
貸金業者	133
瑕疵担保責任	74
過失	9
果実	74
貸付	9
貸付債権	9
貸付信託	74
過失相殺	9
貸主	9

語	頁
（不動産・物品の）貸主	9
過少申告加算税	187
課す	10
貸す	10
（不動産・物品を）貸す	10
課税所得	133
課税標準	133
仮装	133
課徴金	74
課徴金（独占禁止法）	133
合算	133
割賦販売	133
合併	10
合併会社	74
合併契約	10
家庭裁判所	74
過半数	10
株券	10
株券喪失登録簿	188
株券発行会社	74
寡婦控除	188
寡夫控除	188
株式	10
株式移転	74
株式移転計画	133
株式会社	10
株式買取請求権	74
株式交換	74
株式等売渡請求	133
株式分割	74
株式併合	75
株式無償割当て	75
株主	11
株主資本等変動計算書	134
株主総会	11
株主総会参考書類	75
株主名簿	11
株主名簿管理人	75
加盟国	75
貨物引換証	188
借入金	75
仮拘禁	188
仮差押え	75
仮執行	75
仮指定	188
仮釈放	188
仮出場	188
仮処分	75
仮登記	76
借主	11

語	頁
（不動産・物品の）借主	11
仮納付	76
仮払	76
仮放免	188
過料	76
科料	76
為替	11, 49
款	11
簡易公判手続	188
簡易再生	134
簡易裁判所	11
簡易の引渡し	134
簡易配当	134
管轄	11
管轄裁判所	12
管轄違い	76
監禁	188
関係会社	76
関係行政機関	134
関係者	12
監護	134
勧告	76
監査委員	76
監査委員会	134
監査証明	134
観察処分	188
監査等委員会設置会社	76
監査報告	77
監査法人	134
監査役	12
監査役会	12
監査役会設置会社	77
監査役設置会社	77
監視	77, 135
監事	135
慣習	135
慣習法	135
勘定	12
勘定科目	77
関税	77
間接強制	77
完全親会社	12
完全子会社	12
鑑定	135
鑑定書	189
鑑定証人	189
鑑定人	135
鑑定の嘱託	135
鑑定留置	189
鑑定留置状	189

監督 ･･･ 12
監督委員 ･････････････････････････････････ 77
監督機関 ･････････････････････････････････ 12
還付 ･･･ 57
還付加算金 ･････････････････････････････ 189
官報 ･･･････････････････････････････････････ 135
元本 ･･･ 12
勧誘 ･･･ 12
管理 ･･･ 15
関連会社 ････････････････････････････････ 13

き

議案 ･････････････････････････････････････ 13, 78
起因して ････････････････････････････････ 13
帰化 ･････････････････････････････････････ 189
（国や独立した州レベルでの）議会 ････ 78
（地方公共団体の）議会 ･･････････ 136
期間 ･･･ 13
期間の経過後 ･･････････････････････････ 78
期間の計算 ･････････････････････････････ 136
期間の定めのある労働契約 ････････ 78
期間の満了 ･･････････････････････････････ 78
棄却（請求棄却、控訴棄却） ････････ 13
基金 ････････････････････････････････････ 28, 78
議決権 ･･･････････････････････････････････ 13
議決権行使書面 ･･････････････････････ 78
（会社法の）議決権行使代理人 ･･ 47
議決権制限株式 ･･････････････････････ 78
期限 ･････････････････････････････････････ 14, 78
危険運転 ･････････････････････････････ 189
危険負担 ･････････････････････････････ 136
寄港地 ･･･････････････････････････････････ 189
期日外 ･･･････････････････････････････････ 136
期日間整理手続 ･･･････････････････ 136
期日の変更 ･････････････････････････････ 136
期日の呼出し ･････････････････････････ 136
基準債権 ･････････････････････････････ 189
偽証 ･･･････････････････････････････････････ 136
議事録 ･･･････････････････････････････････ 14
規制 ･･･ 14
擬制 ･･･ 78
起訴 ･･･ 14
偽造 ･････････････････････････････････････ 78, 79
規則（法形式が「省令」の場合）･･ 14
基礎控除 ･････････････････････････････ 189
起訴状 ･･･････････････････････････････････ 136
寄託 ･････････････････････････････････････ 136
寄託者 ･･･････････････････････････････････ 137
議長 ･･･ 14

既判力 ･･･････････････････････････････････ 137
忌避する ･････････････････････････････････ 190
寄附金 ･･･････････････････････････････････ 138
寄附行為（財団法人の根本規則） ････ 190
寄附行為（財団法人を設立する行為）･･････ 190
基本的人権 ･････････････････････････････ 14
義務 ･･･ 14
義務（債務一般） ････････････････････ 26
義務付けの訴え ･･･････････････････ 137
記名押印 ･････････････････････････････････ 14
却下 ･･･ 13
休業補償 ･････････････････････････････ 190
休止（それ以上継続させない停止） ････ 79
休止（一時休止） ････････････････････ 14
吸収合併 ･････････････････････････････････ 79
吸収合併消滅会社 ･･･････････････ 137
吸収合併存続会社 ･･･････････････ 137
吸収分割 ･････････････････････････････････ 79
求償権 ･････････････････････････ 15, 79, 137
急速を要する場合 ･･･････････････ 190
急迫不正の侵害 ･･････････････････ 137
給付 ･･･ 18
旧法 ･････････････････････････････････････ 137
休眠会社 ･････････････････････････････ 137
給与所得 ･････････････････････････････････ 79
寄与（例：寄与分） ･･･････････････ 138
共益債権 ･････････････････････････････ 138
共益費用 ･････････････････････････････ 138
境界 ･････････････････････････････････････ 190
恐喝 ･････････････････････････････････････ 138
凶器 ･････････････････････････････････････ 190
協議 ･････････････････････････････････････ 138
（専門家との）協議 ･･････････････････ 79
協議上の離婚 ･････････････････････････ 79
競合 ･･･ 50
強行規定 ･････････････････････････････････ 15
教唆 ･･･････････････････････････････ 79, 138
共済年金 ･････････････････････････････ 190
教唆者 ･･･････････････････････････････････ 138
供述 ･･･ 15
共助 ･････････････････････････････････････ 138
行政 ･･･ 15
行政機関 ･････････････････････････････････ 15
強制競売 ･････････････････････････････････ 15
行政事件訴訟 ･････････････････････････ 79
強制執行 ･････････････････････････････････ 15
行政指導 ･････････････････････････････････ 15
行政処分 ･････････････････････････････････ 15
行政庁 ･･･････････････････････････････････ 79
行政手続 ･････････････････････････････････ 80

行政不服審査	80
強制履行	15
競争上の地位	80
供託	80
供託金	80
供託所	80
共同正犯	138
共同訴訟	138
共同抵当	139
共同根抵当	191
共同不法行為	139
共同保証人	139
業として（反復・継続して）	80
業として（営利目的をもって）	80
強迫	139
脅迫	139
共犯（共犯関係）	139
共犯（共犯である者）	80
業務執行	80
業務執行者	81
業務執行者（会社法の場合）	80
業務執行社員	15
業務執行取締役	81
業務の委託	16
共有	81
享有	139
共有者	81
共有物	139
共有物の分割	139
共有持分	139
供与	81
強要	81, 140, 191
許可	16, 63
許可抗告	191
虚偽表示	16, 81
極度額	191
居住者	16
居住地	16
拒絶	16
拒絶理由通知	140
許諾	16
拒否	16
寄与分	191
記録媒体	81
記録命令付差押え	191
緊急避難	81
禁錮	16
禁止	17
禁止命令	140
近親者	191

金銭債権	81
金銭債務	82
金品	82
金融機関	140
金融商品	82
金融商品仲介業	140
金融商品仲介行為	140
金融商品取引業	82
金融商品取引業協会	140
金融商品取引業者	140
金融商品取引所	82

く

苦情	45
苦情処理	82
区長（特別区の場合）	191
国（地方公共団体と比較する場合）	82
国（例：国の利害に関係のある訴訟についての法務大臣の権限等に関する法律）	82
国の機関	17
（民法上の）組合	17
組合員	82
組合財産	140
繰越し	82

け

刑	17
契印	17
経過	141
経過措置	82
刑期	141
警告	17
掲載	83
警察官	17
計算書類	17
掲示	141
刑事施設	141
刑事訴追	83
軽車両	191
係属	17
競売	17
競売申立人	83
景品類	83
契約	18
契約書	18
激甚災害	191
欠格	141
決議	18

決議について特別の利害関係を有する者	83
決済	18
（窓口での）決済	18
決済（相殺勘定の決済）	141
決算期	83
決算期（決算期末の期日）	18
決算報告	83
決定	18, 38
（裁判形式の）決定	83
決定書	18, 83
原因	92
検疫	191
検閲	141
減価償却（無形固定資産の場合）	192
減価償却資産	192
嫌疑	83
権限	18
権原	84
（信託法等における）権限の委託	126
健康	130
健康で文化的な生活	192
現行犯人	142
原告	19
原告適格	84
減殺	19
現在の危難	142
原裁判所	192
原材料	142
検査機関	192
検索の抗弁	192
原作品	142
検察官	19
検察事務官	192
検察庁	19
検査役	135
検視	192
検事正	192
検事総長	192
現実の引渡し	84
現実の物の引渡し	89
現住建造物	142
原状回復	84
原子力損害	192
源泉徴収	19
源泉徴収税	19
限定承認	192
原動機付自転車	193
現に受けている利益	142
現に受けている利益（現存利益）	84
現に利益を受けている限度において	142

（遺言書の）検認	142
検品	19
現物出資	84
建ぺい率	193
原簿	84
憲法	19
原本	41
権利	19
権利質	142
権利能力	84
権利の濫用	20
権利変動の対抗要件	84
権利を専有する	85
権利を有する者	20

こ

故意	20
項	20
号	20
公安委員会	193
考案者	143
行為	20
合意	20
行為地	85
行為能力	85
公印	20
勾引	127
勾引状	85
公益	143
公益財団法人	143
公益社団法人	143
公益通報	85
公益通報者	85
公益法人	143
公課	85
更改	85
公開会社	86
公開買付け（TOB）	86
交換	11
強姦（不同意性交）	193
綱紀委員会（弁護士法第58条）	193
合議制	143
降給	193
恒久的施設（PE）	86
公共施設	86
工業所有権	86
公共の安全	86
公共の福祉	21
公共の利益	21

項目	頁
航空・鉄道事故調査委員会	193
攻撃防御方法	143
後見	193
後見開始の審判	193
後見監督人	193
後見人	194
航行	194
抗告	86
公告	86
抗告裁判所	143
抗告人	88
抗告訴訟	143
交互計算	194
公債	194
工作物	194
行使	21
行使（偽造文書等の行使）	143
合資会社	86
公示催告	86
公示送達	87
公社債	194
公衆衛生	194
控除	144
交渉	153
公証人	87
控除対象配偶者	194
更新	21
更正	21
更生（会社）	87
更正（税務）	87
更生（犯罪者）	194
公正証書	87, 144
更生手続	144
公正取引	87
公正な	21, 87
公正な慣行	87
公正な競争	87
厚生年金	87
公然と	88
控訴	21
公訴棄却	21
拘束力	21, 88
控訴裁判所	88
公訴事実	21
控訴趣意書	88
控訴状	88
控訴審	88
控訴人	88
後段	22
公聴会	194
強盗	88
強盗（罪名）	88
合同会社	88
高等裁判所	22
口頭弁論	22
口頭弁論調書	22
口頭弁論の期日	22
口頭弁論の終結	22
口頭弁論の全趣旨及び証拠調べの結果	22
降任	144
公認会計士	88
公判期日	22
公判準備	89
公判前整理手続	89
公判調書	22
公判廷	22
公判手続	22
交付	89
交付送達	89
公布の日	22
公文書	23
公平かつ誠実に	144
抗弁	23
合弁企業（JV）	89
（具体的な）公務	23
（性質としての）公務	23
公務員	23
公務執行妨害	195
合名会社	89
拷問	195
小売業	195
勾留	86
勾留状	144
効力	23, 89
効力を失う	23
効力を生ずる	23
効力を有する	50
子会社	23
小切手	195
小切手訴訟	195
国債	195
国際出願	144
国税不服審判所	195
国籍	24
告訴	24
国内	24
国内源泉所得	195
告発	90
国民審査	195
国民年金	195

国有財産	195
国立大学法人	196
個人	24
個人再生委員	196
個人識別情報	144
個人事業者	90
個人情報	24
戸籍	196
国家間の紛争	50
国庫	196
固定資産税	196
異なる種類の株式	90
この法律は…から施行する	144
顧問	144
混同	196
混和	196

さ

災害復旧事業	196
裁決	90
債券	24
債権	24
債権質	145
債権者	24
債権者（金銭債権や倒産法の場合）	24
債権者集会	90
債権者代位権	90
債権者代位訴訟	145
債権者の一般の利益	90
債権者名簿	90
債権者を害する行為	90
債権証書	145
債権届出期間	145
債権の調査及び確定	145
債権の届出	145
再抗告	196
最高裁判所	24
再交付	145
（債務履行の）催告	24
催告の抗弁	145
財産	25
財産開示手続	145
財産権	25
財産分与	90
財産目録	90
最終事業年度（会社法）	91
再審	196
再審開始の決定	197
再審査請求	146
再審の訴え	197
再尋問	91
再生計画	91
再生債務者	91
再生手続	91
細則	91
財団法人	146
裁定	91
（仲裁の場合）裁定	146
在廷	146
最低賃金	197
再任	25
在任する	91
再犯	197
裁判官	25
裁判権	11, 25
裁判所	62
裁判上の請求	146
裁判上の離婚	197
裁判所書記官	91
裁判所調査官	197
裁判長	25
裁判手続	25
裁判の脱漏	197
再販売価格	146
財物	25
債務（金銭債務）	26
債務（債務一般）	26
債務者	26
債務者（金銭債権や倒産法の場合）	26
財務諸表	26
債務超過（無資力）	26
債務の減免	91
債務の承継	100
債務の引受人	58
債務引受	26, 100
債務不履行	26
債務名義	91
罪名（審理対象としての罪名）	27
在留	197
在留期間	197
在留資格	197
在留資格証明書	198
詐害行為取消権	146
詐害行為取消訴訟	146
さかのぼって	27
詐欺	27
先取特権	91
錯誤	27
削除	27

差押え……27
差押禁止……92
差押債権者……92
差押状……27
指図証券（債権）……92
指図による占有移転……27
差戻し……92
査証……146
雑所得……198
殺人……28
雑則……28
査定……147
差別的取扱い……92
参加……92
参加人……147
残存債権者……147

し

死因贈与……198
市街化調整区域……198
時間外労働……28
指揮……28
始期……28
敷金……28
敷地……92
磁気ディスク……28
磁気的方式……93
（商法上の営業に対し会社法上の）事業……5
事業者団体……198
事業所得……198
事業の譲渡……93
事業の譲受け……93
事業報告……129
資金……28
資金決済……147
死刑……28
私権……93
事故……28
次項……29
時効……29
時効（取得時効・消滅時効の両方を含む）……29
時効の停止……147
時効の利益……198
自己株式……93
自己契約……198
事後強盗……198
自己資本……93
自己資本規制比率……198
自己の計算において……29

自己の財産におけるのと同一の注意義務をもって……147
持参人……147
事実……29
事実上……29
事実の認定……29
死者……198
自首する……147
支出……93
次条……29
指針……29
資する……30
下請負人（例：労働基準法第87条）……30
質権……93
質権者……93
質権設定者……94
市町村……94
実演……85
実演家人格権……199
失火……147
疾患……199
（法）執行……30
執行……30
失効……37
実行……30
執行異議……148
執行官……148
執行機関……148
執行抗告……199
執行裁判所……148
執行証書……148
執行停止……148
執行判決（外国裁判所判決）……148
執行文……94
執行役……94
執行猶予……94
失踪の宣告……199
実用新案権……199
私的独占……94
私的録音録画補償金……199
してはならない……30
支店……30
自動公衆送信……199
自動公衆送信装置……199
しなければならない……30
自認……31
支配……31
支配人……94
自白……31
自白（民事）……31

日本語索引

日本語索引	
（窓口での）支払	18
支払期日	31
支払者	148
支払地	94
支払遅延	94
支払調書	148
支払能力	94
支払不能	31
四半期報告書	94
自筆証書	148
事物管轄	199
私文書	149
紙幣	200
私募	95
司法委員	200
司法警察員	200
司法修習生	200
資本	31
資本金	32
資本金の額	95
資本金の額の減少	149
資本準備金	95
事務管理	149
指名委員会	95
指名委員会等設置会社	95
指名債権	95
指紋	149
社員総会	95
社外監査役	32
社外取締役	32
借地権	149
釈放	95
釈明権	95
釈明処分	149
酌量減軽	200
社債	32
社債管理者	95
社債権者	96
社債権者集会	96
社債原簿	149
（株式）社債の償還	99
社団法人	149
受遺者	149, 150
事由	92
収益	149
重加算税	200
就業規則	32
従業者	32
就業場所	200
宗教法人	200
終局決定（非訟事件訴訟法）	96
終局判決	96
重婚	200
住所	32
修正申告	200
重大な過失	32
従たる	96
集中証拠調べ	96
充当	32
（資金・日数を）充当する	180
収入印紙	200
就任	32
従犯	150
（不動産の）従物	201
（動産の）従物	201
十分な理由	150
住民（長期的な定住者）	33
住民税	150
住民票	150
収容	201
縦覧	96
収賄	150
受益権	96
受益者	97
受益証券	201
受寄者	97
受刑者	150
授権	97
主尋問	97
受贈者	150
受託者	97
（委託販売における）受託者	97
（その他の事務における）受託者	97
主たる債務者（金銭債務以外の一般債務の場合）	97
主たる債務者（金銭債務の場合）	97
主たる事務所	33
主張	33
出願	33
（anありの場合）出願公開	150
（anなしの場合）出願公表	150
出願者	33
出願審査	151
出向	33
出資者	97
出資する	30
出資の一部払戻し	7
出資の払戻し	98
出訴期間	98
出頭	98

項目	頁
出版権	151
主登記	151
取得時効	151
取得条項付株式	98
取得条項付新株予約権	98
取得請求権付株式	98
受任者	98
主物	12
主文	151
主務官庁	151
主務大臣	151
主要株主	98
受領遅滞	98
受領能力	151
種類株式	34
種類株式発行会社	99
種類株主	34
種類株主総会	99
種類の株式	99
順位	99
準委任	201
準共有	201
準拠法	34
遵守義務	151
準消費貸借	152
準占有	201
準備金	99
準備書面	34
準備的口頭弁論	99
準用する	34
章	34
条	34
上映	201
承役地	202
上演	202
照会	99
傷害	152
障害年金	202
傷害保険	202
少額訴訟	202
召喚（状）	152
商慣習	34
償却（減価償却）	141
上級審	99
商業登記	34
商業登記簿	34
承継	35
条件	35
証言（する）	100
証券化	215
証言拒絶	152
証拠	35
商号	35
商行為	100
上告	35
上告裁判所	152
上告趣意書	152
上告受理	152
上告受理の申立て	152
上告状	152
上告人	152
証拠収集	100
証拠調べ	35
証拠説明書	100
証拠の取調べ	19
証拠の申出	100
証拠の類型	100
証拠保全	100
使用者	35
招集	72
招集通知	35, 100
証書（契約書など法律的効果を伴う文書）	35
証書（証明書）	35
情状	101
上場会社	36
上申	101
使用貸借	101
承諾	36
承諾（相続や遺贈の承認の場合）	36
譲渡	36, 115, 153
譲渡会社	36
譲渡者	36
譲渡所得	101
譲渡制限株式	153
承認	31, 36, 113, 153
承認（相続や遺贈の承認の場合）	36
証人尋問	36
少年	202
少年院	202
消費寄託	153
消費者	101
消費者契約	101
消費貸借	101
商標	37
商標権	37
傷病手当	202
商標登録	101
商品	37
商品先物取引	153
商品先物取引法	153

日本語索引	
商品投資顧問業	153
商品取引所	153
情報公開	101
情報通信技術	153
小法廷	153
正本	41
抄本	102
証明	37
証明（公的機関による証明）	55
証明予定事実	102
証明力	102
消滅	37, 102
消滅（権利の消滅、知的財産権の消滅）	37
消滅会社	102
消滅時効	102
条約	102
剰余金	103
剰余金の処分	103
剰余金の配当	103
将来の給付の訴え	153
将来の請求権	154
省令	37
書記官	154
嘱託（裁判の嘱託手続）	103
職務発明	103
職務を行う	37
所持	103
所持者	103
所持人	103
書証	103
職権証拠調べ	103
職権調査事項	104
職権で	202
所得税	203
初日	104
処分	37
処分禁止の仮処分	154
処分の取消しの訴え	154
署名	37
書面尋問（民事訴訟手続）	203
書面で	37
所有権	38
所有者	38
思料する	104
知れている債権者	104
侵害	38
侵害訴訟	154
人格権	104
人格のない社団又は財団	154
新株	38
新株の発行	38
新株予約権	38
新株予約権者	104
新株予約権付社債	104
（株式）新株予約権の消却	72
新株予約権無償割当て	104
新規性	104
信義則（信義誠実の原則）	154
審決	154
審決書	154
親権	203
人権	38
親権者	105
進行協議期日	105
申告	15
審査請求	154, 203
心証	38, 105
審尋	38
心神耗弱	154
心神喪失	155
真正な	105
新設合併	105
新設合併契約	155
新設合併消滅会社	155
新設合併設立会社	155
新設分割	105
新設分割会社	155
新設分割計画	155
新設分割設立会社	155
迅速に	39
身体検査	19, 203
身体障害者	203
信託	105
信託契約	105
侵奪	155
診断	105
診断書	105
親等	155
信用格付	155
信用金庫	156
信用状	105
信用取引	156
心裡留保	203

す

随意条件	203
遂行	30
推定	39
推定する	39

推定相続人	203
することができない	39
することができる	39
することを妨げない	39
することを要しない	39
するよう努めなければならない	39

せ

税	39
税額控除	106
生活の本拠	156
税関	77
請求	24, 40
請求異議の訴え	156
請求の原因	40
請求の趣旨	40
請求の追加	106
請求の認諾	40
請求の放棄	40
清算	106
清算株式会社	203
清算機関	204
清算結了	156
清算人	156
清算人会	156
誠実に	40
成人	156
製造	156
製造者	156
製造物	156
製造物責任	106
制定	106
正当な	40
正当な理由	41
正当防衛	106
成年	41
成年後見監督人	157
成年後見人	157
成年被後見人	157
正犯	12
政府	157
政府契約	157
生命保険	157
生命又は身体	106
誓約	93
税理士	204
責任	41
（説明）責任	41
責任限定契約	106
責任追及等の訴え	204
責務	41
施行期日	41
施行規則	41
施行令	42
（具体的）施策	42
（抽象的）施策	42
是正	42
世帯主	204
節	42
接見	42
窃取する	204
窃盗	106
（会社の）設立	42
設立時取締役	157
設立時発行株式	157
責めに帰すべき事由	42
善意取得	42
善意で	40, 42, 43
善意でかつ重大な過失がないとき	43
善意の第三者	43
選挙	43
宣言	43
前項	43
宣告	69
宣告する	57, 157
前条	43
宣誓	43, 157
専属管轄	107
選択債権	157
前段	43
船長	204
選定	43
（ある範疇の者を役職に）選定する	68
（特定の者を役職に）選定する	68
選任	43
全部取得条項付種類株式	158
専門委員	204
占有	44
占有移転	158
占有回収の訴え	158
占有改定	107
占有権	44
占有者	103
占有の訴え	158
占有保持の訴え	158
占有保全の訴え	158
専用実施権	158
専用使用権	158
善良な管理者の注意	44

そ

訴因	107
送還	158, 204
争議行為	204
総合課税	204
相互会社（保険業法）	205
捜査	107
相殺	44
捜索	44
総則	44
相続	44
相続財産の管理人	158
相続人	107
相続分	44
送達	44
送致（する）	159
争点及び証拠の整理手続	159
相当の期間	44
双方代理	205
双務契約	205
贈与	44, 45
贈与者	45
贈与税	205
相隣関係	205
贈賄	159
即時抗告	159
即時取得	159
組織的な犯罪	205
組織変更	205
訴訟	5, 45, 107
訴状	45
訴訟関係人	159
訴訟告知	159
訴訟参加	159
訴訟指揮	159
訴訟代理人	45
訴訟脱退	160
訴訟手続の中止	160
訴訟手続の停止	160
訴訟能力	107
訴訟費用	45
訴訟費用の確定	205
訴訟無能力者	205
措置	42
即決裁判手続	160
続行	160
疎明	107
損益計算書	107
損益分配	45
損壊	128
損害	45
損害賠償	46
損害賠償額の予定	46
損失補てん	160
存続会社	108

た

代位	108
第一審裁判所	46
対価	46, 160
大会社	108
対外直接投資	160
対抗する	108
対抗することができる	108
対抗要件	108
第三債務者	108, 109
第三者のためにする契約	160
貸借対照表	109
退職	46, 205
退職手当	160
退廷する	206
対内直接投資	161
第二審	161
退任	46
滞納処分	206
代表権	47
代表執行役	109
代表者	47
代表清算人	109
代表取締役	46
代物弁済	109
逮捕	46
大法廷	161
逮捕者	161
逮捕状	161
耐用年数	161
代理	46
代理委任状	47
代理権	47
代理者	47
代理占有	109
代理人	47
代理人（任意代理）	47
大量保有	161
宅地建物取引業	206
ただし…	47
ただし書	47
直ちに	47

立会い	161
立入検査	19, 161, 206
（人・物の場所的な）奪取	70
弾劾	206
短期賃貸借	206
単元株式数	109
単元未満株式	109
単元未満株主	109
談合する	49
短時間労働者	206
単純承認	206
団体交渉	206
単独行為	206
担保	48, 109
担保権	110
担保責任	48
担保提供命令	161
担保不動産競売	110

ち

地役権	161
地役権者	161
遅延	110
遅延損害金	110
遅延利息	110
致死	162, 207
地上権	207
遅滞なく	48
地方公共団体	110
地方公務員	110
地方裁判所	48
地方分権	162
致命	207
嫡出である子	207
嫡出でない子	207
注意義務	48
中央労働委員会	207
仲介	110
中間確認の訴え	162
中間配当	162
中間判決	162
仲裁	110
仲裁委員	162
仲裁合意	110
仲裁地	111
仲裁廷	111
仲裁手続	111
仲裁人	111
仲裁判断	162

中止する	48
中止命令	111, 207
中小企業	162
懲役	48
懲戒	48
調書（陳述書）	162
調停	68
帳簿書類	111
直接主義	207
直接に支配する	103
勅令	207
著作権	48
著作権者	48
著作者	49
著作者人格権	111
著作物	49
著作隣接権	207
賃金	49
賃借権	49
賃借人	11
陳述	15
賃貸借	10
賃貸人	9

つ

追加配当	162
追完	162
追徴金（租税等の追徴）	207
追認（民法）	168
通貨	49
通常実施権（特許）	162
通常使用権（商標）	163
通常生ずべき損失	49
通謀する	163
通謀する（民事など）	49
通訳人	49
積立金	111

て

出会送達	163
定款	49
定義	49
定期金	208
停止	14, 50, 163
（支払の）停止	31
停止条件	111
（株式会社以外の）定時総会	50
（株式会社の）定時総会	50

提出期間	111
抵触	50
訂正	21
定着物	163
抵当権	50
抵当権消滅請求	208
抵当権設定者	50
抵当不動産	50
定年	208
定年退職	208
手形	208
手形訴訟	208
適格機関投資家	163
適法な	40, 50
適用	33
適用除外	51
撤回	51
手続	51, 112
手続開始の決定	112
デリバティブ取引	163
電気通信	208
電気通信事業者	208
天災	163
電子公告	163
電子署名	163
転質	112
電磁的記録	163
転借人	51
転貸	51
転貸人	51
天然果実	208
転付命令	208

と

…等	2
同意	36
当該	51
当該者	12
統括安全衛生責任者	184
登記	51
登記事項証明書	51
登記所	51
倒産	26
動産	52
動産質	112
投資	164
投資一任契約	164
投資運用業	164
投資口	164

投資顧問契約	164
投資事業有限責任組合	164
投資者	164
当事者	52
当事者照会	112
当事者訴訟	164
当事者適格	164
当事者能力	164
投資助言業務	164
投資信託	165
投資信託（商品としての投資信託）	208
同時審判	209
投資法人	165
同時履行の抗弁	52
同族会社	165
到達	52, 165
到達（相続や遺贈の承認の場合）	211
投票	52
盗品	209
答弁	52
答弁書	52
謄本	52, 53
盗用	165
とき	53, 165
独占的状態	165
得喪	165
督促	24
督促異議	209
督促手続	209
特に信用すべき情況	209
特に必要があると認める	209
特別支配会社	209
匿名組合	165
匿名組合員	165
特約	112
独立性	53
独立性（第三者性）	165
独立当事者参加	209
土地の所有者	53
特許	53
特許権	53
特許権者	53
特許出願	112
特許請求の範囲	112
特許発明	112
特許無効審判	166
特許を受ける権利	112
都道府県	112
都道府県知事	113
届出	53

賭博	209
富くじ	140
取消し	54
取消権	54, 113
取消訴訟	166
取下げ	54
取締役	54
取締役会	54
取締役会設置会社	113
(参考人・証人等の)取調べ	42
取引条件（T&C）	54
取戻権	166
問屋	208

な

内閣府令	54
内国法人	113
なおその効力を有する	113
仲立ち	110
仲立人	166

に

荷受人	97
〜に応当する日	71
荷送人	3
に限り（限る）	54
に代わる	54
○○に関する法律	54
二次使用	166
日本弁護士連合会	209
に満たない（年齢の場合）	55
に基づく	55
入札	210
入札談合	210
任意規定	113
任意に	55
任意売却	210
認可	16
認可（例：更生計画の認可）	9
任期	55
認証	55
認諾	113
認知	210
認定	153
認定する	166
認否	113

ね

根抵当権	113
根保証	114
年金	114

の

のいずれかに該当する	55
農業協同組合	210
納税義務者	166

は

媒介	110
廃棄	166
配偶者	55
(制度を)廃止する	166
(事業や営業所を)廃止する	166
(規定などを)廃止する	167
排除命令	114
配当（会社の利益の処分）	55
配当（民事執行・配当手続）	114
配当異議	167
配当所得	210
背任	114
売買	5, 55
破棄	167
派遣	56
破産	56, 167
破産管財人	76, 167
破産債権者	167
破産者	167
破産手続	167
罰金	56
罰金刑を科す	56
発行	56
発行価額	56
発行可能株式総数	56
発行可能種類株式総数	114
発行者	56
発行済株式	56
罰条	167
罰則	167
発明	114
発明者	114
払込	18
払込金	56
払込金額	114
払込金額（会社法で用いられる払込金額）	57

払戻し	57
半期報告書	114
判決	18, 57
犯罪	4, 57
犯罪収益	149
犯罪人	114, 115
判事補	210
反訴	115
反対株主	115
判例	57

ひ

非永住者	167
非営利活動法人	211
被害者	13, 57, 115, 167
非課税	168
引受け	58, 115
引受け（手形の場合）	36
引受価額	115
引受人	58, 115, 168
被疑事実	115
被疑者	115
被疑者取調べ	38
非居住者	58
引渡し	115, 211
被後見人	168
被控訴人	168
被告	58
被告人	58
批准	168
被上告人	211
被相続人	168
被担保債権	168
人	58
ひな形	58, 116
否認	16
否認権（倒産法上の否認）	116
否認権（嫡出否認）	211
被保険者	168
被保佐人	168
被補助人	168
秘密	58, 59
秘密保持義務	59
罷免	7
費用	59
表見支配人	168
表見代表執行役	169
表見代表取締役	116
表見代理	169
表示	59, 116, 169
被用者	123
費用の償還	34

ふ

風説	169
不確定期限	211
不可抗力	59
不可分債権	169
不可分債務	169
付記登記	169
復職	169
複製	170
複製権	211
複製物	211
復代理人	116
付合	211
不公正な取引方法	170
不作為	116
不実記載	170
不正競争	170
不正使用	170
不正な	59, 116
附則	212
附属書	116
附帯の	117
負担する	60
負担付遺贈	212
負担付贈与	212
普通裁判籍	117
物権	60, 170
物上代位	170
物上保証人	212
不動産	60
不動産鑑定士	212
不動産質	212
不動産所得	212
不当表示	170
不当利得	170
不特定多数の者	170
賦払金	171
不服申立て	117
不法行為	60
不法行為者	60
扶養義務	212
不利益処分	117
不利益な事実	117
振替	171
分割会社	117

分割債権	171
分割債務	117
分割払い	117
文書提出命令	117
紛争	60
紛争解決機関	60
分配	117

へ

平均賃金	212
併合	118
編	60
変更	73
弁護士	60
弁護士会	171
弁護士法人	213
弁護人（例：刑事訴訟法第31条）	60
弁済	18, 89
弁済期	61
弁済の禁止	118
編集物	171
変造	73
弁理士	213
弁論	33, 61
弁論準備手続	118
弁論準備手続調書	118

ほ

○○法	54
法	61
放火	171
包括遺贈	213
放棄	118
防御権	61
暴行	171
報酬	61
報酬（役員報酬等の場合）	118
報酬委員会	118
幇助	171
方針	42
法人	61, 62
放送権	213
傍聴	213
傍聴人	213
法廷	62
法定果実	213
法定代理人	171
法定地上権	213
法定利息	118
法定利率	118
暴力団	171
暴力団員	171
法令	62
法令又は定款に違反する場合	118
保管者	77
保管する	119, 172
保険	119
保険業	172
保険金	172
保険契約	172, 213
保険契約者	172, 213
保険者	172
保険仲立人	213
保険募集	172
保険募集人	172
保険料	172
保護観察	214
補佐人	172
保佐人	214
保釈（金）	119
募集	12, 172
募集株式	119
募集新株予約権	119
補充送達	173
補償	61
保証	62
保証金	119
保証契約	62
保証債務	62
保証人	58
補助人	119
補正	21
保全異議	173
保全抗告	173
保全執行	173
保全処分	173
保全取消し	173
保全命令	173
保存する	172
発起人（会社の場合）	62
没取	173
本案	62
翻案	214
本案判決	62
本権	84
本籍	119
本店	62
本登記	120

本人確認	120	目論見書	174
本文	62	持株会社	121
翻訳人	49	持ち分	10
		持分	65, 121
		持分会社	121

ま

前払式支払手段	214	物	37, 64
満期	173	者	58
満了	37	物の給付	89
		漏らす	214

み

未決勾留	173	役員	64
未遂	120	約款	64
未成年者	120	やむを得ない（得ず）	121
みだりに	173	やむを得ない事由	121, 122
みなし賃金日額	174		
未満	63		
民事訴訟	63		

や

ゆ

		誘引	138
		誘拐	214

む

無過失	63	有価証券	64, 174
無期禁錮	174	有価証券届出書	174
無記名債権	174	有価証券報告書	174
無権代理	174	有期	175
無効な	63	有給休暇	214
無罪	120	有限責任組合員	175
無償で	120	有限責任事業組合	175
無償割当て	174	有限責任社員	175
		有罪	64
		有償契約	175
		有償行為	175
		優先株式	122
		優先出資	122
		（支払の）猶予	31
		譲受会社	122
		譲受人	64
		譲渡人	36

め

名義書換	174
名誉毀損	120
命令の交付	89
免許	63
免許の交付	89
免除	95, 120
免責	63, 214
免訴	174

よ

養子	175
要旨	175, 214
要旨（概要）	122
養子縁組	175
預金	122
予見可能性	175
予見する	64
余罪	214
予算	64

も

申込み	63
申込者	63
申立て	33, 63
申立人	33, 121
目的	2, 63, 121
目的物	174

預託 ……………………………………… 122
予断 ………………………………………… 73
予納 ……………………………………… 215
予備的 …………………………………… 215

ら

落札者 …………………………………… 215

り

利益相反 ………………………………… 64
利益の処分 …………………………… 122
利害関係人 …………………………… 122
履行 ……………………………………… 65
履行地 …………………………………… 65
履行遅滞 ……………………………… 122
履行不能 ……………………………… 122
離婚 …………………………………… 123
利札 …………………………………… 175
利子 ……………………………………… 65
利息 ……………………………………… 65
立証趣旨 ……………………………… 102
立証する ……………………………… 65
略式手続 ……………………………… 176
略式命令 ……………………………… 176
留置権 ………………………………… 176
流動化 ………………………………… 215
領置 …………………………………… 123
領得する ……………………………… 176
利用の許諾 …………………………… 123
両罰規定 ……………………………… 123

る

累積投票 ……………………………… 176
累犯 …………………………………… 215
流布 …………………………………… 176

れ

令（法形式が政令の場合） …………… 65
令状 ……………………………………… 65

連結計算書類 ………………………… 176
連結子会社 …………………………… 176
連行 ……………………………………… 81
連帯債務 ……………………………… 176
連帯債務者 …………………………… 176
連帯して ……………………………… 65
連帯保証 ……………………………… 176

ろ

漏えい ………………………………… 215
労役場留置 …………………………… 215
労働委員会 …………………………… 215
労働基準 ……………………………… 215
労働基準監督署 ……………………… 215
労働協約 ……………………………… 177
労働組合 ……………………………… 123
労働契約 ……………………………… 65
労働災害 ……………………………… 215
労働時間 ……………………………… 216
労働者 ………………………………… 123
労働者災害補償保険 ………………… 216
労働条件 ……………………………… 177
労働審判 ……………………………… 177
労働争議 ……………………………… 177
労働保険 ……………………………… 216
労務 ……………………………………… 44

わ

わいせつ ……………………………… 177
賄賂 …………………………………… 123
和解 ……………………………………… 65
和解に代わる決定 …………………… 216
割増賃金 ……………………………… 151

を

を超えない …………………………… 65
を超える ……………………………… 66
を除き ………………………………… 66
を除くほか …………………………… 66

高速マスター
法律英単語®Ⅰ 2100 ［第2版］
法律・基礎編

2021年1月14日　初版発行
2025年3月17日　第2版発行

　　　　著　者　　渡　部　友一郎
　　　　発行者　　和　田　　　裕

発行所　　日本加除出版株式会社
本　社　　〒171-8516
　　　　　東京都豊島区南長崎3丁目16番6号

組版・印刷・製本　㈱アイワード

定価はカバー等に表示してあります。
落丁本・乱丁本は当社にてお取替えいたします。
お問合せの他、ご意見・感想等がございましたら、下記まで
お知らせください。

〒171-8516
東京都豊島区南長崎3丁目16番6号
日本加除出版株式会社　営業部
電話　　03-3953-5642
FAX　　03-3953-2061
e-mail　toiawase@kajo.co.jp
URL　　www.kajo.co.jp

【お問合せフォーム】

© Yuichiro Watanabe 2025
Printed in Japan
ISBN978-4-8178-4995-3

〈JCOPY〉〈出版者著作権管理機構　委託出版物〉
本書を無断で複写複製（電子化を含む）することは、著作権法上の例外を除き、禁じられています。複写される場合は、そのつど事前に出版者著作権管理機構（JCOPY）の許諾を得てください。
また本書を代行業者等の第三者に依頼してスキャンやデジタル化することは、たとえ個人や家庭内での利用であっても一切認められておりません。

〈JCOPY〉　HP：https://www.jcopy.or.jp，e-mail：info@jcopy.or.jp
　　　　　電話：03-5244-5088，FAX：03-5244-5089

「英文契約書」の学び始めに最適！
法律英語の単語帳　シリーズ第2弾！

高速マスター
法律英単語®Ⅱ 1000
英文契約書編
弁護士　渡部友一郎 著

2022年6月刊 A5判 184頁 定価1,760円（本体1,600円）978-4-8178-4801-7

本書の特徴

- 「高速マスター 法律英単語®Ⅰ 2100［第2版］法律・基礎編」の姉妹編
- 「英文契約書」を読み解く語彙を培う1000の英単語を収録

―― さらに学習しやすくなった第2弾！ ――

- 読者の声を受け、発音記号・例文を収録！
- アイコンごとに4つの企業間取引のストーリーを想定！
- 例文はネイティブチェック済！
- 特別付録「AIが選ぶ重要英単語（β版）」も収録！

企業イメージ
イラストは
大舞キリコ先生
描きおろし！

フラワーショップ　　植物の卸売事業
部品メーカー　　SNS新興企業　　インターネット企業
自動車メーカー
...and more!

個性豊かな企業と一緒に、英文契約書の旅に出よう！

日本加除出版　〒171-8516　東京都豊島区南長崎3丁目16番6号
営業部　TEL (03) 3953-5642　FAX (03) 3953-2061
www.kajo.co.jp